METAL CLAY FOR
JEWELRY MAKERS

METAL CLAY FOR JEWELRY MAKERS

THE COMPLETE TECHNIQUE GUIDE

SUE HEASER

interweave.com

A QUARTO BOOK
Metal Clay for Jewelry Makers

Copyright © 2012 Quarto Inc

Published in North America by
Interweave Press LLC
201 East Fourth Street
Loveland, CO 80537-5655
www.interweave.com
Conceived, designed, and produced by
Quarto Publishing plc
The Old Brewery
6 Blundell Street
London N7 9BH

QUAR.MCTB

Project Editor: Chelsea Edwards
Art Editor: Joanna Bettles
Designer: Karin Skånberg
Photographer: Phil Wilkins
Picture Researcher: Sarah Bell
Copyeditor: Claire Waite Brown
Proofreader: Lindsay Kaubi
Indexer: Helen Snaith
Art Director: Caroline Guest
Creative Director: Moira Clinch
Publisher: Paul Carslake

Library of Congress Cataloging-in-
Publication Data not available at time
of printing.

ISBN 978-1-59668-713-4

Color separation by Pica Digital Pte Ltd,
Singapore
Printed in China by Hung Hing Off-set
Printing Co. Ltd, China

10 9 8 7 6 5 4 3 2 1

Author's dedication:
To Miles and Oren, wishing them both
happy and creative lives in whatever they
choose to do.

Contents

Introduction   8
About this book   9
Materials   10
Tools   16

CHAPTER 1: BASIC TECHNIQUES   24
Soft clay techniques   26
Keeping clay workable   31
Reclaiming and reconstituting clay   34
Paste techniques   37
Drying techniques   39
Pre-finishing techniques   41
Firing techniques   44
Finishing techniques   50
Findings for metal clay   56
Soldering techniques   64

CHAPTER 2: CLAY SHAPING TECHNIQUES   68
Cutters and templates   70
Applying texture   72
Molds and molding   77
Soft sculpture techniques   82
Weaving, braiding, and knotting   84

Creating with soft clay sheets   86

Paste replicas   88

Hollow core techniques   90

Construction techniques   94

Adding hinges and catches   96

Rivets   102

Links and chains   104

Combining clays   108

Bead making techniques   112

Filigree and syringe techniques   120

Paper clay techniques   124

CHAPTER 3: BANGLE AND RING MAKING TECHNIQUES   130

Bangles and cuffs   132

Ring making   135

CHAPTER 4: EMBELLISHING   144

Engraving, carving, and etching   146

Incorporating gemstones   149

Adding gold   160

Decorative paste techniques   164

Using resin   166

Enameling   170

Embellishing with polymer clay   174

Using glass and ceramics   178

Patinas   183

Resources   186

Index   188

Credits   192

Introduction

Metal clay has become established as an extraordinary metalworking and silversmithing material during the past decade and is now used all over the world by professionals and amateurs alike. Its ease of use has spread the crafting of precious metals far beyond the realms of the silversmith, so that artists in many different genres and media are now using metal clay in their work.

Originally developed in silver and gold, metal clay is now also available in copper, bronze, and other metals and the manufacturers are constantly improving the quality and versatility with new products appearing regularly.

This book contains a comprehensive collection of the metal clay techniques that have been developed by artists, silversmiths, manufacturers, and crafters since the invention of metal clays. Selecting the techniques to include has not been an easy task—there are so many more than can ever be fitted into one volume and inevitably some techniques had to be left, reluctantly, on the cutting room floor. However, I hope that beginners and advanced metal clay enthusiasts alike will find this a rich and inspiring guide. Tried and tested techniques, as well as those on the cutting edge of metal clay creativity, are covered in detail with recent discoveries of my own, and those developed by artists around the world, also being featured.

SUE HEASER

About this book

Designing and making your own metal clay jewelry is an exciting and rewarding pursuit. This book gathers together a vast array of techniques to help you create outstanding pieces.

Finished "apprentice pieces" show what can be achieved using the technique.

Step-by-step instructions guide you through each technique.

Soft sculpture techniques

Sculpting soft metal clay is a rewarding technique for creating original jewelry, and can be as complex or as simple as you wish. Developing sculpting skills is an important part of becoming an accomplished metal clay artist.

Successful soft sculpture is best achieved with metal clay that is well hydrated but has a touch-dry surface. If the surface is wet and slippery, you will find it difficult to control the clay.

The techniques shown here can be used with all kinds of metal clay, both precious metal and base metal. When adding clay to a piece, use a smear of water or paste to ensure a strong join. Copper and bronze clay in particular need firm fixing to avoid pieces coming away during firing.

Freeform
Logs of clay swirled into simple freeform shapes make appealing pieces. See page 84.

Sculptural
Simple organic shapes pressed together make attractive sculptural forms.

Flora
Flowers and leaves are popular jewelry designs and embellishments.

Fauna
Small animal forms can be created from simple shapes and make attractive charms.

Simple organic shapes
Flat-backed shapes are easy forms to sculpt, because you can work on a ceramic tile after making the basic shape. The clay will stick to the tile so that you can shape it without having to hold it.

YOU WILL NEED
Basic tool kit (see page 16)
Polymer clay

▲ THE STRAWBERRY THIEF,
XUELLA ARNOLD
Exquisite sculpting of this delicate bird with fruit, flower, and leaves makes a unique pendant.

STEP 1 Start with a sketch of your design, trying out different shapes. Alternatively, design your piece in polymer clay first. Unlike metal clay, polymer clay does not dry out as you work and will give you time to design in a similar material.

STEP 2 Make sure that your metal clay is well hydrated. Form the piece into a smooth round ball to eliminate any fold lines, then shape it roughly to your design.

STEP 3 Press the shape down onto a ceramic tile. Use tools or fingers to refine the shape further and cut away any surplus clay if required. If the surface dries too quickly and shows cracks, apply water with a paintbrush or wet finger to smooth the surface. Leave until the surface is touch dry before continuing.

Sculpting flowers and leaves
Flowers and leaves are everlastingly popular designs for jewelry. Larger pieces make beautiful earrings and pendants, while smaller pieces can be used as embellishments or charms.

YOU WILL NEED
Basic tool kit (see page 16)

A rose sculpted in copper clay

Bronze leaves

▲ FOOD CHAIN NECKLACE,
TERRY KOVACIK
A beautiful and thought-provoking necklace. An original polymer clay sculpture was used to make a mold for the head of the bird, which was further enhanced by carving when in the plaster dry stage.

STEP 4 To add applied details such as fins on a fish or wings on a bird, press the extra clay piece on the tile to flatten the back. Brush water on the joining surface of the main piece and press the addition to attach it firmly.

STEP 1 To make a rose, roll out a small log of clay about 1" (25 mm) long and point both ends. Roll the log flat on a tile to make a long thin petal. Roll the petal up as shown to form the center of the rose.

STEP 2 Make more logs of a similar size but thicker, and press down on the tile to form larger petals. Cut each petal in half lengthwise. Brush water onto the outside of the rose center and wrap a petal around it, flat edge down, pressing to secure.

STEP 5 Textural details such as fish scales or marks on fins can be applied with a suitable tool. Here, the eye of a needle makes perfect scales on the fish. The eye of an animal could simply be a hole made with a blunt needle.

STEP 3 Continue adding petals on either side of the rose, making them larger as you work outward. Finally, pull the tops of the larger petals outward a little and brush over with water to smooth any rough edges.

STEP 4 To make a leaf, form a small teardrop and press it down on the tile with the end of your finger to flatten it into a leaf shape. Mark veins with a curved knife blade. Remove the leaf from the tile by sliding the blade under it.

Beautiful works by metal clay artists are featured throughout to serve as inspiration.

"You will need" lists detail the tools and materials needed for that particular technique. Most will require the contents of the "basic tool kit" (see page 16).

Materials

The range of different metal clays available has increased dramatically in the past few years and includes: silver, gold, bronze, copper, silver alloys, brass, and steel in a variety of brands and even in different colors, and more clays are sure to follow.

Most of the techniques in this book can be used with all the different types of metal clay, because the main difference between them lies in the firing. Where there are additional differences, these are detailed with the relevant techniques.

SHRINKAGE AND FIRING: PRECIOUS METAL CLAY

To help you choose which clay to use for your projects, this table shows the shrinkage for each type and the recommended firing method. Please note that the information is for guidance only. Refer to the manufacturer's instructions for full firing details.

	Type of clay	Shrinkage (approximate)	Firing method
Gold clays	Art Clay Gold (22k)	15%	Kiln fire only
	PMC Gold (22k)	12%	Blowtorch or kiln
Fine silver clays	Art Clay Silver original	8–10%	Blowtorch, stovetop, or kiln
	Art Clay Silver 650, all kinds	8–10%	Blowtorch, stovetop, or kiln (low fire)
	PMC original	28%	Kiln only
	PMC+	12%	Blowtorch or kiln
	PMC3	12%	Blowtorch, stovetop, or kiln (low fire)
Silver alloy clays	PMC Pro (90% silver; 10% copper)	15–20%	Kiln only—two-part firing in charcoal
	PMC Sterling (92.5% silver; 7.5% copper)	15–20%	Kiln only—two-part firing in charcoal
Paper and sheet clays	Art Clay Silver paper	8–10%	Kiln only
	PMC sheet	12%	Blowtorch or kiln

Precious metal clays

These clays are the most costly, but the silver clay in particular is extremely popular. Rises in the price of precious metals have put gold clay out of the reach of many artists, but silver is more affordable, and fine silver clay is the easiest of all to fire.

Gold clay (1)

Extremely costly, gold clay is fine grained and fires to become 22k gold. The soft clay is easy to shape and the clay can only be fired in a kiln.

Fine silver clays (2)

There are two main brands of silver clay, Art Clay Silver and PMC. Each manufacturer produces clays with different firing temperatures. They vary slightly between each other for feel and drying rate, and which you prefer is down to personal taste. Many of these clays can be fired with a blowtorch or on a gas stovetop, as well as in a kiln. The fired clay is 999 pure silver, relatively soft, and can be hallmarked as 999 silver.

Silver alloy clays

PMC Pro and PMC Sterling silver clays are a new generation of clays introduced as a solution to the soft nature of 999 fine silver clays. They are considerably stronger after firing than the fine silver clays and can be forged and used for delicate pieces where strength is important. Because of their copper content they have to be kiln fired in charcoal in two stages.

Silver sheet and silver paper clay (3)

Silver clay also comes as a ready-made sheet that can be used for a variety of paper techniques. The PMC brand is referred to as sheet and the Art Clay brand as paper clay. Both types have to be kiln fired. Use these products within a year before they become brittle.

Silver clay paste (4)

This is available ready-made for both main brands of silver clay, or you can make your own from lump clay. It is used for attaching findings and repairing cracks and breaks, as well as for making replicas of leaves and seed pods and embellishing. Firing is the same as for the lump clay of the respective brand.

Overlay paste (5)

Art Clay Silver Overlay Paste is another kind of paste that is used to embellish glass and ceramics. It can also be used on fired silver as a low-fire version of Oil paste. Art Clay Gold paste, Accent gold, and PMC Aura gold are all pure gold embellishing pastes used to add gold details to silver clay.

Oil paste (6)

Art Clay Silver Oil Paste is used to mend fired silver pieces or to attach findings to the solid silver. It can be used on fired PMC silver or Art Clay Silver. You can make your own using lavender essential oil and PMC3. Kiln fire.

Syringe-type silver clays (7)

Both Art Clay Silver 650 and PMC3 are available as a ready-made slip in a syringe for filigree techniques. Different sizes of syringe tips or nozzles are available to attach to the syringe.

CLAY QUANTITIES FOR JEWELRY

The following is a rough guide to the quantities of clay required for typical items of jewelry. Some pieces may need more to allow you to roll out the necessary size of sheet for cutting, although not all the clay will be used. The quantities given are for silver clay. Base metal clays will require about 25 per cent less, because they are not as heavy.

Pendant
4 p.c. (1 mm) thick, 1 x ¾" (25 x 20 mm): 7 g

Brooch
4 p.c. (1 mm) thick, 2 x 1½" (50 x 40 mm): 10 g

Woman's band ring
⅜" (10 mm) wide, US size 6½
(UK size N): 7 g

Woman's half-round ring
US size 6½ (UK size N): 10 g

Man's band ring
⅜" (10 mm) wide, US size 10
(UK size T ½): 10 g

Pair of molded cufflinks
¾ x ½ x ¼" (20 x 13 x 6 mm): 13 g

Woman's bracelet
2 ⅜" (61 mm) diameter, 8 p.c. (2 mm) thick, ⅜" (10 mm) wide: 50 g

Woman's cuff
Average size wrist: 50 g

Base metal clays

With the rising cost of precious metals, the recent development of base metal clays is very welcome to metal clay artists. The lower cost of these clays means that larger projects are affordable and, in the case of jewelry, this is particularly so for bangles, cuffs, and large necklaces.

Bronze clays (1)
Bronze was the first base metal clay to be developed, and there are several brands available. The different brands vary considerably in texture and handling quality, so it is worth experimenting to find the one for you. The original bronze clays required lengthy firing schedules, but the new fast-fire clays have shortened this. Some clays are available in powder form so they can be mixed as required to give a lengthy shelf life. Slip can be made as required from lump clay.

Bronze clays have to be fired in a kiln and preferably in charcoal to avoid firestain. They are usually a wonderful golden color after firing and can be treated to give exciting patinas. Bronze is extremely strong after firing.

Copper clays (2)
Similar in use to the bronze clays, copper clays have more problems with oxidation and the soft clay can develop a surface coating of black when stored after opening. Even the powdered clays can blacken

unless used up promptly. Firing is similar to bronze clays with a higher temperature. The fired metal is pure copper, pliable, and strong. Slip is best made in small quantities as required.

Other base metal clays
Steel clay has been developed by Hadar Jacobson as well as rose and white bronze clays. Brass clay is also available. Refer to the manufacturer's instructions for the relevant firings schedules.

Oils and additives (3, 4, and 5)
Light vegetable oil (3) or olive oil is used as lubrication when working with metal clays. Rub a thin coating over your hands, roller, and work surface to prevent sticking. Apply a light coating to clay before pushing into molds or texturing. Lavender oil (4) can be added in small quantities to clay to prevent drying out and in larger quantities to make an oil paste for using with fired silver. Glycerin (5) added to metal clay helps prevent drying and can be used to make flexible clay.

SHRINKAGE AND FIRING: BASE METAL CLAY

The table details the approximate shrinkage and firing requirements of the main brands of bronze and copper clays.

Clay type	Shrinkage	Firing
BronzClay Fastfire, CopprClay	5–10%	Kiln fire in charcoal
Hadar's (powder) quick-fire bronze and copper	10%	Kiln fire in charcoal
Prometheus bronze and copper	6–10%	Kiln fire—open shelf, fiber-cloth wrapped, or in charcoal
MetalMania (powder) bronze and copper	15–19%	Kiln fire—in charcoal or newspaper wrapped in a container
Art Clay Copper	10%	Kiln—open shelf. Can also be fired in charcoal

Other materials

These are the materials used to complete and embellish your jewelry.
Findings are attached to metal clay pieces to transform them into jewelry,
while embellishing materials add color and interest to your work.

Findings and wire (1 and 2)

Findings include fittings for earrings, pendants, brooches, cufflinks, and many more. A large range is available from jewelry making suppliers and they come in gold, fine silver, sterling silver, and base metals. You can also make your own from wire or metal clay.

Wire is indispensable when making jewelry and is available in all the main kinds of metal used in this book. Its thickness is measured by AWG or American Wire Gauge (ga.) in the USA and in millimeters (mm) elsewhere. The most useful gauges for jewelry making are:
18 ga. (1 mm): For making rivets and connecting heavy pieces.
20 ga. (0.8 mm): General all-purpose thickness.
22 ga. (0.6 mm): For delicate pieces, small jump rings, and attaching charms.

Polymer clay (3)

Polymer clay is useful as a design tool, as well as for making molds and embellishing metal clay. Allow the following approximate quantities of polymer clay as a substitute for metal clay when trying out a design:
Silver clays: ¼ teaspoon or ⅝" (15 mm) ball for 10 g
Base metal clays: ½ teaspoon or ¾" (20 mm) ball for 10 g

Putty silicone molding compound (4)

There are many different molding materials on the market, but putty silicone is the easiest to use and is widely available from metal clay suppliers and general hobby and craft suppliers. It makes excellent, detailed and flexible molds, so some undercutting—overhanging parts of the mold—is possible.

Soldering materials (see page 64)

Solder is used to join two pieces of metal together by heating to make a strong bond. Silver solder can be used for all metal types, although copper and bronze solders are available as well. Paste solder is the easiest to use because it contains the required flux to clean and help fuse the metal.

Strip solder comes in long strips to be cut up and needs added flux—a chemical that cleans the metal, helps the solder to flow, and prevents it from oxidizing.

Solders are available as easy (lowest melting point), medium, and hard (highest melting point). Easy solder is the best choice for beginners.

Gemstones (5)

All kinds of gemstones can be incorporated into your metal clay designs, from natural semiprecious stones, pearls, and abalone to lab-created fireable gemstones.

Gold embellishments (6)

A thick 24K gold leaf can be applied to fired silver clay using a technique called keum-boo. Gold paste is available for painting onto fired silver clay (see page 12).

Resins

Epoxy resin is a crystal-clear material sold under a variety of brand names. Resin can be colored with supplied pigments, or with small amounts of oil paints, which give a huge color palette. Resin labeled as "doming" is thicker and can be made to dome.

UV resin is an alternative to epoxy, but it has to be set using an ultraviolet lamp.

Glass and enamels (7 and 8)

If you have a kiln you can fuse your own glass cabochons to add to your jewelry. Fusing glass (7) is available from glass suppliers in many forms, from iridescent dichroic through to colored transparent and opalescent.

Enamels (8)—powdered glass—can be used very successfully with silver metal clay.

Oxidizing materials

Liver of sulfur and Baldwin's patina are mild chemicals used to oxidize metal. Ammonia and vinegar give green and blue colors on bronze and copper.

Tools

One of the advantages of making jewelry with metal clay is the relatively small number of tools needed. A beginner can start with a few simple tools that can be added to over time.

The equipment detailed here is what you will need in order to follow all the main techniques in this book. It is assumed you also have pencil and paper, scissors, and other everyday items to hand. Some embellishing techniques require more specialist equipment, listed with the relevant technique.

BASIC TOOL KIT

To avoid repetition throughout the book, it is assumed that you have the following basic toolkit. Where other tools are needed, they are listed in the technique.

- Work surface
- Ceramic tiles
- Plastic wrap
- Roller and rolling guides
- Ruler
- Craft knife
- Slicer blade
- Paintbrushes
- Water pot
- Simple modeling tools
- Needles
- Drying equipment
- Needle file
- Sanding pads and/or sandpaper
- Stainless steel brush
- Firing equipment
- Burnisher
- Polish and polishing cloth
- Tweezers
- Pliers, round-nosed or needle-nosed
- Wire cutters

Work surfaces
Your work surface needs to be wipe clean. A melamine chopping board, or a sheet of acrylic or glass are all suitable. Avoid wood, which can become ingrained with the clays. Proprietary non-stick mats are available for rolling out clay or you can use a file pocket or piece of Teflon sheet.

Ceramic tiles (1)
Smooth, glazed ceramic tiles, such as those sold for bathroom walls, are invaluable. Clay pieces can be created on them and be placed in an oven still on the tile for drying. Square tiles of 6 or 4" (150 or 100 mm) are ideal.

Rolling tools (2)
Metal clay suppliers stock small, plastic nonstick rollers, or you can use a cake decorating roller. Rolling guides are used on either side of a piece of clay when rolling a sheet and are available in different millimeter sizes. You can improvise with playing cards stacked up instead.

Log roller
This makes rolling smooth and even logs easier. A sheet of clear Perspex, 6" (150 mm) square, is ideal, or use a CD case.

Craft knife (3)
Used for cutting logs, cutting around templates, and cutting small strips of clay. A curved blade is the most versatile.

Slicer or tissue blade (4)
These long blades will cut straight lines and straight-sided strips with ease. They are also available as wavy blades for decorative cuts.

Cutters (5)
Useful for cutting neat shapes in sheets of clay. The open types are easier to position than those with plungers. Tiny cutters make attractive decorative holes. Brush protectors or drinking straws will also cut small round holes.

Needles (6, 7, and 8)
Both a blunt tapestry needle (6) and a sharp darner (7) can be used for making holes in clay. The tapestry needle can double as a sculpting and burnishing tool. A needle tool with a handle (8) is easier to hold.

Paintbrushes (9)
You will need fine paintbrushes for applying paste as well as medium sizes. A large, fluffy brush is also useful for brushing away dust when engraving, sanding, or filing. Paste ruins natural-fiber brushes quickly, so buy good-quality brushes with man-made bristles.

Modeling tools (10 and 11)
Modeling tools range from inexpensive plastic tools to wooden, and stainless steel ones. The latter are best because they do not drag the surface.

A small spatula is useful for mixing and stirring paste as well as applying it.
Ball-headed tools (11) are handy for smoothing clay, creating textures, and burnishing.

Plastic wrap and file pockets
Tightly wrap unused pieces of clay in plastic wrap to keep them moist. File pockets are used to roll clay inside when reconstituting or rehydrating.

Small glass jelly jars
These are very effective for storing plastic-wrapped clay. They have completely watertight lids and keep the clay moist far longer than plastic pots.

Syringe (12)
A plastic syringe, available from pharmacies, can be used for extruding lump clay, adding drops of water to paste, and for adding lavender oil or glycerin in measured drops to lump clay.

Extruders (13)
These come with sets of different dies to extrude lengths of clay of different cross sections. Choose one with a winding handle, which is easier to use than plunger types. Stainless steel is best because it will not react with the clay. Attachments are available to extrude hollow tubes.

Commercial texture sheets and rubber stamps (14)
A variety of these are available from metal clay and craft suppliers. Using handmade texture sheets or found objects will make your work unique.

Molds (15)
Widely available as silicone molds from metal clay suppliers, or you can make your own from molding materials.

Ring and bangle making tools

You will need a few extra tools specifically for making rings or bangles.

Ring mandrel (1)
An inexpensive wooden mandrel is fine for most purposes. A steel mandrel is a more expensive alternative and is calibrated with different ring sizes.

Memo notes are used to cover the ring mandrel so the clay does not stick.

Bangle mandrel (2)
This type of mandrel can be expensive—less so in wood—but you can improvise with a soft drinks can.

Finger gauges (3)
A strip ring sizer is a simple adjustable strip with graduations, or you can use a ring sizing set—a set of rings of all the most common sizes. Cardboard sheet ring gauges are an economical alternative.

Tools for pre-finishing, drying, and finishing

These tools are used for smoothing and refining the clay once it is dried, and also for finishing fired metal clay.

Drying equipment (4)
Using a home oven is the most convenient method for drying metal clay, but for quick drying of paste and added pieces, use a hair-dryer or heat gun. Other methods include a mug warmer, a hot plate, or a food dehydrator.

Rubber block (5)
Used as a support for working on plaster-dry or fired pieces. The surface is forgiving and will not scratch the metal.

Files (6)
A half-round fine needle file is used to smooth any rough areas of clay in the plaster-dry stage, as well as for filing metal. You may want to add a large, fine half-round ring file to your tool kit in time. A medium file cuts through metal faster and is useful for more major smoothing. Clean files frequently using a stainless steel brush.

Drilling tools (7 and 8)
Drill bits (7) are used to make holes in plaster-dry clay and occasionally in fired metal clay. The most useful sizes are 1, 1.5, and 2 mm.

A pin vise (8) is a small tool that is used to clamp the drill bit. You can use a drill bit on its own to drill plaster-dry clay, or put the bit in a pin vise to give more power. Drilling through fired metal clay is much harder and you will need to use a pin vise or a power drill (see Hobby drill, page 22).

Sanding pads (9)
Generally considered indispensable by metal clay artists, these have a sponge layer on the back and a sanding surface on the other side. They bend around curved surfaces and are used to sand plaster-dry clay and to create a mirror polish on fired clay, by sanding with increasingly fine grits. The most useful grits are the three finest ones available:
Superfine (red): 500–600 grit (P1000–P1200), fine
Ultrafine (blue): 800–1000 grit (P1500–P2000), finer
Microfine (green): 1200–1500 grit (P3000–P5000), finest
Sanding pads normally come in sheets 4½ x 5½" (114 x 139 mm), and are best cut into small pieces. Sanding pads used on plaster-dry clay will clog quite quickly, so brush over the surface with a stainless steel brush to clean them. They can be washed clean of the clay powder residue to prolong their life.

Sandpaper (10)
Sandpaper is useful for laying face-up on a work surface to sand the sides of rings or other pieces that need to be flat. A wide variety of grits is available. Sandpaper of 300 or 400 grit is best for rapid sanding of plaster-dry pieces, then refine with sanding pads.

Brushes (11, 12, and 13)
Brass or stainless steel brushes (11) are used to brush the metal clay surface after firing as a first stage of polishing. On silver clay, a brush will smooth down the white surface created by firing. On bronze and copper clay, the brush will normally remove any firestain left from firing in charcoal. Brushes give a pleasing satin finish to fired metal clay, which can be left as the finished surface if desired. Stainless steel brushes can be used dry; brass brushes should be used with soapy water to lubricate the bristles. Small stainless steel brushes are useful for tight areas (12).

Glass fiber pointed bristles held in a pencil-type holder (13) give an even finer finish.

Burnisher (14, 15, and 16)
A burnisher is rubbed over the metal surface to polish it. Any smooth stainless steel tool, such as a blunt wool needle or even a teaspoon, can be used instead.

Stainless steel burnishers are available in small sizes (14) for detailed areas and larger, flatter shapes for bigger pieces (15). They can become scratched with use and will then scratch rather than polish, so take care of them.

Agate burnishers (16) are more expensive but have a lovely smooth surface that is unlikely to scratch. These give a better finish than stainless steel and are traditionally used to burnish gold. If you use one for keum-boo, be careful not to let it get too hot and do not quench it, since it may crack.

Polish and polishing cloths (17)
A soft cloth and silver polish will add the final shine to your jewelry. Any good-quality silver polish can be used. Old T-shirts cut into rags make excellent polishing cloths, but be careful not to let any metal dust from sanding contaminate them, otherwise they will scratch rather than polish.

Firing equipment

Most types of low-fire silver clay can be fired with a simple form of firing, using either a blowtorch or a gas stovetop. Some silver clay techniques can only be fired in a kiln, as detailed in the relevant sections. Base metal clays are best kiln fired for successful results.

Blowtorch (1)

A simple handheld blowtorch will quickly fire pieces of silver clay under 25 g, and can also be used for soldering. Chef's brûlée torches, available from kitchen equipment stores, may work, but an adjustable hand torch such as the one shown is preferable to ensure full firing. Buy one with adjustments for the oxygen/gas mixture that varies the heat of the flame. This type of torch is fueled with widely available cigarette lighter gas, dispensed in aerosol cans.

Plumber's blowtorches are available from hardware stores and building materials suppliers. They are more powerful than the small torches but have less control for delicate work.

Firebrick (2)

You will need a heatproof firebrick to torch the pieces on. Fiber bricks are lightweight, while ceramic bricks are considered longer lasting.

Gas stovetop firing (3)

This is a reliable method of firing small pieces of silver clay and several can be fired at a time. You can use a domestic gas stovetop or a camping gas stove. You will also need a stainless steel mesh (3) to place on the burner.

Kilns

A small jewelry kiln with an internal chamber size of between 6" (150 mm) cubed to 8" (200 mm) cubed is ideal for silver clay. You will need the larger size for clays which have to be fired in a container of charcoal. The kiln needs to have a pyrometer (which measures the temperature) and a digital controller so that it will maintain a specific temperature. Kilns with simple controllers that keep the kiln at a set temperature but do not have built-in timers are perfectly adequate—you use them rather like a domestic oven, heating them up to the required temperature and then using an egg timer to time your pieces. More expensive controllers have firing programs that you can set up to run automatically. They can heat the kiln at so many degrees an hour (the ramp speed), then maintain the top temperature for the required time.

Kiln shelf or firing board (4)

You will need a firing board or kiln shelf to place your silver clay pieces on for firing. These are available as long-lasting ceramic or lightweight fiber that slowly breaks down over time. Do not place the firing board or kiln shelf on the floor of the kiln, but raise it on kiln props, small flowerpots, or pieces of fiberboard, which is better for the kiln's elements. Fire fiber kiln boards at 930°F (500°C) for ten minutes before use in order to remove any impurities from manufacture.

Tongs and protective gloves and goggles (5)

Tongs are used for removing shelves from a hot kiln. Stainless steel kitchen tongs work fine and are suitable in size for small kilns. Protective gloves will save your hands from accidents, and goggles are advisable when looking into a hot kiln.

Charcoal (6)

Base metal clays such as bronze, copper, brass, and steel, as well as sterling silver clay, are normally fired embedded in activated charcoal to exclude oxygen and prevent firestain. Some manufacturers recommend firing on an open shelf, but firestain is often a problem. Activated charcoal is granulated charcoal that has been treated with oxygen to make it exceptionally porous. It is available from metal clay suppliers as both coconut-based and coal-based charcoal. The first is more widely used, while the latter can give interesting colors on the fired metal clay.

Firing containers for base metal clays (7)

Charcoal has to be placed in a container in the kiln. Stainless steel containers are available from metal clay suppliers but you can find suitable containers at a hardware store. Buy good-quality stainless steel, which is less likely to flake when fired. The container needs to fit into your kiln and should be raised slightly from the kiln floor. Some clays require a lid to the container, in which case you can use a kiln shelf or a stainless steel lid.

A small terracotta flowerpot works well, but has to be cooled slowly in the kiln to ensure it does not crack. Fiber cloth or paper folded into a container is another option, but has a limited life. Finally, stainless steel sheet is available from metal clay suppliers to fold into a box.

Ceramic shelf paper (8)

This is used to cover kiln boards to prevent fused glass sticking to them during firing.

Fiber blanket or fiber cloth (9)

This resembles cotton wool and is used for encasing or supporting delicate silver clay pieces during firing.

Vermiculite

Available from gardening stores, this granular material can be put in a terracotta dish for firing delicate pieces of silver clay that need gentle support.

Tweezers (10)

Tweezers have a number of uses, including picking up hot pieces of metal for quenching, holding findings during soldering, and for dipping pieces when oxidizing.

Hammers, pliers, wire cutters, and power tools

These are used for shaping and refining metal after firing.
Pliers and wire cutters are also used for shaping and cutting
wire for findings and attachments.

General-purpose hammer (1)
If you only want to purchase
one hammer, buy a lightweight
hammer from a hardware store
or jewelry tool supplier. One
end should be flat and the other
chisel-shaped if you want to use
it for riveting. This will serve
for all the techniques in this
book. If you need to protect the
metal being struck, cover the
hammer head with masking
tape or hammer through a piece
of fabric.

Plastic hammer (2)
This will not damage soft metal
and is used for shaping rings or
bracelets on a mandrel and for
hammering pieces to flatten or
curve them. Hide hammers are
another version.

Pliers (3 and 4)
These are essential tools for
shaping and bending wire and
making findings. There are many
different shapes, but the ones
most useful for the techniques
in this book are round-nosed or
needle-nosed (3), to make loops
in wire, and snipe-nosed or flat-
nosed (4), for general shaping
and gripping.

Wire cutters (5)
There are many different types
of wire cutter, and they range in
price from economical to costly.
Buy the best you can afford
because the cutting edges of
cheaper ones soon get damaged.
Good-quality cutters will cut
everything from wire and solder
strip to thin sheet and strips of
metal clay.

Hobby drill (6 and 7)
A small hobby drill (6) is not
essential for working in metal
clay, but using one can speed up
some tasks considerably. Many
different types of attachment
for sanding and polishing are
available and are normally
interchangeable between
different brands of hobby drill.
A chuck key (7) is used to open
the jaws of the drill to clamp
the various tools in them. Hobby
drills are only used on fired
metal clay, since plaster-dry clay
is too fragile.

Sanding disks (8)
These make short work of
smoothing rough metal surfaces.

Brass brushes (9)
These brush the metal after
firing and give a satin finish.

Silicone polishing point (10)
Used for preliminary polishing,
these points are available in
different shapes and grits
denoted by their color.

Buffing wheels (11 and 12)
Wool, felt, and cotton wheels and
felt points (11) are used with a
polishing paste such as Tripoli or
jeweler's rouge (12).

Radial bristle brushes (13)
These are invaluable for creating
a mirror finish on silver, copper,
and brass. The color denotes the
grit size embedded in the brush.
They are excellent for reaching
into tight areas.

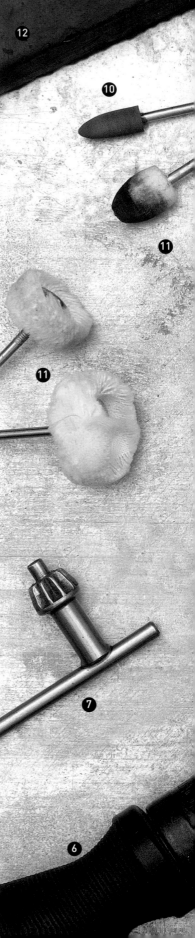

1

Basic
techniques

The basic techniques of working with metal clay involve three different stages: soft clay techniques are methods of shaping the soft clay; pre-finishing techniques are carried out on the plaster-dry clay; and finishing techniques involve working on the solid metal after the clay has been fired.

Soft clay techniques

Soft lump clay is the most widely used type of metal clay, and also the most versatile. Basic techniques are easy to learn and beginners invariably start with simple projects using this type of clay.

The techniques for shaping soft clay are virtually the same whether you are working with precious metal clay, such as silver and gold, or base metal clay, such as copper or bronze. There are small differences between different brands of each type of clay, and it is good to experiment to find what suits you best.

Soft metal clay is best worked with plenty of moisture within it, so that it is soft and pliable, but with a surface that is touch dry. If your clay is too dry, cracks will soon appear and the clay will crumble and become unworkable. If your clay is too wet, it will be difficult to control and your hands will become messy. See pages 31–33 for advice on how to adjust the consistency of your clay by either rehydrating or removing moisture.

Getting started

Before you start shaping the soft clay, check that you have everything to hand, because once you open the packet of clay the contents will begin to dry and you will want to work without interruption. Refer to the techniques over the following pages to find out which tools from the basic toolkit (see page 16) are required.

YOU WILL NEED

Basic tool kit (see page 16)

STEP 1 Open the packet and remove the clay, taking care to include any that is stuck to the inner wrapper.

STEP 2 Although the clay should be in perfect condition, it is a good idea to knead it briefly to ensure that any moisture is well distributed throughout the clay. Some clays require more kneading than others, and some base metal clays only become soft and pliable after firm kneading. If you have hot hands, try kneading inside plastic food wrap to prevent drying.

STEP 3 If you need to pause in your work, cover the clay with a piece of plastic food wrap and smooth it down well to remove all the air. This will delay the drying out of the clay. If your clay begins to feel hard and shows cracks as you work, you will need to rehydrate (see page 32).

STEP 4 ▶ Some clay is sold as a powder, which becomes lump clay when mixed with distilled water. Be guided by the manufacturer's instructions, in combination with the technique for reconstituting dried clay, described on page 35.

Rolling sheets

This technique is the starting point for many different projects. Learn how to roll sheets evenly and well to make your work refined and professional. The best all-round thickness to use for most projects is 4–6 p.c. (1–1.5mm). This gives sufficient strength to the clay when it is dry, and is economical in the use of metal clay. Plastic rolling guides are strips of measured thickness that can be used to aid rolling.

YOU WILL NEED

Basic tool kit (see page 16)

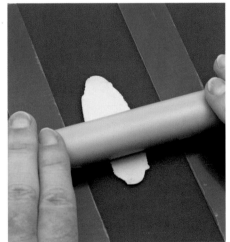

Plastic roller and guides

DEDICATED TOOLS

If you work with both silver and base metal clays, it is a good idea to keep a dedicated set of tools for the silver clay to avoid contamination. After firing, the same tools can be used.

▶ Flatten a piece of clay into a small pancake and place on a nonstick working surface. Put a rolling guide on either side and roll lightly over the clay. Rotate the clay 90 degrees, then roll again firmly until your roller is fully resting on the rolling guides. The sheet should peel away from the working surface easily, but take care not to stretch it. If you are not satisfied, fold in half and roll again.

TIPS FOR WORKING WITH SOFT METAL CLAY

- Always work clean: wipe your hands free of any sticky clay at all times and wipe away drying clay from your work surface and tools.
- Rub a thin smear of vegetable oil over your hands to prevent sticking, but avoid excessive amounts of oil, which will prevent the clay sticking to itself.
- Rehydrate the clay as soon as it shows any signs of drying (see page 32).
- Be careful not to get any foreign materials into the clay (crumbs, animal fur, etc.) because these can cause problems when firing.

PLAYING CARDS AS ROLLING GUIDES

Playing cards (p.c.) are an alternative to rolling guides and are widely used in metal clay work. They are not always consistent in thickness, but you can use the following conversions as a rough guide. Standard playing card thickness is usually 0.28 mm, but may be 0.25 mm to 0.32 mm thick, so commercial millimeter rolling guides are more accurate.

0.25 mm	= 1 p.c.
0.5 mm	= 2 p.c.
0.75 mm	= 3 p.c.
1 mm	= 4 p.c.
1.5 mm	= 6 p.c.
2 mm	= 8 p.c.

Stack the playing cards on either side of your metal clay to use them as rolling guides

TROUBLESHOOTING: ROLLING

The clay sheet has a line across it
The clay was folded badly before being rerolled. Form the clay back into a smooth ball, make a pancake again, checking that there are no fold marks, and reroll.

The clay sheet has small imperfections
The clay was too dry. Rehydrate (see page 32) and reroll.

The clay is not of an even thickness
Check that your nonstick surface is itself on a completely flat surface. Alternatively, you may have let the roller come off the rolling strip on one side.

The sheet cockles or bows when fired
You may be stretching the clay as you roll. To avoid this, roll gently in two directions, as described in Rolling sheets (see page 27), and avoid stretching the clay as you roll.

Cutting strips

Regular strips cut from sheets of clay are useful in many projects, such as to make bails (see page 60), for weaving, and for embellishing.

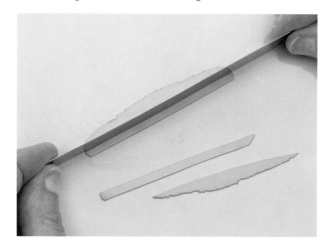

Making balls

Small round balls of clay are useful shapes to master. They can be used as embellishments and are also the starting point for further shapes such as ovals and teardrops. Larger solid balls of clay use up a lot of clay and are best made with a hollow core (see page 90).

STEP 1 Pinch off sufficient clay for the size of ball you wish to make and shape it roughly into a ball. Place the ball on the pad of one forefinger and use the forefinger of your other hand to rotate the lump of clay to make a neat ball. If the ball is not round, adjust the pressure as you roll to find the correct amount to use.

STEP 2 To make larger balls, lay the clay lump on the center of your palm. Use the palm of your other hand to rotate the clay between your hands and form it into a ball.

YOU WILL NEED

Basic tool kit (see page 16)

A clay sheet can be cut into strips using a tissue or slicer blade. Cut a straight edge first, then either cut the strips by eye or make marks in the clay with a ruler to ensure they are the same width all along their lengths. If you want a textured strip, texture the sheet before cutting it out (see pages 72–76).

Ovals

Ovals of clay are also basic shapes that are formed from balls.

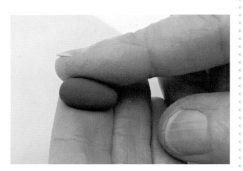

Form a ball of clay, then roll it gently back and forth with your finger to lengthen it into the desired oval shape.

Teardrops

These are useful shapes that can be used as embellishments or as basic elements for small figurative shapes such as birds. Flattened teardrops make small leaves.

Start with a ball of clay. Press gently on one side of the ball between your fingers at the angle shown. Roll the ball back and forth to a point on that side and make a teardrop shape. You can adjust the shape by further rolling to make the point longer.

Flexible clay

Some brands of metal clay can be mixed with glycerin and dried to make flexible clay.

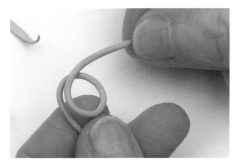

Roll out the clay, smear glycerin over the surface, roll up, and knead inside plastic wrap. Roll into sheets or make logs and leave to dry. The resulting strips, logs, and sheets have an indefinite working time. Test a small piece of clay first—PMC clays and several of Hadar's clays work well, but Art Clay Silver does not remain flexible.

Logs by hand

Long, thin logs of clay have dozens of uses and can be made by hand, with a sheet of plastic or glass, or with a syringe or an extruder.

YOU WILL NEED

Plastic sheet

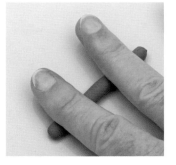

STEP 1 First form a ball of clay and lay it on your work surface. Roll the ball back and forth with your fingers, pressing down lightly to make it first an oval shape, then begin to form a log.

STEP 2 Continue rolling back and forth, rhythmically spreading out your fingers and contracting them as you roll. This will prevent any one finger from pressing in one place for too long, which would cause dents along the log.

STEP 3 Once the log is beginning to form, you can use a small sheet of plastic or glass, or a CD case, to roll the log back and forth. This will make a very even log but it can only be as long as the sheet.

STEP 4 For very thin logs of clay, first roll a thicker log, then hold one end in your nonworking hand. Use the other hand to roll the free end of the clay back and forth, pulling it away from the main log to extend and thin it. With practice, you can make logs less than 4 p.c. (1 mm) thick and about 6" (15 cm) long or more.

Using a syringe

A simple syringe can be used to make longer logs for coiling, plaiting, and winding. It is best to cut off the tip of the syringe to make it wider, so it is easier to extrude the clay.

YOU WILL NEED

Syringe

Glycerin (optional)

Vegetable oil

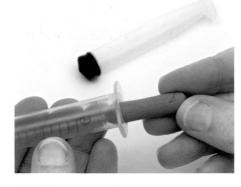

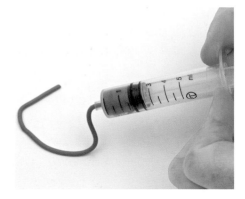

STEP 1 Knead the clay and add some water to make it as soft as possible (see page 32), otherwise the clay will be difficult to extrude. You can add a few drops of glycerin to help prevent it drying too fast. Shape the clay into a log, lightly oil the surface, and insert into the barrel of the syringe.

STEP 2 Press the syringe plunger to extrude the clay, letting the long coil of clay fall gently onto your work surface. If the clay is too stiff to extrude easily, remove it and add more water. The thin logs should be used immediately, before they dry.

These die plates can be attached to an extruder so that you can create a variety of cross section shapes and thicknesses.

Using an extruder

This is a useful gadget for making logs and snakes of different thicknesses and cross sections.

YOU WILL NEED

Extruder

Vegetable oil

Die for the required cross section

Glycerin (optional)

STEP 1 Knead the clay and add water and glycerin to make it as soft as possible and give you a long working time. Oil the clay lightly and smear a thin coat of oil inside the barrel of the extruder.

STEP 2 ▶ Shape the clay into a log and insert it into the barrel of the extruder. Screw on the die of your choice and wind the handle to extrude the clay. After use, clean the extruder thoroughly.

Tube attachments are available for some extruders for making tubes of different diameters, which can then be used to make tube beads. See page 97 for how to make tiny tubes for locket hinges.

Keeping clay workable

Metal clay is at the perfect workable consistency when it is soft and pliable but with a touch-dry surface. The techniques in this section show you how to rehydrate clay that is too dry, remove excess moisture from clay that is too wet, and how to store leftover clay to ensure it will be workable again at a later date.

Creating jewelry with metal clay involves handling small pieces of clay that dry as you work, which can worry beginners. However, learning a few simple strategies for rehydrating the clay soon removes the anxiety, and once you are confident that you can easily return your clay to the moist state, you will work with far greater freedom. The opposite process to rehydrating clay is to remove water from clay that is wet, sticky, and messy.

How to decide if clay needs rehydrating

You can tell if your clay has become too dry to work successfully in several ways. If any of the conditions below apply, your clay is too dry and you need to rehydrate. However, if the clay has become a hard lump that cannot be rolled out or kneaded, you will need to reconstitute it (see page 34).

YOU WILL NEED

Basic tool kit (see page 16)

When you roll out the clay, small patches appear on the surface that rolling does not remove.

The edges of the clay crack or feel hard as you roll or knead.

The body of the clay cracks when a log is bent and the clay crumbles.

Rehydrating

A warm ambient temperature and the heat of your hands will speed the drying process, so learning how to rehydrate metal clay is essential to success in using this material. If you are always rushing to create a piece of jewelry before the clay dries too much to handle, you will never be comfortable in your work.

Rehydrating metal clay is simple to do and is always best achieved when the clay shows the first signs of drying. When this happens, do not spray the clay surface with water, but follow these steps to rehydrate.

A useful tool for rehydrating clay is a plastic file pocket that has been slit open to make a double plastic sheet, inside which you can roll the clay to contain any mess. Alternatively, you can use plastic food wrap, but be careful that it does not break up as you knead, otherwise shreds of plastic may become embedded in the clay.

YOU WILL NEED

Basic tool kit (see page 16)

File pocket cut along the sealed short edge so that it can be fully opened. Alternatively use plastic wrap

Palette knife

Olive or vegetable oil

STEP 1 If the clay is only slightly too dry, you may find that firmly rolling it is sufficient to crush any dry bits and distribute the remaining water in the clay. Roll the clay out as thinly as possible on the nonstick surface; you should be able to roll it paper thin. Fold in half and roll again several times. If it becomes smooth and malleable again you do not need to add any water.

STEP 2 If after rolling and folding several times the clay is still not sufficiently malleable, wet your finger and apply water all over one side of the sheet.

STEP 3 Dry your hands and fold the sheet of clay up so that the water is enclosed.

STEP 4 Open out the file pocket and lightly oil the insides with vegetable oil.

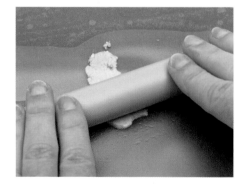

STEP 5 Place the clay in the file pocket and roll it out firmly through the plastic to make a thin sheet again. Any escaping moisture or wet clay is contained inside the pocket.

STEP 6 Open the pocket and fold the clay up, using a palette knife or spatula to scrape it together if necessary. Roll it out again and continue until all signs of wetness have disappeared.

ALTERNATIVE METHOD Instead of using a file pocket, you can knead the wetted clay in a piece of plastic food wrap. Remove the clay and knead it in your hands to check that it is soft and pliable. If necessary, repeat the process to add more water.

Returning wet clay to a workable state

Occasionally, clay straight out of the packet can be too wet and sticky to work with, or you may find you have added too much water when rehydrating dry clay. Nonstick silicone baking parchment is ideal for absorbing excess moisture.

YOU WILL NEED

Basic tool kit (see page 16)

Silicone baking parchment

Some base metal clay, and Art Clay Copper in particular, can become covered with a dark oxidized layer if it is exposed to air for too long, or not wrapped tightly when stored. For this reason, it is best to use it up quickly after opening. If you need to store the soft clay, exclude as much air as possible when wrapping. A drop of lavender oil kneaded into the clay will help reduce oxidation.

Copper and bronze clays that are allowed to dry out and are then ground into powder for recycling can be stored for many weeks in the powder state.

STEP 1 This clay is too wet on the surface. This happens if you spray or brush the clay surface with water when you are forming it with your fingers. If you must spray with water because a piece is only part finished and you need to keep the clay soft, spray, then wait until the surface is touch dry before continuing.

STEP 2 Place the clay lump inside a folded sheet of silicone baking parchment and roll it out thinly inside the paper. The paper will absorb excess moisture and dry the surface of the clay. Peel the clay off the parchment and fold in half.

STEP 3 Repeat if necessary until no stickiness remains. The clay should peel away from the paper, but if any pieces remain attached, rub the main clay over the stuck pieces to gather them up.

An oxidized layer should normally be cut off and discarded before using the clay, but check the manufacturer's instructions. It is also possible to wash the layer off under a running faucet while rubbing gently with a finger.

Storing clay

Leftover scraps of soft clay can be successfully stored for weeks at a time in an airtight container. Clay that has become rock hard will need to be reconstituted (see page 34).

YOU WILL NEED

Basic tool kit (see page 16)

Airtight container

STEP 1 Wrap any scraps of leftover clay tightly in plastic food wrap. Rehydrate them before storing if they are even slightly dry.

STEP 2 ▶ Place in an airtight container: a small glass jelly jar is more airtight than a plastic container. Fill any air space with packed plastic wrap and sprinkle a little water on top before shutting the jar tightly. Clay stored in this way should keep moist for several weeks, but check it periodically to make sure it is not drying out.

Reclaiming and reconstituting clay

Working in any material will always produce waste. With metal clay this may be soft clay scraps, failed projects, or simply a piece that you dislike. This section details the many ways you can make best use of your metal clay with economical practices, recycling, reconstituting, and reclaiming.

The price of precious metal has risen a great deal in recent years, and this has inevitably impacted on the price of metal clay, in particular the precious metal clays. The following tips can substantially reduce the amount of clay that you use.

Roll clay sheets thinly. For many projects, sheets of clay 2 p.c. (0.5 mm) thick will be as successful as thicker sheets. However, it is wise to work at about 4 p.c. (1 mm) thick when you are a beginner to reduce the chances of breaking your work in the plaster-dry stage.

Work smaller. Large, chunky jewelry is great, but so are small and more delicate pieces.

Use mixed media. Pieces do not have to be made entirely of silver, instead try combining it with base metal clays, glass, textiles, wood, and other materials.

Use polymer clay. Choose polymer clay to back or infill pieces after firing so that the precious metal content is reduced. See page 174.

Use hollow core or formers. To avoid working in solid metal, which uses up far more clay, use hollow core techniques or formers. See page 90.

Concave molding. When molding clay, press it into the mold to give a concave back. See page 77.

▲ **TEXTURED BEAD,** *TRACEY SPURGIN*
Making pieces with a hollow core uses less clay and makes jewelry lighter to wear.

Save and reconstitute. Save all your unfired clay scraps for reconstituting. This also applies to dried clay waste from filing or carving, but do not use dust from sanding, which may be contaminated by the grit. See page 35.

Save and recycle. Save any unwanted fired silver for recycling into new pieces. See page 36.

Design for economy. With the above points in mind, design your jewelry carefully, avoiding unnecessary thickness and using other materials for hidden parts, such as the back of a piece.

▲ **MIXED MATERIAL NECKLACE,**
BARBARA SPERLING
Combining silver clay with other materials will make your clay go further. Here polymer clay images framed in silver clay are combined with polymer clay beads to make a luscious whole.

▲ **CUFF,** *MARY ANN NELSON*
Silver clay textured with ammonites embellishes a faux bone cuff.

These dried out pieces are perfect for reconstituting

STEP 1 Put the lumps of clay in a mortar and crush hard with the pestle. Pound hard to break up the lumps, then grind with a circular motion. You need to make a fine powder.

STEP 2 Use a tea strainer to sieve the powder. This is not essential if you grind it really finely. Any lumps in the strainer can be ground further—if they will not grind up, discard them. You can now store the powder for later reconstitution if you wish.

Reconstituting dried-out clay

Any type of metal clay that has been allowed to dry out completely can be ground into a powder and reconstituted remarkably easily. This may apply to a piece that you forgot, which has dried out in its wrapper, a piece that broke too badly for repair in the plaster-dry stage, or that you decided you did not like. You can also use this technique for clay you have collected from filing or carving.

YOU WILL NEED

Small pestle and mortar

Fine tea strainer
(useful but not essential)

Eyedropper or small spray bottle

Palette knife

Glycerin (optional)

File pocket or plastic wrap

STEP 3 Put most of the powder onto a large ceramic tile, but save some for adding if the mix becomes too wet. Use the eyedropper to add a few drops of water (or spray the powder with water) and mix with a palette knife or spatula, scraping the edges into the center as you work.

STEP 4 Only add sufficient water to just moisten the clay, until all the dry powder has gone and the mix is like breadcrumbs. If you add too much water, mix in some of the reserved powder.

STEP 5 Keep mixing and the clay will begin to clump together. You can also add glycerin to aid the water retention of the clay, but use sparingly—about one drop per 10g of clay.

STEP 6 Lightly oil your hands with vegetable oil and gather up the clay. Press it together in your fingers. If it will not hold together, add a little more water.

Continued next page ▶

Recycling soft clay
Save all your scraps of soft clay as you work.

◄ Wrap them in plastic food wrap and store for later use (see page 33), or add them to your paste pot (see page 37). Do not mix different types of clay together when combining scraps of lump clay, because they may have shrinkage and cracking problems when dried and fired. However, you should not have any problems combining different types of one brand of silver clay in paste pots, you just need to fire for the highest schedule required by any of the types in the mix.

STEP 7 Knead the clay well in your fingers. If it feels granular, put it into a plastic file pocket and roll it out very thinly. Fold in half and roll again repeatedly until the lumpiness disappears (see Rehydrating, page 32). Wrap it in plastic food wrap and leave to rest for at least one hour before use.

RECYCLING FIRED SILVER
Fired silver can be sent as scrap to a precious metals dealer or a jewelry supplier that offers this service (see Resources, page 186). Check if there is a charge before you send in your scrap, because if you send in a small amount, the value may not cover the charge.

Alternatively, there are various ways to use your fired scrap silver. As well as the examples shown here, you can create new pieces of jewelry by incorporating scraps into new designs using soldering, riveting, or linking. See pages 64, 102, and 104.

▲ Make rings
Flat pieces of fired metal can be made into exciting and unusual rings. Forge the pieces on a ring mandrel into the correct curve for the required ring size, then join the pieces using oil paste or by soldering. See page 143.

▼ Practice pieces
Use fired pieces for practicing soldering, riveting, and other mechanical techniques. See pages 64 and 102.

▲ Silver balls
Silver scraps can be cut into small pieces and melted with a blowtorch into silver balls to decorate your work.

▲ Embellishing
Use fired pieces to practice embellishment techniques, such as enameling, oxidizing, and keum boo. See pages 160, 170, and 183.

Paste techniques

Paste and slip are two states of lump clay with water added to make it semi-liquid. Paste refers to the stiffer version, while slip is more fluid.

Paste and slip are simple to make and important materials for working with metal clay. While they are mostly used to join clay pieces together, correct blemishes, and fill holes in the plaster-dry state, they are also used for decoration and creating pieces of jewelry.

Oil paste, is used to mend and join fired silver clay pieces, while silver overlay paste is another form that is used mainly for decorating glass and ceramic (see page 180).

Paste and slip can be used for the following:
- To smooth blemishes and fill holes in soft or plaster-dry clay.
- For attaching soft clay to itself—use the slip as a glue to ensure a strong join.
- For attaching soft clay to plaster-dry clay.
- For mending breaks in plaster-dry clay (see page 43).
- For attaching findings to soft clay or plaster-dry clay (see page 56).
- To add texture to soft or dried clay (see page 164).
- Stenciling techniques (see page 165).
- To make leaf and seed pod replicas (see page 88).
- For refilling filigree syringes (see page 123).

Making paste

You can make small quantities of paste as you need it, or make a quantity to keep in an airtight jar for future use.

Silver clay paste is stable and will keep indefinitely in an airtight pot. If it dries out, simply add water to reconstitute. Bronze paste develops a black surface, but this is only due to the tin in the bronze separating out, and so can be stirred in again. Copper paste will oxidize and develop a black surface, so is best only made in small quantities as you need it. If you let copper paste dry out, it will not oxidize and the dried flakes can be stored until they are next needed to make paste.

YOU WILL NEED

Basic tool kit (see page 16)

Palette knife

Airtight container

STEP 1 To make small amounts of paste from lump clay, flatten a small piece of soft clay on a tile and use a brush loaded with water to wet it. Rub with the brush and slip will be dissolved out of the lump. Continue rubbing to make a thicker paste.

STEP 2 When you have finished with the paste, let it dry on the tile, then use a craft knife to scrape the dried flakes off into a paste pot for future use.

STEP 3 To make paste from dried-out metal clay, put the dried pieces into a small jar or pot and just cover them with water. Leave overnight and then stir well. You can add more water if necessary.

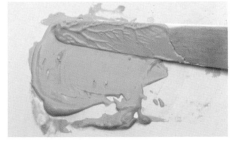

STEP 4 For smoother paste, scoop the wetted clay out onto a tile and use a palette knife to work the clay, pressing hard to crush any lumps and smearing firmly with the knife until smooth. Scrape the paste off the tile and store in an airtight container.

Joining soft clay with paste

Paste is used to attach clay pieces together, both in the soft and the plaster-dry stages. See page 43 for mending plaster-dry clay with paste.

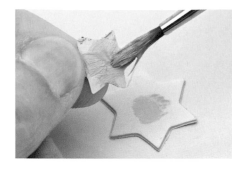

STEP 1 When adding fresh pieces of clay to soft clay, you can simply brush the clay with water before pressing on the new piece. However, brushing with paste will ensure a stronger join. Brush paste over the underside of the piece to be joined. Press the two pieces together and wipe away the excess with a damp paintbrush. Dry fully before firing.

BUZZ BOX,
TERRY KOVALCIK
Paste can also be used as a sophisticated embellishment. Here it is painted on in many layers to create the bee motifs on this pendant. See page 165.

Using silver oil paste

This commercial product is produced by the manufacturers of Art Clay products, but can be used with all types of fired silver clay. It is used to join together two pieces of fired silver to mend breaks, or to attach fine silver findings. It has to be fired in a kiln at 1,470° F (800°C) or higher, so should not be used to attach sterling findings, which break down at this high temperature. It becomes pure 999 silver after firing, so any joins are invisible and can be worked as silver.

Oil paste is diluted as necessary with its accompanying bottle of solvent. Refer to the manufacturer's instructions for full information.

STEP 1 Scoop a small quantity of paste out of the pot and mix with a little solvent if necessary to make a sticky mixture. Apply to the parts to be joined using a metal modeling tool (brushes will be ruined) and press them together. Take care when removing any excess, otherwise the pieces may come apart.

STEP 2 Leave to dry at room temperature or as recommended by the manufacturer. Remove excess oil paste with a cocktail stick. You may need to prop the pieces to keep them from falling apart because the paste is not very sticky. Fire as recommended and file or sand away surplus after firing (see pages 58–61).

HOMEMADE OIL PASTE

You can make your own oil paste by adding pure lavender essential oil to metal clay paste. The recommended quantities are one or two drops per gram of paste. Mix to make a buttery consistency and then use as with commercial oil paste. It is best to test first with your chosen brand of clay, since results may depend on the brand.

Drying techniques

There are many different methods of drying metal clay pieces before firing. The techniques are simple and require no special equipment.

Metal clays must be dried thoroughly before being fired. Any moisture remaining within the clay can lead to cracking and blisters during firing. It is also important that the clay is fully dry before any pre-finishing techniques are used, otherwise the piece is likely to break.

Domestic oven drying

▼ This is a reliable and trouble-free method of drying metal clay. Place the finished pieces on a heatproof cookie sheet or a ceramic tile and put in the oven at 300°F (150°C) for about 30 minutes—a fan oven works particularly well. This ensures that the clay is never overheated and the length of time is enough to dry all pieces under 24 p.c. (6 mm). Thicker pieces can be left in the oven for longer as necessary.

Using a hot plate

An electric hot plate on a low setting can be a reliable method for drying. It is difficult to measure the temperature of a hot plate, but it is important that it does not exceed 480°F (250°C), when the binder will begin to burn off, so using a low setting is imperative.

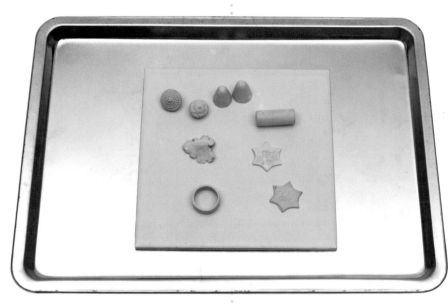

Air drying

Air drying can be unreliable because so many variables affect how quickly the clay dries if left to dry naturally. Pieces left for several days can be assumed to be dry provided they are not left in a cold and damp place; however, it is safest to use a heat source. Placing the piece to be dried in an airing cupboard, over a radiator, or near a stove will speed up the drying considerably, and a piece that is no thicker than about 12 p.c. (3 mm) should dry overnight in such conditions. Slow-dry clay or clay with added glycerin will take longer.

Using a food dehydrator

Expensive but useful if you already have one, a food dehydrator can be used in a similar way to a domestic oven, but the gentle heat makes warping less likely.

Using a kiln

If you own a kiln, it may seem convenient to dry pieces in the kiln before firing but kilns are rarely able to hold a low temperature with any accuracy. If your kiln is able to maintain a temperature of 300°F (150°C) within about 10 degrees then you can use it in the same way as a domestic oven.

Using a hair-dryer

Adding a more concentrated source of heat in the form of a hair-dryer speeds drying further. However this is a noisy and tedious method that takes at least ten minutes, depending on the type of clay. It is best used for drying paste that has been added to a piece that has already been fully dried.

▲ Place the piece to be dried on a stainless steel mesh so that the hot air can pass through it. Hold the hair-dryer about 1" (25 mm) away from the piece and put on full heat and air. Move the hot air over the piece repeatedly for as long as required. Surface drying of paste usually requires about two minutes of hair-dryer heating.

Using a heat gun

A heat gun of the kind used for melting embossing powders is quicker and quieter than a hair-dryer. These guns reach temperatures of up to 660°F (350°C), which is well above the temperature at which the binder in the clay begins to burn off. For this reason, only use a heat gun for short bursts of about 15 seconds at a time. Burning off the binder may result in the piece flaming, or becoming too fragile for any pre-finishing. Like a hair-dryer, a heat gun is most useful for drying paste on the surface of an already dried piece.

▼ Place the piece on a heatproof surface such as a ceramic tile and dry with the heat gun held 1–2" (25–50 mm) away from the clay. There is less air flow than with a hair-dryer and this means the piece is less likely to be blown away.

Using a mug warmer

◄ These are handy gadgets for drying small pieces, but the heat produced varies considerably, so you will need to find out by experience how long items take to dry on one. Mug warmers are useful because they can sit on your table as you work.

AVOIDING WARPING WHILE DRYING

Metal clay can warp during drying, which is best avoided if possible, although warped pieces can be corrected after firing (see page 55). Warping is more likely with thin sheets of metal clay, so dry these naturally for a while before using a heat source.

A good way to prevent warping is to create a piece on a ceramic tile so that it sticks to the tile and is prevented from rising up as it dries. Dry the piece on the tile and after drying it will have freed itself. A tile placed face down on top of a flat piece of clay before placing it in the oven will also prevent warping.

If a piece does warp, spray it lightly with water and leave it to soak in for about five minutes. Check that the surface is touch dry, then cover with a tile as above and dry again.

Pre-finishing techniques

Once the soft lump clay has been shaped and dried, it can be further refined before firing. This is the pre-finishing stage.

Dried clay is normally referred to as plaster dry or greenware, and in this state the clay is fragile, breaking like a cookie if handled roughly. This means that there is a compromise to be made: the dried clay is easier to work than solid silver, but beginners often find that too much working on a fragile plaster-dry piece results in a breakage. It is therefore a matter of personal choice as to whether you prefer to prefinish or to use silversmithing skills after firing (see pages 50–55).

Sanding

This is the most effective way of smoothing and refining metal clay in the plaster-dry state (see page 18 for information on the grits of sandpaper to use for different stages of finishing). Sanding pads are most useful for curved pieces because they can be molded round the shapes. Wash sanding pads periodically in a net bag or old pair of pantyhose in a washing machine and they will last for a long time if only used for plaster-dry clay.

Use sandpaper for pieces that are flat or straight.

Work over a tile or shallow tray so that the sanding powder will be contained, and wear a dust mask. The sanded powder should not be recycled because it will contain particles from the sanding pad or paper.

Superfine sanding pads (500–600 grit) are the most useful for refining plaster dry clay. This is because work done with finer grits will largely be undone during the firing process.

YOU WILL NEED

Basic tool kit (see page 16)

STEP 1 Support the piece to be sanded carefully. Flat pieces should be held in your hand or placed on a flat surface. If you need to work on the edge of a piece, support it well on both sides with the finger and thumb of your nonworking hand.

STEP 2 Support rings from within and rub the sanding pad gently back and forth over the area to be sanded. A small shower of powder will show the sanding pad is cutting and smoothing. Take care over textured areas, since the sanding pad may remove too much clay and spoil the detail.

STEP 3 Sandpaper laid flat on the work surface is useful for sanding any area that needs to be completely flat.

STEP 4 Rotate the piece in a figure of eight on the sandpaper to ensure a smooth finish. This can be used for the sides of a band ring or the two halves of a lentil bead that need to be joined together.

Filing

Some blemishes need more than sanding, so use a fine file to remove rough edges and excess clay at angles or inside rings (see page 52 for filing techniques). Waste clay from filing can be recycled (see page 35).

YOU WILL NEED

Basic tool kit (see page 16)

Support the piece carefully as for sanding. File away from you in smooth strokes, pushing the file lightly over the surface without any pressure, to avoid snapping the piece. If powder is produced, the file is working. After filing, use a sanding pad to further smooth the surface.

Drilling

Whether for attaching findings, embedding stones, or for decoration, the best time to drill holes in metal clay is at the plaster-dry stage. You can make a hole in the soft clay with a needle, but this rarely produces a neat result. Drilling through plaster-dry clay is far easier than through solid fired metal, and if you make a mistake, the hole can be easily filled with paste (refer to page 18 for advice on different sizes of drill bits for drilling metal clay).

YOU WILL NEED

Basic tool kit (see page 16)

Drill bit

STEP 1 A small pilot hole makes drilling far easier, so when the clay is soft, mark the position of the hole with a small dent using a blunt tapestry needle. After drying, support the piece at the back with your finger and twist the drill bit in the hole. Do not use pressure, otherwise the piece may crack.

STEP 2 If the clay is already dry, mark the position of the hole with a pencil and apply a drop of water with the tip of a fine paintbrush to make a soft spot to begin drilling.

ALLOW FOR SHRINKAGE

When making holes for jump rings, drill a hole at least 10 percent larger than the size required. See page 58 for advice on where to position holes for jump rings.

STEP 3 A small shower of powder will confirm that the drill bit is cutting the hole. The bit will only cut when turned clockwise, but it is easier to turn it back and forth in the hole.

STEP 4 When you feel the bit coming through the clay on your finger behind, keep turning until it is fully through. Then remove the bit by twisting gently as you pull it out of the hole.

Joining dried clay with paste

Paste is invaluable for pre-finishing pieces, including joining dried clay pieces together.

YOU WILL NEED

Basic tool kit (see page 16)

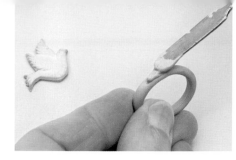

STEP 1 To join dried pieces of clay together, first make sure the pieces fit together snugly, and sand or file the join if necessary. Use a flat modeling tool or small spatula to apply paste generously to one surface.

STEP 2 Press the pieces together and use a damp paintbrush to remove excess paste. Dry thoroughly and sand or file away any further excess.

Caulking

Lump clay is better than paste both for filling larger holes and for spaces between attached elements.

YOU WILL NEED

Basic tool kit (see page 16)

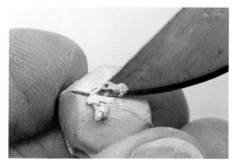

Press soft lump clay into the space, then brush over with water to ensure the fresh clay bonds with the dry clay. Smooth with a tool or with your fingers.

Mending with paste

Use paste to mend broken plaster-dry pieces. After drying and sanding, the original break will be invisible. You should also use paste to fill any small holes and dents in plaster dry clay and to reinforce attached findings and joins.

YOU WILL NEED

Basic tool kit (see page 16)

STEP 1 To mend a snapped plaster-dry piece, apply paste along the broken edge of one piece.

STEP 2 Press the two parts together. If the paste wells up along the crack as the pieces meet, wipe the excess away with a fingertip.

STEP 3 Use a fine paintbrush to add more paste if necessary to fill the crack, taking care to wipe it away from any textured parts. On smooth surfaces, build the paste higher than the surrounding area, because it will shrink during drying and the crack may then reappear.

STEP 4 Dry thoroughly, then sand over the join, which should be invisible. If not, apply more paste, dry, and sand again. Treat the piece gently until it is fired, because mends may be fragile.

Firing techniques

The three main methods of firing metal clay are using a blowtorch, on a gas stovetop, or in a kiln. While a kiln will give the greatest versatility, the other simple methods have much to recommend them.

FIRING DIFFERENT KINDS OF CLAY

Base metal and silver alloy clays

These clays will oxidize during firing, which means that the metal combines with oxygen to produce a black surface called "firestain" or "firescale." Various strategies are used to avoid this. Some brands advise kiln firing in charcoal or a wrapping to exclude oxygen, while other clays must be plunged into water straight from the kiln. However, some types of copper clay can be torch or stovetop fired.

Gold and fine silver clays

These precious metal clays do not oxidize on firing and can be fired on an open kiln shelf. Many silver clays can also be fired on a gas stovetop or with a blowtorch (for full information see Materials, page 10).

Kiln firing is the most versatile method and can be used to fire all types of metal clay, however, a kiln is an expensive piece of equipment and is not essential if you choose clays that can be fired with a blowtorch or on a gas stovetop. It is important to refer to the manufacturer's instructions for your particular clay, since firing techniques vary considerably between brands, clay types, and metal types.

When metal clay is fired it goes through a number of stages. First, the binder burns away. Sintering follows, when the metal particles that make up the clay heat to a point just below their melting point and fuse together. Finally, the piece is cooled, either slowly or by quenching (plunging in cold water).

After firing, the resultant metal is brushed and polished, which hardens and strengthens it.

SAFETY

Firing of any kind involves high temperatures and potential hazards, so observe the following safety rules whenever you fire metal clay:

- Only fire metal clay pieces that have been dried fully.
- Always fire on a heatproof surface. One or two large ceramic floor tiles laid on your work surface are ideal.
- Keep firing away from drapes or fabrics and tie back long hair.
- Wear insulated gloves and use long-handled tongs when removing pieces from a kiln.

- Avoid looking into a kiln when it is glowing red hot—safety glasses should be worn.
- Beware of dropping red-hot pieces onto yourself or onto an unprotected surface. Do not fire with bare feet.
- If you quench hot pieces, listen out for the hiss that indicates that the piece has been cooled: if you have not heard the hiss, the piece may still be very hot.
- Remember that a red-hot piece of metal will instantly burn a hole in a wooden table if dropped, and may start a fire.
- Keep children and animals away from firing processes.

Fireproof gloves protect your hands when removing pieces from a hot kiln

SHRINKAGE

All metal clays shrink during firing, and the amount they shrink by varies between brands and types of clay. The usual amount of shrinkage is between 8 and 12 percent, which is only just noticeable in most metal clay projects. The shrinkage occurs because the clay contracts when the binder in it burns away. Shrinkage becomes important if you are replicating an original piece in metal clay, or when making rings or other jewelry that has to fit a particular size. See the tables on pages 10 and 12 for further information on the shrinkage of different clays. See Ring making on page 135 for details on allowing for ring shrinkage.

Blowtorch firing

Suitable for most fine silver clays (see page 46), blowtorch firing is fast and efficient, although it is only practicable to fire one or two small pieces at a time.

- Use for small projects of suitable silver clays. Though some brands of copper clay can also be fired in this way, ensure you check the manufacturer's instructions and timing requirements.
- Use a blowtorch that will reach 1,470° F (800° C) minimum, and that ideally has an adjustable flame. Chef's brûlée torches may not be hot enough, but you can carry out a test fire first to be sure (see Testing, page 46).
- Take care not to melt silver clay while firing (see Step 4, page 46).
- Blowtorch firing is not suitable for pieces that include glass, or gemstones larger than 5 mm in diameter.

Parts of a small, hand-held blowtorch

The controls for gas, oxygen, and ignition indicated on the blowtorch below may be different to yours but will serve the same function.

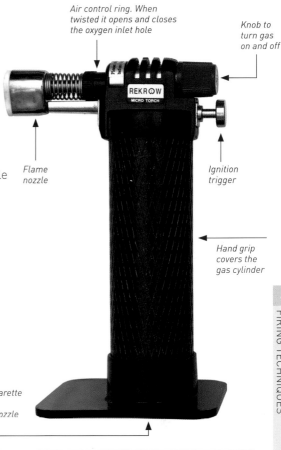

Air control ring. When twisted it opens and closes the oxygen inlet hole

Knob to turn gas on and off

Flame nozzle

Ignition trigger

Hand grip covers the gas cylinder

Fill with cigarette lighter gas through a nozzle in the base

Know your flame

Familiarize yourself with the various flame settings on your blowtorch.

Cool flame: This flame is mostly gas, because the oxygen control has been set to minimum.

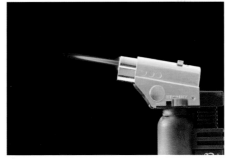

Hot flame: Here, the oxygen flow is turned to maximum. The flame is all blue with a sharp point, and is called a "pencil flame." This is the hottest setting and the one to use when lighting your torch.

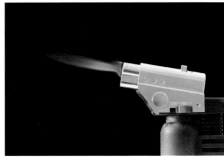

Medium flame: This is the ideal flame for firing metal clay. The oxygen control has been turned up full and then turned down until the flame is softer and feathery.

45

FIRING TECHNIQUES

Firing with a blowtorch

Blowtorch firing is quick, simple, and ideal for rapid firing of small pieces.

YOU WILL NEED:

Basic tool kit (see page 16)

Blowtorch

Firebrick

Kitchen timer

STEP 1 Place the dried clay piece on a firebrick. Light the torch and adjust the air flow so that the flame is midway between the oxygenated blue pencil flame (very hot) and the yellow pure gas flame (cooler).

STEP 2 Begin to heat the piece with a waving motion, holding the torch at an angle so that the flame strokes over the piece. After a few moments, flames will come from the clay, showing that the binder is burning off.

STEP 3 Continue heating and the piece will blacken then turn white as the sintering begins. You may notice it will shrink at this point.

STEP 4 When the piece reaches a pale orange glow, begin timing and fire as detailed in the table below. Keep the color at the same pale orange, pulling the torch away if it glows too hot. If a silver surface begins to show, pull the torch away, as the silver is beginning to melt.

STEP 5 When the time is up, you can either leave the piece to cool for at least 20 minutes, or quench it by grasping it with tweezers and plunging it into a ceramic or glass bowl of cool water. Make sure the piece gives a strong hiss as you quench it, if not it may not be fully cool. Do not quench pieces that contain stones or other inclusions, since they may shatter.

TIMINGS FOR BLOWTORCH AND GAS STOVETOP FIRING OF SUITABLE SILVER CLAYS

	Firing time	Maximum size
Blowtorch	All Art Clay Silver clays: Small pieces: 4 p.c. (1 mm) thick or less: 1–1½ minutes Thicker pieces: up to 2½ minutes PMC+: All pieces at least 5 minutes PMC3: All pieces at least 2 minutes	25 g 1½" (40 mm) diameter
Gas stovetop	Art Clay (all types): 5 minutes PMC3: 10 minutes	30 g 2" long x 1¼" wide x ¾" high (50 x 30 x 20 mm) The piece must fit in the red-hot glowing area

TESTING

It is highly recommended to fire small test pieces of clay when using a blowtorch or gas stovetop to fire for the first time.

Make some small strips of silver clay about 1" long x ⅛" wide x 1/32" thick (25 x 3 x 1 mm). Fire as recommended for the clay and cool. Try to break the fired pieces. They should bend into a "U" before snapping, and ideally should be capable of being bent back and forth several times before breaking. If they break, then they were either not fired hot enough or long enough.

Gas stovetop firing

This is a reliable method of firing many types of silver clay. All types of Art Clay Silver and PMC3 can be fired successfully in this way. It is an economical method of firing and ideal for those who do not want the expense of a kiln, or do not want to use a blowtorch.

- Can be used for PMC3 Silver clay and all types of Art Clay Silver.
- Suitable for small pieces of 30 grams or less.
- The piece or pieces to be fired should fit inside the red-hot glowing area on the stainless steel mesh.
- Do not use to fire pieces that incorporate glass or gemstones larger than 5 mm in diameter.
- Camping gas or domestic gas stovetops are both suitable for use.
- Use the hottest burner on a domestic hob and full setting during firing.
- Some gas stoves may not reach a high enough temperature to fully fire the piece (see Testing, page 46).
- It is best to fire at night for the first time, so that you can dim the lights and see the pale orange glow more easily, since it is not as intense as it is with a blowtorch.

YOU WILL NEED:

Basic tool kit (see page 16)

Gas stovetop or camping gas stove

Stainless steel mesh (available from metal clay suppliers or enameling suppliers)

Kitchen timer

STEP 1 Place a stainless steel mesh on the burner. If you are using a domestic gas stovetop, use the largest burner. Turn on the gas burner and note where the mesh glows red hot. These are the areas where the clay pieces must be placed to ensure that they are fully fired.

STEP 2 Turn off the gas and use tweezers to place the fully dried pieces on the areas that glowed red hot. You can fire several pieces at a time as long as the whole of each piece is in a red-hot area.

STEP 3 Turn on the gas again, and after a few moments the pieces will begin to give off small flames. This is the binder burning away.

STEP 4 Continue heating and the pieces will turn white, then begin to glow a pale orange. At this point begin timing and keep heating on full for the time given in the table on page 46. When the time is up, turn off the gas and leave the pieces to cool, or quench them (see Step 5 of Firing with a blowtorch, opposite).

Kiln firing

There are many different kilns available, and choosing one can be a bewildering process for the uninitiated. For firing any type of metal clay, the kiln must have the ability to hold the temperature at a particular heat. This is usually done with a digital controller that is built into the kiln, along with a pyrometer to monitor the temperature inside the chamber.

Tips for kiln firing fine silver clay:

• Pieces that are made purely of fine silver clay and that contain no stones or other inclusions can be placed in a kiln that is at the firing temperature.

• Hollow core items should be placed in a cold kiln and ramped slowly to avoid the core burnout overheating the silver.

• Fire silver clay at the highest temperature recommended by the manufacturers for a strong result.

Kiln firing silver clay

Fine silver metal clay is the easiest type to fire because it is pure 999 silver and there are no concerns about firescale. It can be fired on an open shelf for a relatively short time. Silver alloy clays should be fired as per base metal clays opposite.

YOU WILL NEED

Fiber firing board

Fiber blanket

Long-handled tongs

Insulated gloves

STEP 1 Make sure that the pieces to be fired are completely dry and lay them on a fiber or ceramic firing board. Leave a small gap between pieces, although they are unlikely to stick together even if they do touch.

STEP 2 Pieces that are irregularly shaped can be fired on fiber blanket with small pieces torn off and placed strategically to support them. Hollow core items should have a circle of fiber blanket enclosing them but be open at the top. This is to protect adjacent pieces from the burning core.

STEP 3 Place small pieces of fiberboard or kiln props on the floor of the kiln and put the board on top of these. This allows the heat to circulate and is better for the kiln. Program the kiln to ramp (heat up) at full speed and set the temperature. It is always best to fire silver clay at its highest recommended temperature for as long as possible—refer to the manufacturer's instructions—to ensure maximum strength of the pieces.

STEP 4 After the firing time, turn off the kiln and allow to cool a little before removing the board. Remove using long-handled tongs and insulated gloves. You can leave the pieces to cool down naturally or quench them (see Step 5 of Firing with a blowtorch, page 46).

Kiln firing base metal clays

There are many different kinds of base metal clay available, and their manufacturers give a variety of firing requirements. Follow the instructions carefully when firing these clays. Most clays need to be fired in charcoal to prevent oxidation and some manufacturers recommend two firings: the first at a lower temperature uncovered by charcoal to burn off the binder; the second in charcoal to sinter the clay. Other types can be fired on an open shelf and then quenched immediately to prevent oxidation.

YOU WILL NEED

Basic tool kit (see page 16)

Firing container

Charcoal

Ceramic paper

STEP 1 ▲ When firing with charcoal you will need a container. You can improvise with a small clay flowerpot, or use a stainless steel container such as this sugar bowl from a kitchen equipment store. Stainless steel containers can be cooled quickly. Alternatively, you can make a container using fiber paper or a pet food can.

MAKING A FIBER BOX

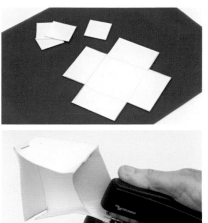

To make this alternative container, cut a sheet of fiber paper into a cross shape. After folding up the sides, staple them together. This will only last for a few firings.

STEP 2 Put a ½" (13 mm) layer of acid-washed charcoal in the bottom of the container—a flowerpot in this case. Place the dried clay pieces on top of the charcoal, keeping them away from the sides and each other.

STEP 3 Cover the pieces with a layer of charcoal, at least ½" (13mm) thick. Some clays need to be covered so use a piece of fiberboard kiln shelf to cover the container if required.

STEP 4 Place the pot on supports inside the kiln, positioning it furthest from the door in a front loader to be in the hottest part of the kiln. There should be at least 1" (25 mm) all round to allow air flow. Follow the firing temperature and schedule instructions for the type of clay you are using. Cool slowly, otherwise the pot may crack.

STEP 5 ◄ To fire pieces that are suitable for doing so on an open shelf, place the pieces on a kiln board covered with a sheet of ceramic paper to prevent sticking. Fire in the kiln for the required time, then drop the red-hot pieces immediately into cold water to prevent oxidation. They may need pickling to remove any firescale (see page 51).

These pieces are ready to be fired on an open shelf in the kiln

Finishing techniques

Once metal clay is fired, it is solid metal and can be polished, filed, soldered, and worked using normal metalworking techniques. Here are the main techniques for finishing jewelry pieces both by hand and with simple electric tools.

After firing, metal clay pieces should be strong and durable, although they are not as strong as their cast metal equivalents because the sintering process leaves the metal slightly porous. You can improve the strength of fired metal clay by polishing and hammering it.

50

BASIC TECHNIQUES

Hand polishing on silver clay

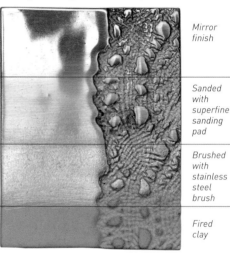

Mirror finish

Sanded with superfine sanding pad

Brushed with stainless steel brush

Fired clay

Burnishing on silver clay

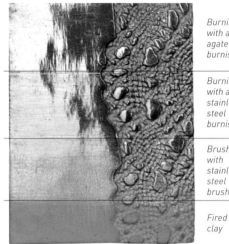

Burnished with an agate burnisher

Burnished with a stainless steel burnisher

Brushed with stainless steel brush

Fired clay

Filing on silver clay

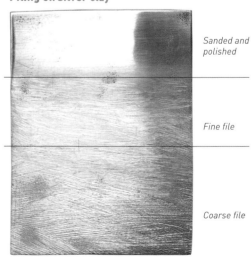

Sanded and polished

Fine file

Coarse file

Using a power tool on bronze clay

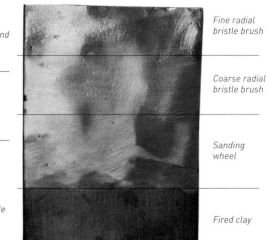

Fine radial bristle brush

Coarse radial bristle brush

Sanding wheel

Fired clay

HALLMARKING PRECIOUS METALS

If you sell your jewelry you should make yourself aware of the laws of your country on the hallmarking of precious metals. The laws vary between countries and there is no international standard.

USA, Australia, New Zealand, Canada: There is no compulsory hallmarking. You may mark your own silver clay pieces "999" and also mark your own logo or initials as you wish.

UK: All silver and gold jewelry that is offered for sale has to be hallmarked by an assay office. Silver pieces under 7.78 grams and gold pieces under 1 gram are exempt.

European countries: France, Austria, The Netherlands, and Switzerland have their own laws.

The International Hallmarking Convention has information on its website for all the countries belonging to it: www.hallmarkingconvention.org

WORKING WITH DIFFERENT METALS

You can use the same tools to file, sand, and polish fired silver, copper, bronze, and other metals. There is no need for separate tools.

Brushing

After firing, all metal clays are best brushed with either a dry stainless steel or a soft brass brush and soapy water. Silver clay will have a white crystalline surface that needs to be smoothed before the bright silver will show (see pages 18–19 for finishing equipment required). The base metals may have a black surface from oxidation, which can be removed by pickling if severe (see below) or by brushing if slight.

YOU WILL NEED

Basic tool kit (see page 16)

STEP 1 For silver clay, brush firmly over the piece to lay down the white crystalline surface. The result is a pleasing satin finish. Use water and nonabrasive soap if you use a brass brush to prevent it leaving marks on the silver.

STEP 2 Bronze and copper clays should be brushed to remove any traces of oxidation.

STEP 3 Use a small wire brush to get into crevices and indented areas.

STEP 4 Alternatively, you can use a fiberglass pencil brush to get into these detailed areas.

Pickling

This is the technique used to remove the black layer of firestain caused by the oxidation of the surface of the metal during firing or soldering. Pure 999 silver clay does not oxidize during firing, but bronze and copper clays will, and may need pickling if they are very black. You may also need to pickle after soldering sterling silver findings.

Pickle is an acidic solution that will remove firestain when the metal is immersed in it. It is a simple process and proprietary safety pickles are available from jewelry making suppliers. Alternatively, you can make your own nontoxic pickle:

Homemade pickle 1:
1 tablespoon salt
½ cup (150 ml) vinegar

Homemade pickle 2:
2 tablespoons citric acid
½ cup (150 ml) water

STEP 1 Mix up the pickle in a glass or plastic pot and heat in the microwave for 30 seconds for ½ of a cup (150 ml), or by placing the container in a saucepan of boiling water. Pickle works best when kept warm, and you can use a small crock pot or a mug warmer to maintain the temperature of about 120°F (50°C).

STEP 2 Immerse the metal in the pickle and leave until it is clean, then remove with either brass or plastic tweezers, or a plastic spoon. Most firestain will be removed in ten to 30 minutes, but homemade pickle may take longer. Rinse the pieces thoroughly, or neutralize in a hot or boiling solution of baking soda.

YOU WILL NEED

Basic tool kit (see page 16)

Pickle solution

Filing

If you have prefinished your piece successfully there will be very little work needed to polish and finish it. However, if there are rough areas that need removing, or you have mended with oil paste, you will need to file. A half-round file is the most versatile and can be used for most tasks. Use a small needle file for delicate filing.

YOU WILL NEED

Basic tool kit (see page 16)

TUMBLING

You can tumble your fired pieces in a rock tumbler to polish them, but this will not give as high a polish as hand polishing with sanding pads or a power tool. Tumblers are a useful time saver if you make a lot of jewelry, and tumbling will work-harden the metal and compact the surface. However, it should not be used for delicate pieces or those with very subtle textures. Use stainless steel shot and tumbling solution as recommended by the tumbler manufacturers.

STEP 1 Support the piece well on a rubber block or jeweler's peg. Hold the file firmly and with a light pressure on the piece, push the file away from you. The file only cuts as it is pushed away, so lift it at the end of the stroke and bring it back for the next stroke.

STEP 2 Use a needle file to cut into detailed areas that need smoothing. A coarser file will remove more metal but will leave deeper marks than a fine file. You will then need to go over the filed area with a fine file to smooth it enough for sanding.

STEP 3 Use the flat side of a half-round file for flat or convex surfaces, and the curved side for inside rings or concave surfaces. After filing the surface will need sanding to remove the file marks (see opposite).

STEP 4 ◄ Always use the largest file practical for the job. Here, a large half-round file is used to smooth rough edges on the side of a copper bangle.

Burnishing

Burnishing compacts the surface of metal to give it a shine. On softer metals, such as silver and copper, it will leave visible marks, so is best used only on textured areas or for difficult corners.

YOU WILL NEED

Basic tool kit (see page 16)

STEP 1 Rub over the surface of the metal with the side of a burnishing tool, taking care not to scratch the metal surface with the point. Any smooth stainless steel surface, such as a wool needle or even a teaspoon, can be used to burnish.

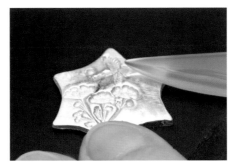

STEP 2 An agate burnisher has a larger smoothing area to use on flatter surfaces and is less likely to leave lines.

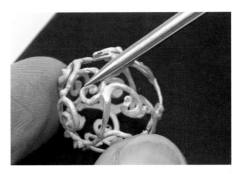

STEP 3 Burnish pieces such as filigree or paper clay, which are too fragile or intricate to sand.

Sanding

Sanding the metal surface by hand will give a variety of finishes, from satin smooth to mirror polish. It is the best way to achieve a smooth and beautiful surface on flat undecorated areas of metal. The steps show sanding with sponge sanding pads, which are easy to use and bend round curves. Alternatively, you can use wet and dry sandpaper in similar grits to those given.

YOU WILL NEED

Basic tool kit (see page 16)

STEP 1 Support the piece on a rubber block or jeweler's peg. Begin sanding with a superfine pad (500–600 grit/P1000–P1200). Press the pad hard against the metal and rub firmly. At first the pad will make a hissing sound as it cuts, then become almost silent as it smooths the surface. The surface will now have a satin finish, and if you wish to polish further, change to a finer pad.

STEP 2 Sand again with the medium, ultrafine pad (800–1000 grit/P1500–P2000) and the fine, microfine pad (1200–1500 grit/P3000–P5000). Each time continue until the pad makes no sound on the metal and the feel becomes slippery. Finally, polish with metal polish and a soft cloth to bring out the mirror finish.

STEP 3 A true mirror finish means that you can see a clear reflection of an object placed against the metal.

Using a hobby drill

A small hobby drill with its various attachments can be used to brush, sand, and polish finished pieces quickly and thoroughly. There are a bewildering number of attachments available for small drills (see page 22) and these steps show some of the most useful for metal clays.

YOU WILL NEED

Hobby drill and attachments

Sanding disk

STEP 1 This attachment is used for sanding smooth a flat surface, such as the back of a piece. Peel off the paper on the back of the disk and press the sticky side to the rubber mandrel.

STEP 2 Open the chuck of the drill with the chuck key and insert the mandrel shank into the jaws. Tighten the chuck to clamp the shank firmly in the drill chuck.

STEP 3 Hold the piece firmly on a block or jeweler's peg and lightly press the upper part of the disk against the piece. Work over the surface to smooth and refine.

Brass brush

A brass brush makes short work of brushing into detailed areas of a high-relief piece. Lubricate with soapy water to avoid black marks.

Silicone polisher

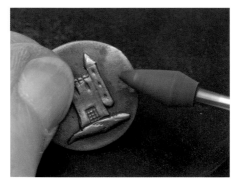

Made of silicon impregnated with silicon carbide abrasive in different grits, silicone polishers come in different colors to indicate the grit. Use for gentle sanding and firestain removal. Using light pressure and a low speed, work in a circular motion over the surface of the piece. Pointed cone polishers can reach into difficult areas.

Radial bristle disk

These disks are color coded for different grits and can be used for light sanding through to mirror polishing. They are excellent for reaching into nooks and crannies. Use a slow speed for the coarser disks, increasing the speed as you move up through the grits to the finer disks. The finest disk will achieve a high mirror polish.

Felt polishing wheels and points

Felt wheels and points are for final polishing to a mirror finish, and calico and wool wheels can be used instead. They should all be used in conjunction with a polishing paste such as tripoli or jeweler's rouge.

YOU WILL NEED

Felt point and polishing paste

Hobby drill

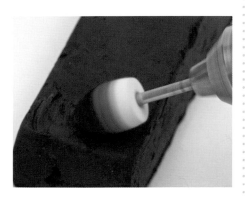

STEP 1 Clamp the shank of the felt point in the drill chuck and turn on at a slow speed. Hold the felt point or wheel against the polishing paste to coat it.

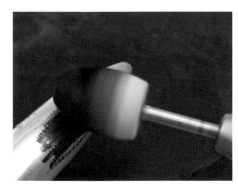

STEP 2 Turn up the drill speed and polish the piece. It will produce a black coating as it polishes, which you then remove with soapy water and a toothbrush.

Hammering warped pieces

Thin pieces of metal clay may warp as they are fired. This is more common with stovetop and blowtorch firing and is usually caused by the wet clay being stretched when rolled out. It is not difficult to flatten a piece of metal after firing.

YOU WILL NEED

Hammer

Rubber block

STEP 1 Do not brush or sand the piece, since it is softest when it is newly fired and quenched. Lay the piece on a rubber block and tap gently with a hammer to flatten it. The piece will harden as you tap, so if it begins to feel hard and stiff before you have flattened it, anneal it (heat to pale orange glow again and quench) to keep it soft enough to work on.

STEP 2 To correct a ring that is not round, put it back on the mandrel and tap it gently while pulling the ring toward the wider end of the mandrel. This will also strengthen the ring.

Hammering to strengthen

Fired metal clay is relatively soft after firing but any working of the surface (brushing, sanding, and filing) will harden and strengthen it. Hammering gently will strengthen it further. Excessive hammering will make the metal brittle and it may split, so it is important to hammer only until the piece feels hardened.

YOU WILL NEED

Hammer

Jump rings, brooch pins, and other findings that need strength should be hammered lightly on a flat surface. Cover them with a piece of soft leather or a folded sheet of paper to stop them jumping as you hammer.

MIRROR IMAGE EARRINGS,
HADAR JACOBSON
Strengthened findings will make your jewelry last.

Findings for metal clay

Findings are the various metal elements used to connect parts of a piece of jewelry and fix the finished piece in place. From earring fittings to brooch backs, pendant bails to jump rings, findings are essential to jewelry making.

The findings you use should make the jewelry practical and comfortable to wear while also complementing or enhancing the piece. They can be hidden and subtle, or form an integral part of the design. The variety of findings available is vast, whether you chose to buy them ready-made or make your own to add individuality to your work—and for economy.

The metal clay jeweler shares many types of findings techniques with those used by conventional metalsmiths, but has the advantage of also being able to embed findings in soft clay and fire them into the piece. Findings can be added to metal clay pieces during any of the following three stages of work:

• Embedded in soft clay.
• Added during pre-finishing using paste.
• Added after firing using oil paste or soldering.

POD NECKLACE,
HATTIE SANDERSON
The necklace closure has the starring role in this lavish piece.

Bail for a pendant
A purchased bail soldered on the back of a pendant. See page 65.

Earwires for drop earrings
Handmade earwires. See page 61.

Necklace clasp
Toggle-and-ring clasp for a necklace. See page 63.

Brooch pin
Handmade brooch pin. See page 62.

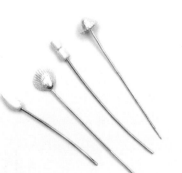

Head pins
Assorted head pins for a variety of uses including earwires. See page 58.

Pendant loop
Simple pendant loop for embedding or soldering. See page 59.

Making jump rings

These small rings are used to link components and hang charms or pendants, and should be made using a wire that matches the type of clay used. For ³⁄₁₆" (5 mm) diameter jump rings and larger, a good general-purpose wire thickness is 20 ga (0.8 mm), whereas 22 ga (0.6 mm) thickness is best for smaller jump rings.

YOU WILL NEED

Basic tool kit (see page 16)

Wire, in the metal and thickness of your choice

Knitting needle or piece of dowel of the diameter required

STEP 1 Use the thumb of one hand to hold one end of the wire against the knitting needle, and use the other hand to wind the wire tightly around it, making sure each coil touches the previous one.

STEP 2 Slide the coil off the needle and use wire cutters to cut each jump ring off the coil one at a time. Cut each ring in the same place so that the jump ring is a complete circle.

STEP 3 To use a jump ring, open it by pushing the two ends apart sideways. Thread the ring through the hole and push the ends back together in the same way. This ensures that the jump ring is not distorted. Jump rings can be soldered closed, but this is meticulous work with small jump rings and it is not normally necessary.

Jump rings can be made oval or hexagonal in shape by using a former of the desired cross section.

FINE SILVER VERSUS STERLING SILVER

When using either purchased silver findings or making your own, you have a choice between Sterling silver (925) and fine silver (999). Each has its own advantages and disadvantages.

FINE SILVER

For

• Can be embedded into silver clay before firing and fired with a blowtorch or gas stovetop as well as in a kiln.

• Does not produce firestain when fired or soldered.

• Is relatively slow to tarnish.

• Unlikely to cause allergies.

Against

• Is not as strong as sterling silver.

• Fine silver wire is too soft to be used for brooch pins and findings that need to retain their spring.

STERLING SILVER

For

• Relatively strong and should be used whenever strength is needed, therefore for earring stud posts, jump rings, and brooch pins.

Against

• Should not be embedded into silver before firing unless firing in a kiln at 1,200°F (650°C), because it will break down.

• When fired or soldered sterling silver produces firestain, which requires sanding or pickling to remove.

• Tarnishes faster than fine silver.

• More likely to cause allergies.

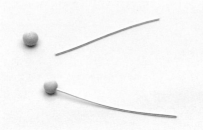

Small modeled shapes or molded beads can be used as the heads instead of plain balls.

Making head pins

These pins have a round or decorative head and are used to hang beads and dangles, or shaped into earring hooks. In their own right, with a sharpened point, they make stickpins, which can be worn on scarves. Use 20 ga (0.8mm) wire or above for strength.

YOU WILL NEED

Basic tool kit (see page 16)

Rubber block

Wire

STEP 1 Form small balls of metal clay and pierce them with wire of your chosen thickness. Dry and fire. Alternatively, make holes in the clay balls for the pins to be soldered into after firing. Hammer gently to work harden, or twist the wire by 360 degrees.

STEP 2 To sharpen the end of the wire to make a point, first file a groove in a rubber block or wooden jeweler's peg. Lay the end of the wire in the groove and file the end as you rotate the head pin. Sand to complete the point. See page 66 for balling the end of wire to make simple head pins.

Pendant holes

The simplest way of attaching a pendant is to use a hole. Large holes can be made in soft clay using a tiny cutter of any shape that removes the clay and makes a neat and decorative finish. Holes drilled with a drill bit are best for smaller pieces where a bail would be too large. You can also drill holes in plaster-dry clay during pre-finishing, as detailed on page 42. Holes are most often used in conjunction with jump rings.

YOU WILL NEED

Basic tool kit (see page 16)

Pin vise or hobby drill

Small cutter

TIPS FOR MAKING HOLES

• Position the hole so the piece hangs correctly and is not off-center on a symmetrical piece.

• Leave sufficient clay between the hole and the edge of the piece for strength. A minimum of 1/16" (1.5 mm) in a 4 p.c. (1 mm) thick metal clay piece is advisable.

• The hole needs to be large enough to take the thickness of the wire of the jump ring after firing. Holes that shrink too much can be re-drilled after firing.

STEP 1 For decorative cutout holes, use a small cutter, a brush protector, or a drinking straw in soft clay. Here, a pin is used to remove the cutout clay neatly. After drying, the hole can be refined with a needle file.

STEP 2 If you need to drill a hole in solid silver, a pin vise gives good control. First make a small dent by striking a nail or punch into the metal. Hold the rotating end of the vise in your palm and twist the lower part with your fingers while pressing down lightly on the drill. Small burrs of silver show the bit is cutting. Do not press too hard, otherwise the bit will break. This method takes a lot longer than drilling plaster-dry clay.

STEP 3 If you have one, a hobby drill is quicker for drilling holes in thick pieces of solid metal. Copper and silver are relatively easy to drill, bronze takes much longer and it is advisable to wet the piece as you drill to keep it cool.

Small loop-and-peg finding

This type of loop is used to attach pieces to a chain or to other pieces. Proprietary loops are available from metal clay suppliers (often called "screw eyes") but it is easy and economical to make your own loops to embed in metal clay.

Use fine silver wire for embedding in silver clay and copper wire for embedding in copper and bronze clays. For small loops use a wire thickness of 20 ga (0.8 mm), while 18 ga (1 mm) or more is suitable for larger loops.

YOU WILL NEED

Basic tool kit (see page 16)

Wire

Hammer

STEP 1 First make a loop in the end of the wire using round-nosed pliers. Grip the end of the wire in the pliers at the appropriate point in the graduated jaws for the size of loop required, and turn the pliers away from you to make a complete loop.

STEP 2 Grasp the base of the loop in the pliers and kink it slightly in the other direction to center the loop on the wire.

STEP 3 Cut the wire about ¼" (6 mm) from the base of the loop.

STEP 4 Hammer the straight part (the peg) on an anvil or flat surface to flatten it into a blade. This makes the blade slide into the clay more easily.

STEP 5 Push the blade part into soft clay just far enough to embed the base of the loop. Press the clay round the blade to secure, and add paste if necessary.

WORK HARDENING WIRE

After wire has been heated by firing or soldering it will become softened and more flexible. In order to give it strength and firmness again you need to work harden it. One way to do this is to gently hammer the wire. Alternatively, grasp one end of the wire in pliers and use a second pair of pliers at the other end to twist the wire by at least 180 degrees. Longer pieces of wire will need to be twisted at least 360 degrees.

To make jump rings stronger, work harden by hammering them lightly with a plastic hammer (see page 55), or place them inside a newspaper to hammer them with a metal hammer.

STEP 6 After firing, the clay will have shrunk around the blade making a secure loop that can be connected to a jump ring.

ALTERNATIVE METHOD Loop-and-peg findings can also be added to the back of a dried metal clay piece by applying paste, pressing on the blade part, and pasting over. Ensure that the blade is completely covered with paste. After drying, sand the area into a smooth dome before firing.

Making U-loops

These are stronger than loop-and-peg findings and are used for cuff links and any other jewelry that needs a strong connection.

YOU WILL NEED

Basic tool kit (see page 16)

Wire

Hammer

STEP 1 To make a U-loop, cut a piece of wire about 1" (25 mm) long and hammer each end flat into a blade.

STEP 2 Shape the wire into a U by pulling the ends down over the jaws of a pair of round-nosed pliers.

STEP 3 Push both blades of the U-loop into soft clay for a secure attachment point. This is useful for cufflink bars and other pieces where a strong loop is required.

Making bails

There are many different ways to make bails, either using the metal clay itself, or by shaping wire.

Making your own bails with metal clay gives complete freedom of design. You can texture the piece to match the pendant or leave it smooth. Most bails should be made about 2 p.c.–4p.c. (0.5 mm–1 mm) thick, depending on the size of the pendant.

You will need a former around which to create the bail. Choose one that will result in a large enough hole for your chosen chain or cord. A thick wool needle, a drinking straw, knitting needles, pencils, or toothpicks all make good formers.

YOU WILL NEED

Basic tool kit (see page 16)

STEP 1 Cut a strip from a rolled sheet of soft clay and curve it round the former to make a loop. Use paste to attach the end of the loop to the strip.

STEP 2 After drying, attach the bail to the back of the plaster-dry pendant using paste. Alternatively, fire the bail and solder to a fired pendant (see page 65).

BAIL VARIATIONS

Purchased bails can be added to pendants at the plaster-dry stage using paste, or be soldered on after firing. Fine silver bails can be added to fired silver clay pieces using oil paste.

You can also make your own bails using fine silver flat wire shaped with pliers. Attach to plaster-dry or fired pieces in the usual ways.

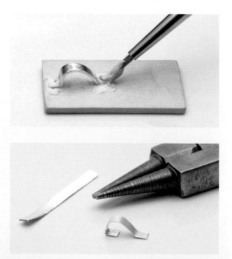

Making earwires for drop earrings

Earring findings are simple to make using metal wire, and give wonderful freedom of design. Use sterling silver for strength. Copper wire is suitable for using with base metal clay earrings, but may cause allergies in some people. A good general thickness for earring hooks and studs is 20 ga (0.8 mm).

YOU WILL NEED

Basic tool kit (see page 16)

20 ga (0.8 mm) wire, in the metal of your choice

Wooden dowel, ½" (13 mm) diameter, or use a pen of similar thickness

Hammer

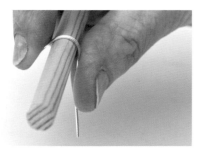

STEP 1 Cut the wire into two 2" (5 cm) lengths. Hold both wires together. Lay them over the dowel, 1½" (38 mm) from one end, and bend both together into the same U-bend.

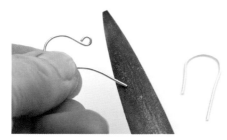

STEP 2 Turn a loop in the shorter end of each wire and use your fingers to bend the longer ends simultaneously into a gentle curve outward, ensuring you match the curve. File the ends smooth.

STEP 3 Finally, hammer the earrings gently to flatten and strengthen them over the top of the curve. Attach a drop earring to each of the loops.

EARWIRE VARIATIONS

Make a pair of decorative head pins (see page 58) and use these to make the hooks.

Melt a ball on one end of each piece of wire (see page 66) and thread the drop earring on from the other end after shaping. Turn the ball back on itself to trap the earring.

Making stud earrings

A universal favorite, stud earrings have posts attached to the back of the earring.

YOU WILL NEED

Basic tool kit (see page 16)

20 ga (0.8 mm) fine silver wire, or use sterling silver wire and fire in a kiln at 1,200°F (650°C)

Drill and 1 mm drill bit

Earstud scrolls—available from jewelry suppliers

STEP 1 Cut the wire into two ¾" (20 mm) lengths. Drill a hole in the center back of each earring with a 1 mm drill bit, ⅛" (3 mm) deep. Apply paste to one end of each wire and insert into the hole, secure with more paste. Dry, sand if necessary, and fire.

STEP 2 Sand away any firestain on the wire posts or pickle. Trim the posts to ½" (13 mm) and file each end smooth. Use round-nosed pliers to pinch a groove ⅛" (3 mm) from the end of each as a stop for the earstud scroll.

ALTERNATIVE METHOD Purchased earstud findings, either with a flat pad or a simple post, can be soldered to the back of fired pieces.

Attaching a purchased fine silver brooch finding

There are various commercial brooch fittings available with separate parts that can be embedded in the clay or soldered on after firing. The pin is added after firing or soldering. Do not add it before or it will soften and be difficult to work harden sufficiently. A commercial fine silver brooch finding has a sterling pin to provide strength and spring.

STEP 1 Attach the fine silver joint and catch with paste at the plaster-dry stage, ensuring that the attachment points are well embedded in the paste. Dry, then sand to smooth any rough areas and fire.

STEP 2 Nip the pin joint around the pin base with pliers. Cut the pin to size and file to sharpen the point. You can also add brooch fittings after firing by soldering or by using oil paste and firing again.

> **TIPS FOR USING BROOCH PINS**
> Always attach a brooch fitting to the top third of your piece, otherwise the brooch will sag forward during wear.

Making a brooch pin

Handmade brooch pins are simple to make. Use sweat soldering to attach the wires.

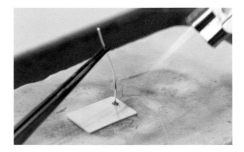

STEP 1 Cut one piece of wire the required length of the pin plus 2" (5 cm). Cut another piece of wire ⅜" (10 mm) long.

STEP 2 Solder the longer piece of wire to the first mounting point (see page 66). This will form the pin and coil spring.

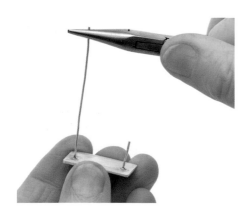

STEP 3 Solder the smaller piece of wire to the second mounting point, ensuring it is in line with the first. Twist each wire 360 degrees to work harden it and test the joins.

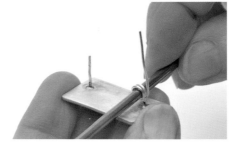

STEP 4 Shape the longer length into three coils by winding the wire around a knitting needle or rod as shown. The free end should emerge from over the top of the coil.

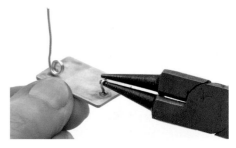

STEP 5 Shape the shorter wire into a curve to catch the pin, trimming it if necessary.

STEP 6 ▶ Trim the pin to length—it should protrude about ⅛" (3 mm). File the end into a point.

Making a toggle-and-ring clasp

There are many different types of catches and clasps available from jewelry making suppliers that can be used to finish your jewelry. Alternatively, it is rewarding to make your own, and they can be embellished or designed to match the piece they are to be attached to. Toggle-and-ring clasps are some of the easiest kinds to make in metal clay.

YOU WILL NEED

Basic tool kit (see page 16)

Two circle cutters of different sizes, here ¾" (20 mm) and ⅜" (10 mm)

Two loop-and-peg findings

STEP 1 Roll out a sheet of clay, 4 p.c. (1 mm) thick, and texture if desired. Lay the clay sheet on a tile and cut out a circle with the larger cutter. Pull away the waste clay, then use the other cutter to cut out a smaller circle inside it to make the ring.

STEP 2 Make a loop-and-peg finding from the wire (see page 59). With the clay ring still on the tile, push the blade of the finding into the edge of the circle. Allow to dry. If the blade is visible on the back after drying, cover it with paste and sand smooth.

STEP 3 Roll some clay into a ⅛" (3 mm) thick log and cut a length of ¾" (20 mm). The best length for the toggle bar is equal to twice the diameter of the central hole. Make another loop-and-peg finding and insert the blade into the middle of the toggle bar.

Making cufflinks

The simplest type of cufflink to make is a bar and chain.

YOU WILL NEED

Basic tool kit (see page 16)

Two loop-and-peg findings (see page 59)

Two U-loops (see page 60)

Strong chain, medium belcher chain is ideal

Four jump rings with the ends overlapped for extra strength

STEP 1 Make the cufflink pieces from metal clay. Embed a loop-and-peg finding into the back of each piece while the clay is soft.

STEP 2 Make the bars by rolling clay out 12 p.c. (3 mm) thick and cutting the bars ⅛" (3 mm) wide with a straight blade. They should be about ¾" (20 mm) long.

STEP 3 Embed a U-loop in the center back of each bar while the clay is still soft. Dry and fire.

STEP 4 Attach a ⅝" (15 mm) length of chain to each U-loop with the overlapped jump rings.

ALTERNATIVE METHOD Commercial cufflink findings can be soldered to the backs of cufflinks after firing.

Soldering techniques

Soldering is not a difficult technique to learn, and it allows you to add findings to your pieces after firing them. It only requires a small butane blowtorch and a few simple materials.

Learning simple soldering skills will help your metal clay work to advance and flourish. Soldering is the best way to add many types of findings and creative elements to jewelry, and soldered joints are normally much stronger than a joint made with clay products.

It is certainly possible to work successfully in metal clay without learning simple soldering, but you may find yourself using convoluted techniques of firing and refiring work to avoid a few minutes of soldering. It is not rational to use a kiln for one hour instead of a blowtorch for three minutes, both environmentally and in the use of your time.

The techniques described here are an introduction to soldering and will serve for most basic needs with metal clay.

TOOLS FOR SOLDERING

You will need only a small collection of simple tools and materials to solder your metal clay pieces.

1 Cross-lock tweezers grip pieces being soldered without the need to hold them closed (you can improvise with ordinary tweezers held shut with a twist of wire) 2 Flux— used with strip solder 3 Syringe of paste solder (contains added flux) 4 Paintbrush for applying flux 5 Solder strip 6 Blow torch 7 Firing brick 8 Strong wire cutters for cutting strip solder

SOLDERING SILVER

- Soldering is a useful technique if you do not possess a kiln. If you are already firing your silver clay with a blowtorch, you can use your torch for soldering.

- If you fire with a gas stovetop, then a blowtorch is a relatively small expense.

- Soldering enables you to use strong and less expensive sterling silver findings in your jewelry.

- Soldered joints are normally much stronger than a joint made with silver clay products.

- After soldering, the piece will have firestain on any sterling silver parts—these can be sanded clean or pickled.

- Sterling silver solder paste is the easiest type to use on silver.

SOLDERING COPPER AND BRONZE

- Copper is a little more difficult to solder than silver— you will need to use a hotter flame with your torch and more generous amounts of solder.

- Bronze is the most difficult as it requires a very hot flame that a small torch cannot provide. Use a plumbers' torch from a DIY store instead. In addition, you may need to use flux and solder pallions instead of paste because these are better for heavy duty soldering (see page 67).

- It is normal to use silver solder for base metals and the piece will need pickling after soldering to remove firestain. Copper- and bronze-colored solders are available but are not usually as easy to use as silver solder.

- If the silver color of the solder shows, oxidize the solder to darken it.

Soldering a bail

Adding a bail after firing using soldering is quicker than using metal clay paste in the plaster-dry stage.

YOU WILL NEED

Basic tool kit (see page 16)

Newly fired silver metal clay piece, unpolished

Bail

Silver solder paste in a syringe—easy solder (solder with the lowest melting point)

Firebrick

Blowtorch

Pickle (see page 00)

STEP 1 The surfaces to be joined should be clean and free of grease. If they are not newly fired, heat them with the blow torch to pale orange and then quench. They should also fit tightly together because solder will not fill gaps. File the joining surfaces of the fired piece and the bail to clean and smooth them.

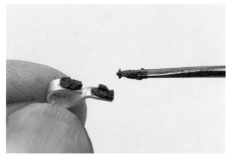

STEP 2 Squeeze out some of the solder paste onto a tile and use a small spatula or cocktail stick to spread it on flat parts of the bail that are to be joined to the piece. Cover the areas with a 1/32" (1 mm) thick coating and scrape off any excess that overhangs.

STEP 3 Place the fired piece face down on the firebrick and press the bail onto the center of the back. The paste may seep out a little as you press down. If there is a lot of seepage, scrape away the excess but leave some visible so you can watch it heating. Use a pair of tweezers—or other metal tool—to hold the bail while heating, otherwise it will shift as the solder bubbles.

STEP 4 Light the blowtorch and adjust to a medium flame (see Step 1 of Firing with a blowtorch, page 46). The pendant is the largest element, so aim the flame of the torch at this and move it around to heat it up first. Then aim the torch at the bail and the solder, but keep the flame moving around the whole piece as well.

STEP 5 Watch carefully, and after a few moments the paste will bubble. This is the flux boiling away.

STEP 6 ◄ Continue heating until you see the solder flow in a sudden shine of liquid silver. Pull the flame away immediately, otherwise you will overheat the solder.

STEP 7 ► Quench the piece in cold water and test the join by pulling it hard with pliers. If you are not happy with the joint, you can heat the piece and pull away the bail when the solder flows to try again. Pickle and rinse or sand away any firestain. The piece is now ready to polish.

Sweat soldering wire

This is a useful technique for soldering wire to the back of a piece, such as earstuds or handmade brooch pins. You will need to grip the wire in a pair of tweezers. Use cross-locking tweezers (see page 64), or improvise with a coil of scrap wire to hold the tweezers closed.

YOU WILL NEED

Basic tool kit (see page 16)

Wire

Firebrick

Blowtorch

Solder paste

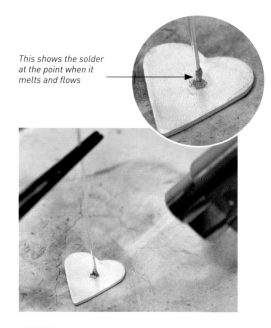

This shows the solder at the point when it melts and flows

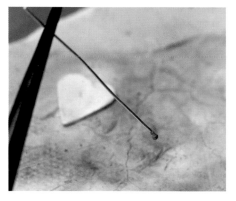

STEP 1 Cut a piece of wire longer than required—it is easier to cut it after soldering. Apply solder paste to the end of the piece of wire to be soldered and heat with a medium flame (see Step 1 of Firing with a blowtorch, page 46) until it bubbles and forms a blob on the end.

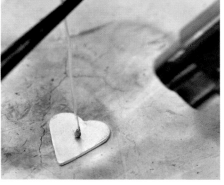

STEP 2 Lay the fired clay piece face down on the firebrick. Hold the wire in the tweezers and position the blob of solder on the back of the clay piece.

STEP 3 Heat until the solder flows, then quench immediately.

STEP 4 ▼ To test the joint, grip the wire in pliers and twist it 360 degrees. This will also work harden the wire. Pickle or sand away any firestain if necessary, then trim and shape the wire as required.

BALLING WIRE

The end of silver or copper wire can be melted using a blowtorch to form a small ball. This is useful for making simple headpins, for earwires and for decorative hinges.

To ball the end of silver or copper wire to make a head pin, hold the wire in tweezers over a heatproof surface and aim the hot flame of a blowtorch at the end of the wire. It will glow orange then ball up. Quench the wire. Pickle or sand it if necessary to remove firestain.

Soldering with solder strip and flux

Instead of using solder paste, you can use solder strip and flux. This technique can be used for silver, and is preferable for soldering copper and bronze or for soldering different metals together.

The soldered silver and copper pieces, pickled and ready for polishing

STEP 1 Hammer the end of the solder strip to flatten it and cut small pieces, called "pallions," off the end with wire cutters. The pallions should be about 1/16" (2 mm) square.

STEP 2 File the joining surfaces to ensure a good fit. Paint flux all over the surfaces to be joined as well as over the pallions of solder. Flux helps to prevent firestain so be liberal over the copper piece.

STEP 3 On a firebrick, place several pallions on the point where the silver piece is to be attached. Fired copper and bronze metal clay is quite porous so you will need generous amounts of solder, as shown. Place the silver piece on top and hold it in place with tweezers.

STEP 4 Begin by heating the copper piece with a medium flame (see Step 1 of Firing with a blowtorch, page 46). The flux will bubble and then clear. The piece will begin to glow pale orange. Move the flame to the smaller piece and continue heating.

STEP 5 When the solder flows you will feel the upper piece drop onto the copper piece below. You may see liquid silver solder emerge at the edges. Pull away the flame as soon as this happens.

STEP 6 Quench the piece and test the join with pliers. This shows the back of the piece. Pickle to remove the firestain and polish the piece as required.

2

Clay
shaping
techniques

Soft metal clay is a malleable and finely grained material. It can be rolled into sheets, formed into balls and logs, extruded, molded, textured, and sculpted. After shaping and drying, it can then be carved, joined, added to, refined, and worked on in many ways before it is fired.

Cutters and templates

One of the joys of working in metal clay is the ease with which it can be rolled into sheets and cut out into various shapes using cutters and templates.

Traditional metalworking techniques require the laborious sawing of sheet metal, and these metal clay techniques for soft clay sheets are valuable alternatives. Cutters and templates are used for creating precise cutout shapes with smooth edges, and for the repeat cutting out of a single design.

Commercial cutter
A textured star cut out using a commercial cutter.

Pendant
Frame pendant cut out using hand-cut templates.

Brooch
Silver fish brooch cut out using a handmade cutter.

Box pendant
Bird-box pendant made using templates created on graph paper. See pages 71 and 94.

Earrings
Drop earrings made using a hand-cut template.

Bead
Silver bead made using a round commercial cutter. See page 115.

Using cutters
Cutters are pressed down on a sheet of soft clay to cut out a shape.

YOU WILL NEED

Basic tool kit (see page 16)

Cutter

Ceramic tile

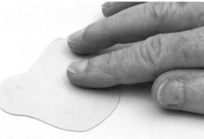

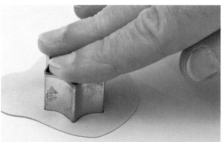

STEP 1 Roll out the clay into a sheet of the required thickness (see page 27) and texture if required (see page 72). Place the sheet on a ceramic tile and stroke the surface gently to ensure that it is stuck to the tile.

STEP 2 Press down firmly with the cutter until it meets the tile. A slight circular motion when the cutter is fully pressed down emphasizes the cut and makes it easier to remove the waste clay. Remove the cutter. If the piece comes away in the cutter, push it out with a fingertip or blunt tool to avoid marking the surface.

STEP 3 Pull away the waste clay from around the piece. It can now be removed from the tile by sliding under it with a flat blade, or preferably dried on the tile without moving it to prevent distortion.

Making cutters

To make your work individual, you can create your own cutters from thin metal sheet. Use metal cut from aluminum cans or the sheet copper sold for metal embossing.

YOU WILL NEED

Basic tool kit (see page 16)

Metal sheet

Strong glue

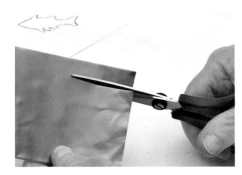

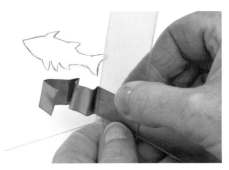

STEP 1 Draw on paper, and to size, the shape you wish to make into a cutter. Use simple curves or straight lines. Use an old pair of scissors to cut a straight strip of metal about ¾" (20 mm) wide and long enough to go right around the drawn line.

STEP 2 Bend the strip to shape following your design. Use a straight edge or snipe-nosed pliers to bend the sharp angles and round-nosed pliers or a round pencil for the curves. If your strip is not long enough, glue on more metal with strong glue.

STEP 3 Overlap the ends by about ¼" (6 mm) and trim the excess strip. Position the inside overlap edge on a corner so it will not show when cutting out clay, and glue with strong glue. Adjust the shape if necessary; the cutter must lie perfectly flat to cut well.

Using templates

Templates are another way of cutting out shapes. You can use purchased templates or make your own.

Roll out the clay and lay it on a tile. Place your template on the clay and use a craft knife, held vertically, to cut round the shape. If the shape is very intricate, use a fine needle to do the cutting. Remove the waste clay and stroke along all the cut edges with your finger to smooth them.

YOU WILL NEED

Basic tool kit (see page 16)

Template—commercial or homemade

Making templates

Making your own templates is not difficult, and will add individuality to your work. Thin cardstock is ideal for templates, or for more permanent templates, use acetate or thin plastic sheet. You can draw your own designs or use a drawing program on a computer. For symmetrical templates, draw half the design on paper or graph paper, fold along the midway mark, and cut out both sides together. Transfer the shape by tracing around it onto the template material and cut out.

YOU WILL NEED

Basic tool kit (see page 16)

Thin cardstock

Pencil

Vegetable oil

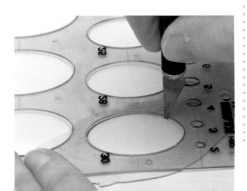

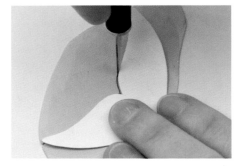

STEP 1 Draw or trace the outline shape onto thin cardstock or plastic. Cut out the shape and, if you are using card, rub with vegetable oil to prevent it absorbing moisture from the clay.

STEP 2 Homemade templates are used in the same way as commercial templates except that it is easier to cut around the outside of the template.

Applying texture

Soft metal clay takes impressions extremely well and with far less effort than in conventional silversmithing. This opens up a wonderful world of creativity, and you will soon discover all kinds of materials that can be pressed into the clay to make your jewelry unique.

To begin, there are natural materials in abundance to try. Fresh and dried leaves and flowers, textured pebbles, seashells and coral, and grasses and bark all create fascinating textures and patterns. Commercial texture sheets and rubber stamps, often intended for other crafts, can be adapted for metal clay. You can also make your own texture sheets and stamps to give your pieces more originality. Finally, you could try one of several exciting techniques for using metal clay paste to texture and embellish the clay surface.

Lace
Handmade lace rolled into clay.

Fern leaves
Leaves were laid onto the oiled surface of a clay sheet and rolled in. See opposite.

Rubber stamp impression
Small, commercially available rubber stamps were used here. See page 75.

Feathers
Small (budgerigar) feathers were rolled into the surface of the oiled clay sheet.

Candle wax impression
The ship design was drawn onto a smooth candle surface with an engraving tool. The oiled clay was then pressed onto the drawing to make a relief image that is ideal for embellishing with enameling or resin. See page 76.

Cuttlefish impression
The oiled clay sheet was pressed on to a cuttlefish bone to create this effect. See page 73.

Text impressions
From top to bottom: polymer clay reversed stamp made from a candle wax engraving; candle wax engraving written in reverse; commercially available letter stamps.

Commercial texture sheet
The oiled clay sheet was pressed onto a commercial rubber texture sheet. See page 74.

Impressing with fine materials

Fine materials such as leaves, feathers, and grasses give lovely subtle textures when rolled into metal clay. The aim is to keep any untextured area between the impressions as smooth as possible, and using rolling guides is the best way to do this. This method is best used for materials that are less than 1/32" (1 mm) thick.

YOU WILL NEED

Basic tool kit (see page 16)

Vegetable oil

Leaves

STEP 1 Lay the impressing material on the rolled out clay and roll between the rolling guides so that the leaves are pressed firmly into the surface. It is best to roll from the center outward in each direction.

STEP 2 Peel away the leaves to reveal the texturing. Any small leaf pieces that remain can be left to burn away during firing.

Impressing with thicker materials

If the material to be used for texturing is more substantial and cannot be rolled into the clay, then the clay needs be pressed onto the material. This applies to chunks of stone, pieces of wood and bark, coral, granite, and cuttlefish bone, as shown here. This technique does not give such a smooth back to the clay sheet as with thinner materials, but a piece of fabric or leather pressed onto the back will give it a more professional finish.

STEP 1 Roll out the clay to the desired thickness for the project using rolling guides. Oil the surface of the clay lightly to create a faint sheen.

STEP 3 Press a piece of fabric or leather over the lightly oiled back of the clay in order to remove fingerprints and give a uniform effect.

YOU WILL NEED

Basic tool kit (see page 16)

Vegetable oil

Cuttlefish bone

Piece of soft leather or fabric

STEP 2 Press the oiled side of the clay sheet firmly against the most interesting part of the texturing material. Work over the back of the sheet, pressing firmly with the flat pad of your finger to ensure that all the clay is textured.

STEP 4 Carefully peel the clay away from the texturing material and pat down lightly on a tile to flatten it.

**TURTLE LAGOON
PENDANT,**
SUE HEASER
Silver clay textured with
granite and cuttlefish
bone provide the
background for a hand-
sculpted turtle in this
colorful pendant.

KESTRELS NECKLACE,
SUE HEASER
Copper clay sheets
textured with a cockle
shell were used for the
cutout bird silhouettes
and the beads in this
lively piece.

Using texture sheets

Many different commercial texture
sheets are available, and this is a good
way to use them.

YOU WILL NEED

Basic tool kit (see
page 16)

Texture sheet

Vegetable oil

Piece of lace or fabric

STEP 1 Roll out the clay to the required
thickness and fold the sheet in half.

STEP 2 Oil the surface of the clay lightly
and lay it on the texture sheet. Place rolling
guides on the texture sheet on either side of
the clay and firmly roll over the clay.

STEP 3 The clay will be pushed down
onto the texture sheet and revert to the
original thickness again while taking
the impression. Peel off the clay to reveal
the texturing.

ALTERNATIVE METHOD Another way that
controls the depth of the texture is to roll
out the sheet using rolling guides of the
required thickness plus an extra pair of
0.5 mm guides (or 2 additional p.c.). Then
lay the clay on the texture sheet as above
but this time without the extra 0.5 mm guides.
This will give an impression 0.5 mm deep.

ALTERNATIVE METHOD To texture both
sides of a clay sheet, lay a piece of lace
or other thin material over the back of
the sheet before rolling it down on the
texture sheet.

Further texturing techniques

There are many other ways of adding texture and impressions to metal clay. You will also find objects in your home such as engraved cutlery, jewelry, lace, and textiles that can be used for interesting textures.

Fingerprints

This is a popular technique for family mementoes. Knead the clay lightly and form a thick patty. Oil the clay surface. Now press the child's finger into the clay firmly and remove it carefully to avoid smudging the impression. The child's name can then be scribed in the soft clay surface with a needle. Oxidizing will enhance the detail in the print.

Texturing with paper cutters

Cut shapes out of textured or smooth paper, by hand or using a paper punch. Lay the cutout shapes on the oiled clay surface and roll in. This makes attractive areas for filling with resin or enamel.

Embossing with stencils

Brass and plastic stencils used for paper embossing and parchment craft can be used with soft clay sheets. Press the oiled sheet into the stencil with a fingertip from behind.

Using stamps

Metal clays will take detailed impressions from stamps. Use commercial rubber stamps or wooden stamps, as here. You can make your own stamps by carving polymer clay, soft wood, or even an eraser.

Making your own textures

To be truly original in your jewelry making, you can use your own textures. Use any of the techniques described to make an impressing material that can be used to texture metal clay in the ways described above.

YOU WILL NEED

Basic tool kit (see page 16)

Putty silicone

Polymer clay

Talcum powder

Piece of lace, ribbons, or fabric

Candle

Woodcutting tools

Vegetable oil

Putty silcone

Putty silicone makes flexible sheets with fine detail. Combine the two putties supplied by the manufacturer, as described on page 78. Roll out a 12 p.c. (3 mm) thick sheet of the compound and press onto the textured surface you wish to replicate. Leave to set and peel away.

Polymer clay

This can be used in a similar way to putty silicone and is good for making texture sheets from fine materials. Roll out a sheet on a tile, brush with talcum powder, then press or roll on lace, ribbons, or fabric. Remove the fabric and bake the clay on the tile according to the manufacturer's instructions.

Soap and wax

Smooth pieces of soap or candle wax can be carved with engraving tools or fine woodcutting tools. The oiled sheet of metal clay is then pressed onto the surface. This produces good embossed outlines that can be filled with enamel or resin.

Photopolymer sheets

These are available as commercial kits to help you make your own texture sheets from drawings and prints from your computer. The kits are relatively expensive but creating your own textures opens up exciting new design possibilities.

CHINESE PENDANT REVERSE,
CHRIS PATE
A handmade polymer clay stamp was used to create the texture on this stylish reversible pendant.

Molds and molding

Molding is one of the easiest metal clay techniques, and is a delight for beginners. However, it is also a very useful technique for advanced designer–makers who want to replicate their own original sculpts.

At a beginner level, using molds with metal clays enables the artist to replicate objects such as shells or small pieces of jewelry. The original is pushed into the molding material, such as putty silicone or polymer clay, to make a simple one-part mold. After the mold is hardened, metal clay is pushed into the mold, removed, and the resulting piece dried, refined, and fired.

At a more advanced level, molding can sidestep laborious lost wax techniques to duplicate original pieces in precious or base metals. Sculpts in polymer clay, wax, metal clay, or other sculpting materials can have molds made from them to replicate a whole piece or to make embellishments for jewelry. Two-part molds can be made for three-dimensional pieces.

A huge variety of commercial molds is also available, for those who do not wish to make their own.

See page 117 for techniques for molding beads.

Molded shell pendant with tiny molded shells and a molded miniature turtle.

Tiny charms sculpted, in polymer clay and molded in silver clay.

Dragon cufflinks made using sprigging techniques (see page 81).

One-part silicone mold
This poppy head was molded in a one-part silicone mold. See page 79.

One-part polymer clay mold
Silver button molded in a one-part polymer clay mold. See page 78.

Two-part silicone mold
Bronze coins molded in a two-part silicone mold. See page 79.

Molded brooch
Molded copper disk brooch—the original piece was sculpted in polymer clay.

Making a one-part mold using putty silicone

These are the simplest types of mold and are often called push-molds. They consist of a single cavity into which soft clay is pressed. The resulting piece will have a flat, unmolded back. There are many different molding materials on the market, but putty silicone is the most popular.

YOU WILL NEED

Basic tool kit (see page 16)

Putty silicone

Object to mold

MIDNIGHT FEAST,
LYNDA CHENEY
Molds taken from tiny bones and a carved mouse *netsuke* were used to create this fabulous pendant.

STEP 1 Take equal quantities of each of the two colors of putty silicone, allowing sufficient in total to embed the original. You can shape these into balls to judge equal amounts, or weigh them with a jeweler's scale for greater accuracy.

STEP 2 Mix them together until all streakiness has disappeared. The mixture will normally have up to five minutes working time after mixing. Form into a ball and press onto a tile to make a patty large enough to mold the original.

STEP 3 Press the original onto the patty, pushing it down until it is embedded and the top is just below the top surface of the molding compound. If you are using a three-dimensional object, push it into the compound up to the widest part. Leave for five to ten minutes to set, then remove the original from the mold.

Making a one-part mold using polymer clay

Polymer clay can also be used as a molding material, although it makes a more rigid mold so is best used for shallow moldings.

YOU WILL NEED

Basic tool kit (see page 16)

Polymer clay

Talcum powder

Object to mold

STEP 1 Make a patty of polymer clay and smear talcum powder over the surface. Press in the original and ease out carefully.

STEP 2 Bake the mold on the tile to harden it. If the original can withstand the heat of baking, it can be left in place and removed after baking.

Molding with a one-part mold

In this example, a poppy head has been used to make a mold from putty silicone. Alternatively, you can use a ready-made mold.

YOU WILL NEED

Basic tool kit (see page 16)

Silicone mold, commercial or make your own (see opposite)

Object to mold

Vegetable oil

Lace or textured sheet

STEP 1 Form the metal clay into a smooth ball with no folds or cracks. Add water if it shows any signs of dryness. Shape the clay into a similar shape to the mold cavity and smear the surface with vegetable oil.

STEP 2 Push the clay into the center of the mold, pressing it into all the details of the cavity. The clay should just fill the mold cavity—if there is too much, pinch off some clay and remold. You should be able to see the beginning of the molded cavity all round.

STEP 3 Press a texture sheet or piece of lace onto the back of the clay to remove fingerprints and give a decorative finish.

STEP 4 Leave the piece to dry in the mold for about five minutes, or use a heat gun on the clay for a few seconds. Flex the mold and turn the piece out. Any rough edges can be trimmed off with a knife or filed once dry.

STEP 5 If the piece will not come out easily, or you are using a polymer clay mold that is not flexible, pierce the clay with a needle and ease it out of the mold. The small hole from the needle can then be smoothed away.

Making a two-part mold

Two-part molds are used for molding three-dimensional objects, or for molding both sides of a coin. Use putty silicone to make the mold.

YOU WILL NEED

Basic tool kit (see page 16)

Putty silicone

Object to mold

Vegetable oil

Toothpick

STEP 1 Make a one-part mold (see making a one-part mold, left), and when the original is pressed into the soft compound, push small lengths of toothpick into the surface of the mold around the object. Make a registration mark with a knife on the side of the mold.

STEP 2 When the compound has set, remove the toothpick, but leave the original in the mold.

Continued next page ▶

STEP 3 Smear vegetable oil over the set part of the mold to prevent sticking. Make up some more compound and shape into a patty to cover the first mold. Press the patty down over the original and the top of the bottom mold, pushing the soft putty down well to ensure that it fills all gaps and is forced down into the toothpick registration holes.

Molding with a two-part mold
Use a two-part mold for making pieces where the back will be seen, such as charms for charm bracelets or dangling earrings.

STEP 4 Make a mark on the fresh compound to match the registration mark on the bottom mold. Leave to set.

STEP 1 Form metal clay into a shape roughly the size of the total mold cavity of both halves of the mold. Make sure that there are no folds or lines in the clay. Press the clay firmly into the lower mold cavity.

STEP 2 Place the upper half of the mold over the lower half, aligning the registration pegs with their respective holes as well as the outer registration mark. Press the upper mold down firmly onto the lower mold, working over it to make sure it is fully pressed down.

STEP 5 Pull off the upper mold, which will now have the impression of the top of the original and have registration pegs to match the holes below. The mold is now ready to use.

STEP 3 Open the mold and remove the molding. If there is a lot of excess clay—known as "flashing"—that has appeared round the edges, remove it and remold using the remaining piece of metal clay, which will now be the correct amount. A small amount of flashing can be trimmed with a knife or filed during pre-finishing.

Making sprigs

A sprig is a ceramics term that refers to a small molded embellishment. Tiny flat-backed sculpts in metal clay are molded to create embellishments that can then be applied to a clay surface. Alternatively, a flat back can be applied to the back of the sprigs while they are still in the mold, for a neat result.

STEP 1 To make a sprig mold, place the original face up on a tile and press a generous amount of putty silicone over it and leave to set. This creates a mold with a wide, flat surface surrounding the cavity.

STEP 2 Press metal clay firmly into the mold cavity to make a sprig.

STEP 3 Use a knife or scraper to sheer off any excess clay. The clay should be leveled so it is flush with the surrounding mold. The piece can now be unmolded and applied as a decoration to another piece of clay. If applied when soft it can be curved to match the surface it is applied to, such as a ring.

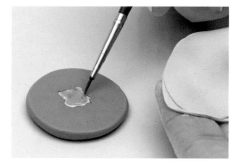

STEP 4 To attach a backing to a sprig while it is still in the mold, roll out a sheet of clay of the required thickness and texture (see page 72) or leave smooth. Wet the back of the sprig with a paintbrush.

STEP 5 Press the clay sheet onto the back of the sprig, pushing down well to join. Remove any fingerprints by pressing on a texture sheet or piece of leather.

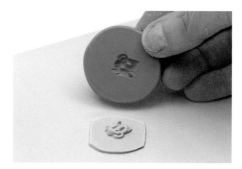

STEP 6 Unmold the clay. The sprig is now a relief decoration on a background sheet of clay, which can be used as required.

STEP 7 Use a cutter to cut out the shape (see page 70), ensuring that the sprig is positioned well. This technique is good for making cufflinks, buttons, stud earrings, and ring heads.

ALTERNATIVE METHOD Polymer clay can also be used to make detailed sprig molds. Roll out a thick, smooth sheet of polymer clay, smear talcum powder over it, and press the original face down onto it. Remove the original and bake.

Soft sculpture techniques

Sculpting soft metal clay is a rewarding technique for creating original jewelry, and can be as complex or as simple as you wish. Developing sculpting skills is an important part of becoming an accomplished metal clay artist.

Successful soft sculpture is best achieved with metal clay that is well hydrated but has a touch-dry surface. If the surface is wet and slippery, you will find it difficult to control the clay.

The techniques shown here can be used with all kinds of metal clay, both precious metal and base metal. When adding clay to a piece, use a smear of water or paste to ensure a strong join. Copper and bronze clay in particular need firm fixing to avoid pieces coming away during firing.

Freeform
Logs of clay swirled into simple freeform shapes make appealing pieces. See page 84.

Sculptural
Simple organic shapes pressed together make attractive sculptural forms.

Flora
Flowers and leaves are popular jewelry designs and embellishments.

Fauna
Small animal forms can be created from simple shapes and make attractive charms.

▲ **THE STRAWBERRY THIEF,**
XUELLA ARNOLD
Exquisite sculpting of this delicate bird with fruit, flower, and leaves makes a unique pendant.

Simple organic shapes

Flat-backed shapes are easy forms to sculpt, because you can work on a ceramic tile after making the basic shape. The clay will stick to the tile so that you can shape it without having to hold it.

YOU WILL NEED

Basic tool kit (see page 16)

Polymer clay

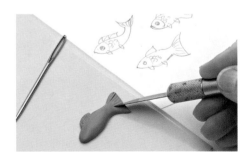

STEP 1 Start with a sketch of your design, trying out different shapes. Alternatively, design your piece in polymer clay first. Unlike metal clay, polymer clay does not dry out as you work and will give you time to design in a similar material.

STEP 2 Make sure that your metal clay is well hydrated. Form the piece into a smooth round ball to eliminate any fold lines, then shape it roughly to your design.

STEP 3 Press the shape down onto a ceramic tile. Use tools or fingers to refine the shape further and cut away any surplus clay if required. If the surface dries too quickly and shows cracks, apply water with a paintbrush or wet finger to smooth the surface. Leave until the surface is touch dry before continuing.

Sculpting flowers and leaves

Flowers and leaves are everlastingly popular designs for jewelry. Larger pieces make beautiful earrings and pendants, while smaller pieces can be used as embellishments or charms.

YOU WILL NEED

Basic tool kit (see page 16)

A rose sculpted in copper clay

Bronze leaves

▲ **FOOD CHAIN NECKLACE,** *TERRY KOVACIK*
A beautiful and thought-provoking necklace. An original polymer clay sculpture was used to make a mold for the head of the bird, which was further enhanced by carving when in the plaster dry stage.

STEP 4 To add applied details such as fins on a fish or wings on a bird, press the extra clay piece on the tile to flatten the back. Brush water on the joining surface of the main piece and press on the addition to attach it firmly.

STEP 1 To make a rose, roll out a small log of clay about 1" (25 mm) long and point both ends. Roll the log flat on a tile to make a long thin petal. Roll the petal up as shown to form the center of the rose.

STEP 2 Make more logs of a similar size but thicker, and press down on the tile to form larger petals. Cut each petal in half lengthwise. Brush water onto the outside of the rose center and wrap a petal around it, flat edge down, pressing to secure.

STEP 5 Textural details such as fish scales or marks on fins can be applied with a suitable tool. Here, the eye of a needle makes perfect scales on the fish. The eye of an animal could simply be a hole made with a blunt needle.

STEP 3 Continue adding petals on either side of the rose, making them larger as you work outward. Finally, pull the tops of the larger petals outward a little and brush over with water to smooth any rough edges.

STEP 4 To make a leaf, form a small teardrop and press it down on the tile with the end of your finger to flatten it into a leaf shape. Mark veins with a curved knife blade. Remove the leaf from the tile by sliding the blade under it.

Weaving, braiding, and knotting

Cords and strips of metal clay can be woven, braided, and knotted to make unusual and beautiful jewelry.

These metal clay techniques are often seen as challenging because of the concerns with clay drying during the process. The solution is to hydrate the clay well before you start and to plan your designs using polymer clay. Glycerin or vegetable oil kneaded into the clay also helps slow drying.

These techniques stem mainly from fiber crafts and basketry, and if you enjoy them you can find further inspiration in books on knotting, weaving, and canework.

Braids
Silver clay braided to form strips and rings.

Knots
Cords of clay tied in a love knot.

Looped designs
Cords of clay can be looped to create freeform or symmetrical designs.

Weaving
Woven panel of flat strips of copper clay.

CLAY CORDS

Long cords of clay used for braiding and to make ropes, loops, and knots can be rolled by hand, rolled with a log roller, or extruded using an extruder or syringe. Cords made with an extruder can be made with a variety of cross sections.

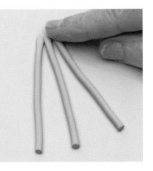

Braiding

Work on a ceramic tile so that you can stick the ends of the clay cords to the tile to prevent unraveling.

YOU WILL NEED

Basic tool kit (see page 16)

STEP 1 Lay three cords of clay side by side on the tile and press the top of each down onto the tile to anchor it. Spread out the outer two cords as shown.

STEP 2 Begin braiding by passing the left outer cord over the inner cord. Then pass the right outer cord over the new inner cord. Continue in the same way, moving the cords as you work to keep them splayed out.

STEP 3 When you reach the end, lightly squeeze the three cords together. You can now shape the braid further to make bangles, rings, or other jewelry.

Twisting

Twisted cords can be used as decorative ropes to surround gemstones.

Fold a long cord in half and twist together to make a delicate rope that can also serve as an attractive dangle.

Freeform and symmetrical loops

Try twisting soft cords of clay into looped shapes.

YOU WILL NEED

Basic tool kit (see page 16)

Graph paper

STEP 1 Brush water or paste onto the places the cords touch to stick them firmly together.

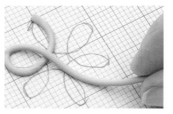

ALTERNATIVE METHOD Anchor the clay cord and follow your drawn design. Apply paste where the cords cross.

Knots

Making knot jewelry has been a maritime craft for centuries, and you can replicate this in metal clay. The following steps create a love knot formed from a traditional reef knot.

YOU WILL NEED

Basic tool kit (see page 16)

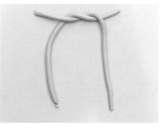

STEP 1 Make two cords and anchor one end of each down on a tile, spacing them about 3" (75 mm) apart. Tie a single knot by passing the right-hand cord over the left one.

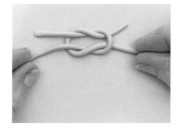

STEP 2 Now tie a second single knot, this time passing the left cord over the right. Pull gently to tighten the knot as required.

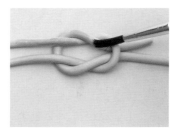

STEP 3 Brush over the cords with a wet paintbrush to remove any stress marks or cracking, and trim the ends as required.

Weaving

Woven strips of metal clay make unusual pieces of jewelry. They can also be draped over formers or used to cover a combustible core for three-dimensional pieces.

YOU WILL NEED

Basic tool kit (see page 16)

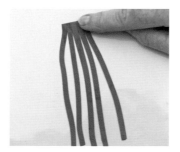

STEP 1 Cut strips from thin sheets of clay. Lay the desired number of strips side by side on a tile and press the tops of the strips down to anchor them.

STEP 2 Fold back alternate vertical strips, then lay a horizontal strip across the remaining flat strips.

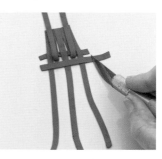

STEP 3 Replace the folded strips and fold back the other alternate strips, then place the next horizontal strip.

STEP 4 Continue the piece, then trim the ends. The clay can be dried on the tile before firing, or be removed while still soft and draped over a former.

Creating with soft clay sheets

Rolled out sheets of soft clay can be the starting point for many different, and versatile, jewelry designs.

Texturing and cutting out flat sheets of clay make good basic beginners' projects, but sheets of clay are also useful elements for more elaborate jewelry. They can be rolled out thin or thick, textured or smooth, and be shaped in many different ways. Thicker sheets will add strength to pieces, but will use considerably more clay.

86

CLAY SHAPING TECHNIQUES

Crumple
A crumpled and freeform design formed from a 1 p.c. (0.25 mm) thick sheet.

Curling
A 2 p.c. (0.5 mm) thick sheet gives more control for curling and shaping.

Formers
A 2 p.c. (0.5 mm) thick sheet is good for draping over formers and for combustible core jewelry. See page 90.

Thick
A thicker, 4 p.c. (1 mm) sheet, has more strength, and can be used for rings and larger pieces of jewelry.

Freeform sheets

Use sheets to make attractive, loose shapes that are simple to make in metal clay but would be difficult to replicate in conventional metalworking. The clay sheet should be about 1 p.c. (0.25 mm) thick.

YOU WILL NEED

Basic tool kit (see page 16)

Cutter

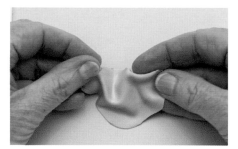

STEP 1 Roll out a sheet of clay 1 p.c. (0.25 mm) thick on a nonstick surface or inside a file pocket. The clay is easiest to control when it is slightly dry but before it begins to crack. Lay the sheet on a tile. Gather the sheet up into crumpled folds, tucking the edges underneath or leaving them visible if you wish.

STEP 2 Use a cutter to cut a neat shape in the piece.

STEP 3 Pull away the scrap clay and dry on the tile. After drying, a thicker sheet can be pasted to the back to hold a brooch back or pendant bail after firing.

Shaping sheets over formers

Three-dimensional forms can be created by shaping strips or sheets over formers. Glass and glazed ceramic or stainless steel make the best formers because the dried clay is easier to remove from these surfaces.

YOU WILL NEED

Basic tool kit (see page 16)

Former—here a knitting needle

FOLDED PENDANT, *LYNDA CHENEY* Textured clay sheets have been shaped over a former; the top piece appears to peel back to reveal the interior dangle.

Cutting and shaping sheets

Sheets of clay lend themselves to being cut and formed into exciting shapes. You can find great ideas in books on papercrafts. Experiment with polymer clay first. In this instance the sheets should be 2 p.c. to 4 p.c. (0.5 to 1 mm) thick.

YOU WILL NEED

Basic tool kit (see page 16)

Cutter

Polymer clay

STEP 1 Cut out the required shape from a soft clay sheet on a tile. Texturing one side of the sheet adds interest to this technique. It is easier to create flaps if the clay is fairly firm, but not cracking.

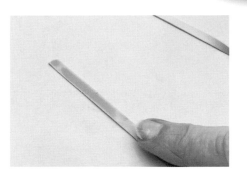

STEP 1 Use a 2 p.c. (0.5 mm) thick sheet, textured on one side if you wish. Cut a strip of clay and wet one side to help it stick to the former.

STEP 2 Place the wet side of one end at an angle on the former and wind the strip around and down.

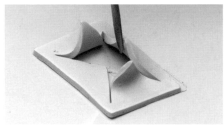

STEP 2 Pull up the flaps of clay and curl them over in the directions required. Use small scraps of polymer clay to weight them in place. Alternatively, use paste to attach them in their new position.

STEP 3 Dry on the former then gently ease it off. These twirls make attractive pendants and drop earrings.

ALTERNATIVE METHOD To make domed shapes, cut out the required shapes from a sheet of clay and press these onto a glass marble or piece of dowel. Lightbulbs can be used for larger pieces. When made in pairs, these can be pasted together after drying to make hollow lentil beads.

STEP 3 After drying and firing, the piece can be further embellished by backing with polymer clay for a peephole effect.

Paste replicas

Metal clay paste or slip is mainly used as a joining and mending material, but it can also be used to create beautiful jewelry. Paste is the most fragile form of metal clay but if used thickly enough it can be remarkably durable.

An exciting technique for creating jewelry with paste is to make replica leaves by coating the underside of a leaf with layers of paste, then drying and firing. The original leaf burns away and a beautiful metal clay leaf results.

Paste leaves
Replica leaves made from a variety of herb leaves.

TIPS FOR SUCCESSFUL REPLICA LEAVES
- Choose a leaf that is fairly stiff and can therefore tolerate being coated with paste without collapsing.
- Check the underside of the leaf: it should have a good strong texture in the veins.
- Avoid leaves that are hairy, because the hairs will interfere with the texture.
- Remember that metal clay paste does not produce as strong a metal as lump clay. If you want to make a strong piece, apply extra coats of paste.

◀ Strength
Successful leaves are strong herb leaves such as sage and lemon balm. Scented geranium leaves are excellent as well as blackberry and raspberry leaves.

▶ Avoid fragility
These leaves will not work well with paste because they lack strong veining and are fragile and thin.

Making replica leaves with paste
All types of metal clay paste can be used to replicate leaves, with silver, copper, and bronze pastes producing gorgeous results in a variety of colors.

YOU WILL NEED

Basic tool kit (see page 16)
Suitable leaf
Paste—about 7 g for a 1" (25 mm) leaf
Mesh
Cotton swab

STEP 1 Scoop some paste onto a tile and add water to make a consistency of thin cream. This will be used for the first layer. Brush the paste all over the back of the leaf, working it into the crevices between the veins.

STEP 2 Dry with a hair-dryer or heat gun until the paste goes pale and matte, and looks dry.

STEP 3 Now apply undiluted paste in a thick layer with a small spatula, again covering the whole of the back of the leaf and working the paste up to all the edges.

STEP 4 Dry again and repeat. The paste layer just applied will become thinner as it dries, so you need to build up the layers in several coats.

STEP 5 After about four thick applications, the paste layer on the leaf should be about 1/32" (1 mm) thick, and the veins completely covered. Support the center of the leaf with a file to preserve its natural shape and dry thoroughly on a mesh.

STEP 6 Use a paintbrush to smooth the back if required and reinforce any thin areas with more paste. Leave the piece to dry completely overnight or in a low oven (210°F/100°C).

STEP 7 Use a damp cotton swab to remove any paste from the top of the leaf. Fire using a blowtorch, stovetop, or in a kiln and the natural leaf will burn away leaving a beautiful replica.

STEP 8 Brush all over the replica to remove any ash from the burnt away leaf. Use a gentle touch to avoid breaking the leaf. Burnish lightly to bring out areas of sparkle in the natural texture.

REPLICA VARIATIONS

Pods and seedheads
Use the same technique to make replicas of seedpods, but apply paste to only half of the pod so that the surface detail of the original is visible after firing. These can be combined into elaborate pieces or be used on their own.

Aquilegia seed head

Flowering Judas tree pod

Maple tree seed

Catananche seed head

Forging
The replica leaves can be annealed and forged into curved shapes to make rings and bangles.

Forged leaves ready for soldering into rings

Hollow core techniques

Hollow core techniques give you freedom to create larger and lighter pieces in metal clay, with the clay pieces made over a combustible core—also sometimes referred to as a "sacrificial core"—that burns away during firing.

Hollow core techniques open up amazing methods of making three-dimensional jewelry. Some of the advantages of hollow form jewelry are:

• It is lighter to wear.
• The amount of metal clay in the piece is reduced and so is more economical.
• Larger three-dimensional forms can be achieved that would be difficult or inappropriate to make in solid clay.
• Interesting designs elements can be created with filigree or openwork where the sacrificial core provides support until fired.

Fine silver and gold metal clay both work well with combustible cores. Metal clays that need to be fired in charcoal are more problematic because there is insufficient oxygen to burn out the core. To work around this, pieces may be fired twice—first at a lower temperature to burn off the core, then embed in charcoal for a full firing. Refer to the manufacturer's instructions. The three main methods of covering a core are with sheets of clay, with syringing, and with paste.

Syringe
Syringed hollow core pendant. See page 92.

Silver pendants made with a combustible core
The right-hand heart had a loop attached by inserting it into the core before covering the rest of the core with silver clay. The left-hand piece has a wire inserted through its hole after firing with a loop made at each end. See page 92.

Core materials

Cork clay
Cork clay is available from metal clay suppliers. It burns away completely but gives off unpleasant fumes when fired, so it is advisable to only use it with a kiln that will contain the fumes.

Wood clay
As for cork clay but with a finer finish. Nontoxic when fired.

Paper, wood, and card
Shapes made from these materials do not need drying as cork and wood clay do.

Pasta
Pasta shapes work well as combustible cores. They come in a great many shapes and burn away completely.

Soft toilet paper
Toilet paper can be wetted and molded to make freeform shapes. However, it is difficult to achieve a smooth finish. White breadcrumbs moistened with water are also successful and similar to use.

Creating the core

Shape core materials with your fingers or with modeling tools. The same basic techniques for shaping metal clay are used for the cores. See page 26.

YOU WILL NEED

Basic tool kit (see page 16)

Core material

STEP 1 Model the core material into the desired shapes just as you would with metal clay. Pieces may be joined by wetting the joining area well and pressing on the fresh piece. Remember that the fired piece will be larger than the core so allow for this.

STEP 2 Wood clay has a finer grain than cork clay and a smoother finish is possible. Work on a tile for flat-backed pieces. You can use cutters to cut the clay into a basic shape, here a round cutter is used to shape a crescent.

STEP 3 Use damp fingers to smooth and refine the shape. There is no point in making fine detail on the core because it will not show through the applied metal clay layer.

STEP 4 If wood clay feels too dry to model easily, flatten it into a pancake and apply a film of water. Fold this inside the piece and knead well. Water can also be added to cork clay in the same way.

STEP 5 A heart shape is popular for pendants. Make a teardrop shape and press it down onto a tile. Use a tool to shape the top of the heart and then smooth and refine the shape.

STEP 6 The core pieces should be left to dry thoroughly, as any moisture left in the material may expand with steam during firing and damage the metal clay covering. Cork and wood clay take 24 hours in an airing cupboard or warm place. Slow drying is preferable to prevent cracking and warping. Alternatively, use a gentle heat of 210°F (100°C) in a domestic oven for at least two hours.

STEP 7 Sand over the dried core with sandpaper to smooth it and remove any lumps or large blemishes. Wood clay can be successfully carved. Any large cracks can be filled with more material and dried again.

HOLLOW CORE VARIATION

Hollow forms can also be made in two halves over formers and dried. The formers are removed and the halves joined before firing. This technique is suitable for stovetop or torch firing because there is no burnout of the core material. It is also best for base metal clay that must be fired in charcoal. This type of hollow core formation is detailed on page 115.

Covering the core with a clay sheet

Clay sheet gives the smoothest result and guarantees sufficient thickness of the hollow form walls. The method given here is rather like putting the peel back on an orange and ensures an even covering.

STEP 1 Roll the clay to a thickness of 2 p.c. to 4 p.c. (0.5 to 1 mm) and cut a piece large enough to cover the core. Lightly dampen the sheet and wrap the wet side of the clay around the thickest part of the core.

STEP 2 Pinch the sheet together where it forms natural folds and use scissors to trim away excess sheet. Aim to cover the core with a single layer of sheet, overlapping joins slightly for strength.

STEP 3 Brush water over the joining edges of clay and smooth over. Work around the piece until it is fully covered and smoothed.

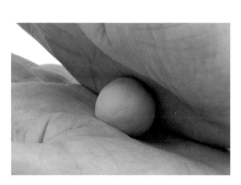

STEP 4 Round shapes can be rolled in your hands to smooth further.

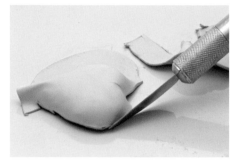

STEP 5 Cover flat-backed shapes by laying over a wetted sheet of clay and tucking it in all round, trimming as required. The piece can be left with an open back, or dried and then another sheet applied to the back in the same way, smoothing the joins.

STORING CORK AND WOOD CLAY

These clays need to be kept moist, so wrap them well in plastic food wrap and keep in an airtight container. Cork clay can show black patches of mold over time but this does not affect its properties.

Covering the core with filigree

Use filigree techniques (see pages 120–123) with combustible cores to make ethereal jewelry. Here, a loop has been inserted into the core as a hanging point. Ensure that the syringed lines connect to each other all over with no gaps. They should also connect on all sides to the loop.

Covering the core with paste

Push a toothpick into the core as a handle and apply multiple layers of paste, drying between each, to build up to at least 1/32" (1 mm) thick.

COVERING PASTA SHAPES

Wrapping cords of clay around pasta shapes is one way to make large-holed bead charms for threading on a chain.

The basic beads can be decorated in many ways

BANGLE OF THE BRIDE,
ELIF ACAR
A wood clay combustible core was used to shape this fabulous Turkish bangle.

Drying and firing

Most large pieces with a combustible core need careful firing in a kiln to contain the smoke from the burnout. However, you can blowtorch or stovetop fire small pieces in silver clay if you fire outdoors. Fire pieces slowly at first with a low flame to burn away the core. Base metal combustible core pieces should be fired as recommended by the clay manufacturer.

YOU WILL NEED

Basic tool kit (see page 16)

Fiber cloth

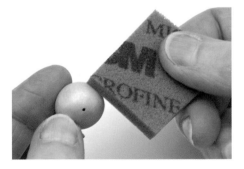

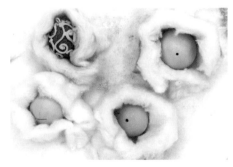

STEP 1 Dry the clay over the core using a gentle heat in an oven at 210°F (100°C). Sand to remove blemishes and add findings using paste if required. It is advisable to make a small, inconspicuous hole in the clay to allow the core gases to escape when burning.

STEP 2 Fire combustible core pieces in a kiln using a nest of fiber cloth (see page 48). The burning out of the core may raise the temperature high enough to melt the metal, so ramp slowly and fire at the lowest temperature recommended for the clay. Do not open the kiln door during firing, otherwise the core will flare. Pieces that are only part covered in clay should be placed with the metal clay downward so that the heat of the burning core escapes upward.

STEP 3 After firing, cool the piece and use a needle to remove any ash left from the core, or rinse under running water.

Construction techniques

Plaster-dry pieces of metal clay can be assembled using slip to make three-dimensional jewelry pieces. This technique produces precision pieces for lockets and other hinged jewelry.

There are many types of jewelry that have the added interest of a hollow interior, be it a locket, box frame, amulet holder, novelty pendant, or ring. Plaster-stage construction techniques are a successful way of creating pieces such as these. The simplest types of three-dimensional objects to make using this technique are flat-sided geometric shapes. For organic and rounded shapes, combustible core techniques are often preferable.

Hollow form jewelry such as lockets or amulets can be further enhanced with hinges (see pages 96–101).

Sheet construction
This bird-box pendant has been created by fixing plaster-dry elements together with paste.

Bronze clay locket made with a cutter
A cutter was used in the making of this locket, and a simple wire loop forms the hinge.

Hinged locket
An oval locket formed using a cutter with a hinge and catch. See pages 95 and 100–101.

Making box forms
Clay sheets cut to a pattern, dried, and assembled using paste make all kinds of interesting three-dimensional shapes. This demonstration makes a hollow bird-box pendant.

YOU WILL NEED

Basic tool kit (see page 16)

Graph paper

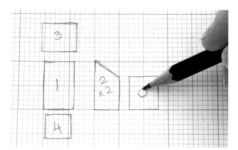

STEP 1 Draw a template for your piece on graph paper, lining up the various parts to ensure they are the correct size to fit together. Allow for the thickness of the clay sheet in your templates, and label each piece to identify it. Try making the piece in cardstock first, which you can then adjust as necessary before making the piece in clay.

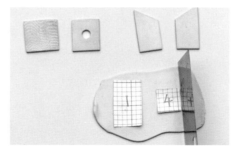

STEP 2 Roll out the clay sheet between 2 p.c. and 4 p.c. (0.5 and 1 mm) thick for smaller pieces, and over 4 p.c. (1 mm) thick for larger pieces that will have unsupported walls more than 1" (25 mm) across. Cut out the pieces on a tile using the templates (see page 71). To avoid warping, dry on the tile without added heat for an hour, you can then add heat as desired after this time.

STEP 3 Apply paste along one edge of a piece and press it against an adjacent piece. Use the end of a rolling guide to ensure that pieces are at right angles.

STEP 4 Continue to assemble the piece in the same way, building extra paste inside to reinforce. Accuracy at each step is important when fitting the pieces together. If any piece does not fit well, rub the edge on sandpaper to correct it.

STEP 5 Paste on the final piece—here the roof of the bird box. Dry the piece thoroughly. If you are making a sealed box without openings, drill a hole in an unobtrusive place before firing to avoid cracking during firing.

STEP 6 Sand away any excess paste and use paste to fill any gaps. Dry and sand again as necessary. Add a pendant loop or other findings as required. Fire the piece whichever way gives maximum support to minimize sagging of any larger unsupported walls. These pieces will fire successfully on a stovetop or with a torch.

Making lockets using cutters

Use a metal cutter as a former to make lockets and other box-type jewelry. The shape of the cutter determines the shape of the piece.

YOU WILL NEED

Basic tool kit (see page 16)

Cutter

Hinge and catch

STEP 1 Choose a cutter. Roll out a sheet of clay between 2 p.c. and 4 p.c. (0.5 and 1 mm) thick as required. Cut a strip of about ¼" (6 mm); the width of the strip will be the depth of the locket. Apply the strip round the cutting edge of the cutter.

STEP 2 Make a butt joint by cutting through the two ends together and removing the waste clay, but do not join the ends, which will make removal easier after drying. Dry on the cutter.

STEP 3 Remove the dried clay piece from the cutter and paste the two ends together. Dry and sand. You now have the sides of the locket in the shape of the cutter.

STEP 4 Roll out another sheet of clay and place on a tile to make the locket back. Wet the surface and press the locket sides onto the sheet of clay. Trim round the sides and remove the scrap clay.

STEP 5 Dry on the tile, then sand the base to smooth the cut edges.

STEP 6 To make the locket front, lay the locket on another sheet of clay and cut around about ¹⁄₃₂" (1 mm) away from the sides.

STEP 7 Dry and sand the front edges so that they fit the locket base, and follow the instructions on pages 100–101 to add a hinge and catch.

Adding hinges and catches

Hinges are an attractive element when added to certain types of jewelry. A small door that opens to reveal a hidden interior can be a delightful feature in a pendant or ring, while a hinged bracelet is durable and stylish.

Making tiny hinges for jewelry is one of the more challenging techniques in metal clay, but one that is within the capabilities of most if taken one step at a time. The following method of creating small tubes for hinges should soon be achievable with a little practice. The clay is rolled into a log around a needle, then dried to make fine tubes. These are attached to the two pieces to be hinged and, after firing, the hinge is assembled with the appropriate size of wire as the hinge pin.

Molded acorn locket
This locket is molded in two halves from a real acorn and then hinged. See pages 78–79.

Hinge and catch locket
Hinged jewelry often needs catches to hold the elements in place when shut. This locket has a hinge and catch. See pages 100–101.

Friction catch
The catch is a chip of silver that holds the door shut by friction when it is closed.

Wire hinge
A locket with a wire loop making a simple swinging hinge.

NEEDLES AND WIRE

You will need a long darning needle of the correct thickness for the size of hinge required and the thickness of wire used. A good size for small jewelry hinges made from metal clay that shrinks by about 10 percent is a needle 1/32" (1 mm) thick and wire 20 to 19 ga (0.8 to 0.9 mm) thick. After firing, the tube will shrink to an internal diameter correct for the wire. A tube made from a 1/16" (1.5 mm) thick needle will need wire of about 16 ga (1.3 mm) thick. Do not use fired logs of metal clay instead of wire, because they will not be strong enough.

BLUE MOON BRACELET,
SUZANNE REUBEN
Hinges link the curved elements of this gem-studded bracelet.

Making the hinge tubes

These tubes form the basis of all the hinges detailed in the following techniques.

YOU WILL NEED

Basic tool kit (see page 16)

Needle of the required diameter

Sheet of Perspex

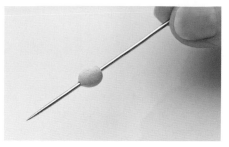

STEP 1 Pinch off a small lump of metal clay that is well moistened. Form it into a small ball and pierce it with the needle.

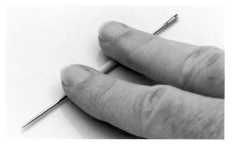

STEP 2 Lay the needle on your work surface and roll it back and forth so that the ball forms a log and extends along the needle in both directions.

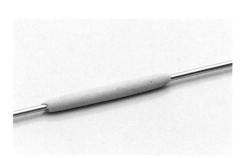

STEP 3 Continue until the log becomes a thin tube around the needle. If you feel that the clay is getting floppy it means it is pulling away from the needle. Pinch the log all along its length to exclude the air inside and attach it to the needle again.

STEP 4 Give the clay a final gentle roll with a sheet of Perspex to make the tube more even. Check the thickness of the log: it should be no more than double the thickness of the needle or about ¹⁄₁₆" (2 mm) thick.

STEP 5 Hold a sharp blade against the clay tube and rotate the needle to cut the tube into sections. Their lengths will depend on the size of the piece to be hinged. You will need three lengths of tube for a hinge, so measure the total length of hinge required and divide by three. A ½" (12 mm) hinge will require three ⁵⁄₃₂" (4 mm) lengths. Cut the lengths oversize to allow for sanding after drying, and cut more than you need for spares.

STEP 6 You can leave some of the tube uncut, since it can be cut up for future hinges with a sharp blade when dry. Dry the tube thoroughly on the needle and when dry, slide it off the needle.

STEP 7 Sand the ends of each length on a flat piece of sandpaper, holding the clay tube exactly upright to ensure the ends are straight. Reassemble on the needle to check they fit together tightly, and sand to adjust if necessary. The tube is now ready to be made into a hinge.

Making a flat hinge

This is the easiest type of hinge to make. Two flat pieces of metal have a hinge along one side. This can be used for joining the links of a bracelet.

STEP 1 With the hinge tubes assembled on their needle, place them alongside the point where they are to be attached to both flat clay pieces and mark their position on the flat pieces with a pencil. Positioning is important for the hinge to work well, so be accurate in your marks.

STEP 2 Apply paste to the edge of the piece where the two outer tubes will be attached. The central tube will be attached to the other flat piece to make the hinge.

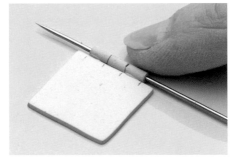

STEP 3 Press the outer hinge tubes, still on the needle, onto the paste, taking care that no paste touches the central tube. Dry with a heat gun or hair-dryer.

STEP 4 Now apply paste to the central point of the second flat piece where the central tube will be attached.

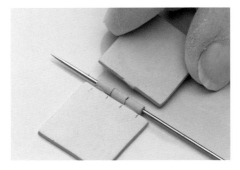

STEP 5 Press the second flat piece against the hinges, positioning it carefully so that the paste only contacts the central tube. Dry as before.

STEP 6 Carefully remove the needle and separate the two hinged pieces. Apply paste all around the joins to reinforce them, then dry and sand the whole piece. Check that the reassembled hinge moves easily with the needle in place, then remove the needle to fire and cool.

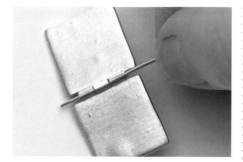

STEP 7 Assemble the hinge with wire instead of the needle. If it is too tight to insert, use a thinner gauge of wire. If it is not a tight fit, use a larger gauge of wire. If necessary, file away any metal that prevents free movement of the hinge. Cut the wire so that it is about 1/32" (1 mm) longer than the hinge.

STEP 8 Position the hinge on the edge of an anvil or hard surface and rivet the ends of the wire to secure the hinge, following the instructions on pages 102–103.

STEP 9 The finished hinge should work freely and give at least 90 degrees of movement in both directions.

Making a book hinge

This type of hinge is used when the two metal pieces to be hinged must lie flat when closed together. The two pieces are offset so that the hinge lies in the right angle between them. This type of hinge makes an attractive miniature book pendant.

YOU WILL NEED

Basic tool kit (see page 16)

Three hinge tubes to make up the total length required, plaster dry (see page 97)

Two pieces of plaster-dry clay to be hinged together

Wire

Hammer

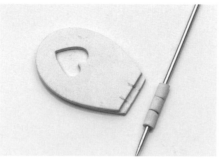

STEP 1 Make three hinge tubes (see page 97) and reassemble them on the needle after drying and sanding. Place the two plaster-dried pieces of metal clay together, one on top of the other, with the lower one protruding above the upper one as shown.

STEP 2 Attach the two outer hinge tubes to the top piece with paste. Attach the central hinge tube to the center of the lower piece. Reinforce the join with paste and dry. Check that the hinge opens and shuts, then remove the needle and reinforce the pasting around the joins. Dry and sand smooth. After firing, assemble the hinge with riveted wire or alternatively use an ornate hinge pin (see below).

ALTERNATIVE HINGE PIN

You can make an ornate hinge pin instead of a rivet. Cut the wire long enough to make a decorative coil at either end and shape the ends into spirals with pliers. A chain can be attached to the coils.

Make open coils for attaching a chain

Making a locket hinge

Locket or box hinges are made at the edge of a locket and lie at right angles when closed. The locket to be hinged should be in the plaster-dry state.

The finished locket shown open. The hinge should be tight but still move freely

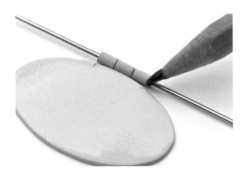

STEP 1 Make three hinge tubes (see page 97). Lay the tubes against the locket front and mark their position on the locket.

STEP 2 File the side straight where the hinges will be attached.

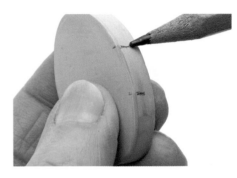

STEP 3 Place the front piece on the locket. Transfer the markings on the top to the side of the locket, matching them accurately.

STEP 4 Roll out a small 4 p.c. (1 mm) thick sheet of clay and cut a rectangle to reinforce the locket side where the hinge is to be added. A decorative lower edge adds interest. Paste the sheet onto the side of the locket, flush with the top edge of the locket base.

STEP 5 With the locket front in place to ensure accuracy when attaching the hinge, paste the two outer hinge tubes to the top of the added piece on the locket base. Allow to dry.

STEP 6 File a flat notch in the locket front between the marks so that the bottom hinges can move freely when opening the lid.

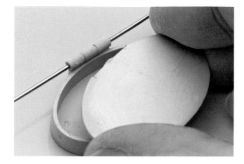

STEP 7 Apply paste to the center of the lid notch and press it against the central hinge still held in place on the needle next to the outer hinges.

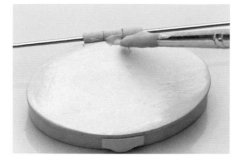

STEP 8 Reinforce the join with paste and dry. Check that the hinge opens and shuts, then remove the needle and reinforce the pasting round the joins. Dry and sand smooth. Add a hanging loop to the locket and a catch before firing (see below). After firing, assemble the hinge with wire, and rivet (see page 102).

Making a locket catch

Hinged jewelry often needs a catch to hold the hinged part shut. While there are many complex types of catches for jewelry, the following simple catch is relatively easy to make and will serve for most types of locket.

YOU WILL NEED

Basic tool kit (see page 16)

Plaster-dry locket with hinge in place

1 mm drill bit

Balled end piece of 20 ga (0.8 mm) wire (see balling wire in Findings, page 66)

³⁄₁₆" (5 mm) length of plaster-dry hinge tube (see page 97)

Wire

PANEL RING,
TERRY KOVALCIK
Hand-carved openwork panels are linked with neat hinges in this unusual ring.

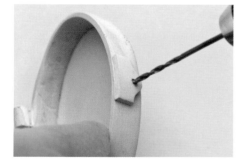

STEP 1 Decide the point where the catch is to be attached and reinforce the side of the locket with a decorative sheet of clay, as for the locket hinge, above. Drill a hole in the lower center for the balled wire. Trim the wire end to about ¹⁄₃₂" (1 mm) from the ball and use paste to embed it with the balled end protruding to make the catch knob.

STEP 2 Attach the hinge tube with paste to the side of the locket front so that it will sit directly above the catch knob when the front is closed. Fire the locket and rivet the hinge as described on page 102.

STEP 3 Measure the distance from the tube to the knob and cut a piece of wire three times this length. Form this into a triangle with the join in the center of the top of the triangle and insert the ends into the tube. Push the wire triangle down over the knob. Use pliers to nip the wire together around the knob until it is a tight fit and snaps over the knob to close. Take care not to lever against the tube, otherwise it may fracture.

Rivets

Rivets are used to connect fired pieces of metal clay together, and are often a decorative element as well. They are useful for joining pieces when either soldering or firing is not appropriate.

Rivets can be used to connect different materials together, such as different types of fired metal clay that are difficult to join using other means. They can also be used to join metal pieces to polymer clay, paper, card, plastic, glass, or fabric, because no heat is involved.

Riveting is a secure method of connecting jewelry mechanically. It can also be used to make movable parts by riveting pieces together using card as packing, so that when the packing is torn away, the connections provide free movement.

IF I COULD FLY,
HOLLY GAGE
Rivets are part of the decoration around the perimeter of this brooch.

Basic riveting
A silver flower is topped with a copper washer and riveted to a bronze backing.

Bail
A copper clay bail is riveted to a polymer clay piece.

Ring
This polymer clay bead is riveted to a silver clay ring and topped with a textured silver washer.

Compass
This ceramic compass card with a silver clay compass needle is riveted to a copper clay backing.

RIVETING THEORY

A rivet is a short length of wire or metal that is inserted into a hole drilled through two or more elements that are to be joined together. Gentle tapping with a hammer creates a head at each end of the wire to capture the pieces into a whole. The wire must fit tightly in the hole, otherwise it will bend during the tapping process.

Basic riveting

When making pieces to be riveted in metal clay, drill the hole at the plaster-dry stage, then drill again with the same drill bit after firing to enlarge the hole to the correct diameter for the wire used. Use the same drill bit to drill the rivet hole in all of the other elements.

YOU WILL NEED

Basic tool kit (see page 16)

Fired pieces to be riveted together, with holes drilled at plaster-dry stage

1/32" (1 mm) drill bit in a pin vise

18 ga (1 mm) wire, in the metal of your choice—copper wire is used here

Hammer with a chisel end (see page 22)

Rubber block or anvil

STEP 1 Redrill the holes in the fired metal clay pieces, because they will have shrunk during firing. Other materials should be drilled with the same drill bit.

STEP 2 Stack the elements to be riveted and push the end of the wire through the holes in each layer.

File each end of the wire flat

STEP 3 Trim the wire to ¹/₃₂" (1 mm)—or one wire width if greater—above the washer and file both ends of the wire to ensure they are completely flat. Place the pile on a hammering surface.

The finished rivet heads should lie snug against the metal on each side

STEP 4 Hold everything tightly together and use the chisel end of the hammer to tap the protruding end of the wire until it just begins to spread outward. Rotate the piece as you tap to ensure an even result.

STEP 5 Flip the stack and push the elements onto the flattened rivet. Trim the wire again if it is protruding more than ¹/₆₄" (0.5 mm), and tap again. Rotate the stack as you hammer to spread the end of the wire and make a second rivet head.

STEP 6 Finally, hammer the ends of the rivets on both sides with the flat head of the hammer to flatten them and consolidate the whole.

Captured rivet

This type of riveting involves embedding a wire in the bottom layer of a stack of elements to be riveted and using this wire as the rivet. It can be used to make interesting rings.

YOU WILL NEED

Basic tool kit (see page 16)

Plaster dry metal clay ring

Wire

Bead and metal clay washer

Mandrel

Hammer

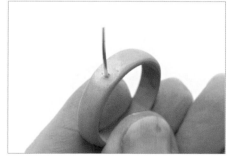

STEP 1 Embed the wire in the plaster-dry metal clay—here in the top of a ring shank—before firing.

STEP 2 To attach a feature bead to the top of a ring with a captured rivet, thread the bead on the wire and top with a washer. Trim the wire as with basic riveting and put the ring on a mandrel to support it. Tap the end of the wire until the pieces are held tightly together. There is no need to tap the other side, which is embedded in the ring.

Links and chains

Linking pieces of fired metal clay together enables you to work larger and create articulated jewelry that moves with the body. This section shows you how to link in a variety of ways for bracelets and necklets, as well as how to make your own chunky chains from metal clays.

Links are used mainly for making bracelets and necklaces, and are a fascinating area of jewelry making. Links can be identical and geometric in shape or random, organic, and varied. They can be flat sections joined with jump rings or lengths of chain; or curved links joined with wire connections. Variations on linking can also be used to connect pieces for elaborate dangling earrings.

Chains are made by cutting or shaping pieces into loops and interlocking them together.

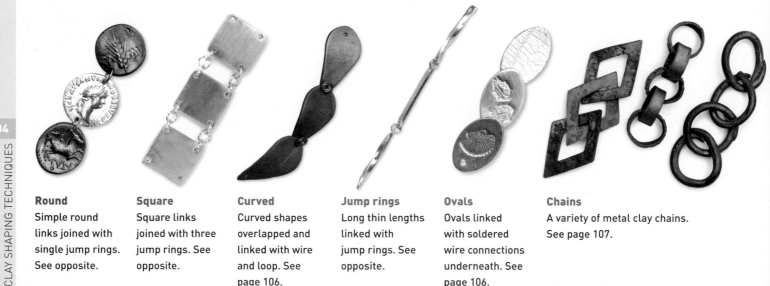

Round
Simple round links joined with single jump rings. See opposite.

Square
Square links joined with three jump rings. See opposite.

Curved
Curved shapes overlapped and linked with wire and loop. See page 106.

Jump rings
Long thin lengths linked with jump rings. See opposite.

Ovals
Ovals linked with soldered wire connections underneath. See page 106.

Chains
A variety of metal clay chains. See page 107.

TEXTURED TILE BRACELET,
SUZANNE REUBEN
Intricate textures embellish this ornately linked bracelet.

Joining links with jump rings

This is one of the easiest ways of connecting elements into a bracelet, and uses a single jump ring between each pair of links. Attach relevant findings, such as catches or clasps, when all the elements are linked (see pages 57–63).

YOU WILL NEED

Basic tool kit (see page 16)

Graph paper

1mm drill bit or suitable size to make holes to take jump rings

Jump rings (see page 57)

CHAIN BRACELET,
EMMA BAIRD
A simple chain bracelet in fine silver with round textured links.

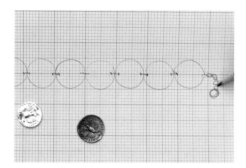

STEP 1 First, calculate how many links you will need for the bracelet. The average woman's bracelet is about 8" (20 cm) long. The clay pieces will shrink depending on clay type and brand, so make a sketch of the bracelet to scale allowing for this, and mark the distance between the links for the jump rings. Draw in the catch to be used as well.

STEP 2 Make the elements to be linked. Here, simple one-part molds have been used to mold replica coins. Mark the position of the jump ring holes with a blunt needle. The holes should be at least 1/16" (2 mm) from the edge for strength. You can position them farther in but remember to allow for the size of jump ring that you will be using to link the pieces.

STEP 3 Dry the pieces and then drill the holes at the points marked. After firing and polishing, connect all the links together by threading with jump rings (see page 57).

JUMP RING JOIN VARIATIONS

Using square links and three jump rings together at each corner gives more space between the links. You could use a larger jump ring between two smaller ones, and small dangles or charms can be hung from the jump rings to add further interest.

Cut long bars of clay—1" (25 mm) or more—from a thick sheet, flatten the ends of each bar, and make a hole, then, after firing, connect the bars with jump rings. For variety, some bars can be twisted.

Hammer jump rings to strengthen them before attaching (see page 55)

Joining links with wire

This type of connection uses lengths of wire to attach links together. The result is an articulated piece with decorative connections. Use curved links for bracelets so they will sit comfortably on the wrist, and attach relevant findings, such as catches or clasps, when all the elements are linked (see pages 57–63).

YOU WILL NEED

Basic tool kit (see page 16)

1 mm drill bit or suitable size to take wire gauge used

Drinks can

Wire—20 ga to 18 ga (0.8 mm to 1 mm) is a suitable size. Use a larger gauge for heavier pieces.

STEP 1 Make the required number of links by cutting out the shapes from a sheet of clay. This example has been textured with feathers. Mark the position of a single hole in each end of each link with a blunt needle, at least ¹⁄₁₆" (2 mm) from the edge for strength and allowing an overlap of about ¼" (6mm) or more for a heavier bracelet. Dry the pieces on a drinks can to curve them for a bracelet, then drill the holes at the points marked. Fire and polish.

WIRE JOIN VARIATION

In this type of link the connecting wire is hidden under the bracelet.

Instead of using a balled end on each wire, you can embed or solder the wire to the underside of one end of each link. Drill a hole in the other end. Thread the wire through the link below and curve it over to just touch the first link as shown. It should be just long enough to allow free movement.

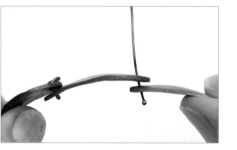

STEP 2 Cut the wire into 1" (25 mm) lengths and use a blowtorch to ball one end of each (see page 66). Alternatively, turn a small loop on one end of each wire instead. Thread the wire through adjacent links so they overlap as shown, with the balled end underneath.

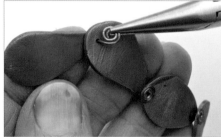

STEP 3 Use pliers to twist the protruding end of the wire into a decorative coil on the top of the upper link. Repeat for as many links as required. Bracelets made with this technique move well and sit comfortably around the wrist because of the curved links.

When the links are viewed from the right side, the linking wires are invisible. Here, identical oval links decorated in different ways, form the components of a bracelet.

WHITE BRONZE HEADBAND,
SABINE ALIENOR SINGERY
Textured leaves of bronze are linked with black thonging for a beautiful headband.

Chains

Dramatic jewelry can be created by making chains of openwork metal clay links. The clay is shaped into large links that are interlocked with each other in the plaster-dry stage before firing. Links can be cut from sheets of clay or extruded and joined.

There are various ways of connecting chain links, but the following is one of the easiest to accomplish.

YOU WILL NEED

Basic tool kit (see page 16)

Cutters or templates

STEP 1 Roll out a sheet of clay at least 4 p.c. (1 mm) thick and use cutters or templates to cut out the required number of links. Cut out the center of each link using a smaller identical shape, or a different one. Chain links with larger holes tend to lie better.

STEP 2 Dry the pieces and sand smooth. Hold a piece firmly on a flat surface and cut through the clay with a sharp blade. Most plaster-dry clays will cut well without cracking, but they vary between metal type and brand. If the clay link breaks in two with the first cut, proceed to the next step and mend as you join.

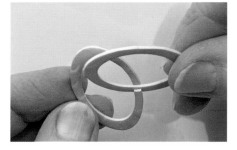

STEP 3 Ease open the link, which should be flexible enough for the purpose, and loop it through two other links to give three in a row.

STEP 4 Apply water or paste to the cut edges and press together. Smooth over the join with a fingertip and apply more paste if required to ensure a strong joint. Repeat to connect the next two links to the chain, cutting one free link and using it to attach the other to the chain. This means that you only have to cut half the links.

STEP 5 Fire the whole chain—the links should not stick together. Take care if you plan to polish with a mini drill, and hold the chain tightly around a piece of wood to prevent snagging.

CHAIN VARIATIONS

Extruded or rolled lengths of clay can be made into rings, figures of eight, or S-shapes. When dry, make more rings in soft clay and use them to connect the dry rings.

Charm bracelets are eternally popular and you can make your own charms in metal clay. These can be shapes cut out from sheets of clay or molded from original sculpts, buttons, or other objects. Make your own chain from small links, or use a purchased one. Attach the charms to the bracelet using jump rings.

CHAIN MAKING TIP
Use plenty of paste when joining bronze and copper clay chain links, otherwise they may crack during firing.

Combining clays

Ever since the appearance of base metal clays, metal clay artists have been experimenting with combining clays of different colored metals in one piece. The different firing temperatures required have made this a challenge, but new solutions are being found all the time.

MY PRIMARY COLORS,
HADAR JACOBSON
Extruded, multicolored metal clays are showcased in this colorful pendant.

Caning
Stripes in silver and copper. Stacked layers are rolled into a sheet. See page 110.

Feathering
Feathering in silver and copper. See page 110.

Appliqué
Appliqué in bronze and copper. See page 111.

Inlay
Inlay of silver into copper. See page 111.

Mokumé gané effect
Wood grain effects in silver and copper. See opposite.

More caning
Stripes in copper and bronze.

Many beautiful effects can be achieved by combining different types of metal in a single piece.

Metal clays can be combined in four main ways:
- During the soft clay stage by partially mixing clays together as shown here.
- By embellishing the surface of one type of clay with another. (See Appliqué on page 111).
- Adding soft clay of lower firing clay to a fired piece of a different type. The whole is then fired at the temperature required for the added clay.
- After firing, using links, soldering, and riveting (see pages 64, 102, and 104).

The first method is the most difficult because of the different firing requirements of different clays. Charcoal firing in a kiln is required to prevent the base metal clays from oxidizing. Careful temperature regimes are also needed so that clays of different firing temperatures are fully sintered in a combined firing.

RUNNING HORSES BROOCH,
CHRIS PATE
Silver, bronze, and copper clays are all used to make this atmospheric brooch.

CLAY SHAPING TECHNIQUES

Metal clay caning

Caning is a way of organizing metal clay colors within a block of clay that is then sliced to reveal patterns. The results are similar to the metalwork technique of laminating different metals, called "mokumé gané."

Use different color clays, but with similar firing schedules, preferably from the same manufacturer (see the box on page 111).

YOU WILL NEED

Basic tool kit (see page 16)

Fast-fire copper metal clay and fast-fire bronze metal clay, preferably of the same brand

Small rectangular cutter or template, about ¾ x 1" (20 x 25 mm)

Wavy tissue blade

Firing container and charcoal (see page 49)

AVOIDING WASTE

You will inevitably have scraps of clay left over from combined projects, and the cost of silver clay makes it desirable to use the silver and copper scraps. If the scraps consist of approximately 50 percent each of silver and copper/silver alloy, you can make them into 75 percent/25 percent copper/silver alloy again by adding two parts pure copper clay to one part of the mixture. Use for the silver/copper technique on page 111.

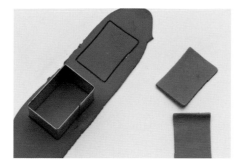

STEP 1 Roll out separate sheets of the bronze and copper clay to 4 p.c. (1 mm) thick and use a rectangular cutter to cut out several pieces from each sheet.

STEP 2 Stack alternate types into a small loaf. A light smear of water between each layer helps the two different clays to stick together, but do not use too much, otherwise the loaf will be too wet to cut.

STEP 3 Compress the stack a little, cut in half, and stack again to give double the layers. These should be about 2 p.c. (0.5mm) thick after compressing.

STEP 4 Stand the stack on one edge so that the layers inside are vertical and shape into a slight curve. Use a wavy tissue blade to cut thin slices from the stack. You will find that the slices will have a variety of loops and patterns that you can alter by distorting the stack in different ways.

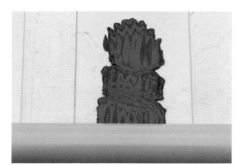

STEP 5 Lay the slices on a nonstick surface and roll them out thinly using a roller and roller guides. This will flatten the corrugations caused by the blade and make a smooth veneer.

STEP 6 The veneer can now be cut to shape with cutters, as here, applied to formers, or backed with a sheet of copper or bronze clay to make rings and other jewelry.

STEP 7 Fire in a kiln using the firing instructions detailed on page 111 for the appropriate clay mix used. Apply Baldwin's patina to bring out the contrasting colors of the fired copper and bronze (see page 185).

Feathering effects with copper and silver

This technique is relatively easy to do and is borrowed from cake icing methods. To ensure proper sintering of the copper clay, it is first mixed with 25 percent fine silver clay to make an alloy. This technique can be practiced first with two different colors of polymer clay.

YOU WILL NEED

Basic tool kit (see page 16)

Fast-fire copper clay and low-fire fine silver clay

Small rectangular cutter or template, about ¾ x 1" (20 x 25 mm)

Toothpick

Firing container and charcoal (see page 49)

STEP 1 To make the copper alloy, roll sheets of copper and silver clay 4 p.c. (1 mm) thick. Cut out three rectangles of copper and one of silver clay.

STEP 2 Mix the two clays together thoroughly by rolling them thin and folding them in half repeatedly until all streakiness has disappeared.

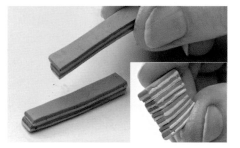

STEP 3 Roll out 4 p.c. (1 mm) sheets of the mixed clay and more of the fine silver clay. Cut out rectangles with the cutter (keep all scraps separate for future projects) and stack as for caning (see page 109).

STEP 4 Cut the stack in half lengthwise and stack again, then press down so that the stripes are thinner. Repeat to make a thin, tall stack.

STEP 5 Place the stack on a nonstick surface and lay 8 p.c. (2 mm rolling guides) on either side. Roll flat along the direction of the lines. Use this as a finished pattern or continue to create the feathering.

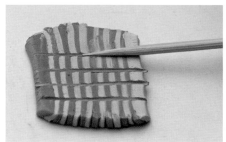

STEP 6 Lay the piece on a tile and smooth it down. Drag the point of a toothpick over the surface in lines about ⅛" (3 mm) apart, all in one direction. Do not mark too deeply, the objective is to disturb the lines on the surface, not cut into the sheet.

STEP 7 Now repeat, dragging the toothpick in the opposite direction between the first lines to make a feathered pattern.

STEP 8 Finally, lay 4 p.c. (1 mm roller guides) on either side of the piece and roll across the pattern to accentuate it. Cut out shapes with cutters or use as required. Dry thoroughly and fire using the instructions detailed opposite for silver and copper alloy clays combined.

Firing silver clays with copper/silver alloys

Best results are achieved if the clay is first fired with a blowtorch or on an open kiln shelf to burn off the binder. Full firing in charcoal then sinters the clays.

COMBINATION VARIATIONS

► To make spirals, try rolling together a sheet each of copper and bronze like a jelly roll (Swiss roll). Cut slices to apply to a sheet of copper clay and roll thinly to make a veneer.

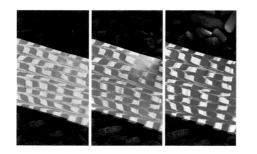

STEP 1 Lay the piece on a ½" (13 mm) deep layer of charcoal in a suitable firing container. Heat the piece with a blowtorch until it flames and the binder has burned away (see page 46). The silver will look white and copper parts will look black. Alternatively, fire on an open shelf in a kiln at 1,110°F (600°C) for ten minutes.

STEP 2 Cover with at least ½" (13 mm) of charcoal and fire as detailed in the table below. Leave the piece to cool in the charcoal or remove and quench immediately. The metal should be smooth on the surface and strong with both types fully sintered. See Patinas on page 183 for how to emphasize the different colors.

► To appliqué a clay motif onto a clay base, first make the base piece in bronze clay and dry. Add cutout shapes of copper clay, using paste to attach them.

Firing combined clays

These firing schedules are for a small front loading muffle kiln with an internal chamber size of 5½ x 4 x 6½" (14 x 10 x 17 cm). The schedules can only be an approximation, because kilns vary considerably in their internal temperatures, so test small pieces first to find the correct temperature for your kiln. You should also refer to the clay manufacturer's instructions.

These combining techniques have been tested using the following types of clay: Base metal clays: Fast-fire or quick-fire clays that fire in less than two hours. Low fire silver clays: Art Clay Silver 650 clays and PMC3.

It is advisable to do a test firing of combined clays. If there is any sign of the metal crumbling, fire using the second phase again at 20°F (10°C) higher. If there is blistering, fire at 20°F (10°C) lower.

▲ To inlay metal clay, make a background sheet of copper/silver alloy mixture and stamp or texture (see pages 72–76). Dry, then fill the recesses with silver clay paste. Dry and sand back.

FIRING COMBINED CLAYS

Clay combination	First phase (to burn off the binder)	Second phase
Fast-fire copper clay with fast-fire bronze clay	On an open kiln board or in charcoal: Full ramp to 1,110°F (600°C) Hold 10 minutes then proceed at once to phase two	In a container with charcoal covering, no lid necessary: Full ramp to 1,560°F (850°C) Hold 90 minutes
Fast-fire copper (75%) and low-fire fine silver (25%) alloy mixture with low-fire fine silver clay	Torch fire on top of charcoal or fire on an open kiln board: 1,110°F (600°C) for 10 minutes Proceed at once to phase two	In a container with charcoal covering, no lid necessary: Full ramp to 1,330°F (720°C) Hold 90 minutes

Bead making techniques

Bead making is a favorite technique for many metal clay artists, and one that the clays lend themselves to beautifully. This section features bead-making techniques of all kinds.

You can use metal clay to make large feature beads or tiny bead caps, which can be decorated with a wide variety of techniques. Making lots of tiny beads in metal clay is not a worthwhile undertaking because purchasing commercially made beads is less costly in both time and materials. However, making your own large feature beads or beads that match a theme in a piece of jewelry is an exciting process that is not difficult.

There are five main ways to make beads using metal clay:
• Forming a bead in solid clay by hand or using a mold.
• Making flat and disk beads from strips and sheets.
• Using a combustible core for hollow beads.
• Making beads in two halves over a former or in a mold.
• Making tube beads on a former.

AFRICAN DRUM BEADS,
STANLEY MICALLEF
These beads were formed over cork clay. They have been decorated with applied clay, carving, and gemstones.

Hand-formed small beads
Heart, bicones, and melon beads. See pages 113 and 114.

Silver flat beads from sheets
See page 114.

Silver filigree beads using combustible core
See page 92.

Bronze, copper, and silver molded beads
See page 117.

Lentil beads from marbles
Silver hollow core lentil beads. See page 115.

Tube beads from needles
Silver hollow core beads made on knitting needles. See page 116.

Copper bead caps and bead cone
See page 119.

Hand-forming solid, round beads

While solid beads are the simplest beads to make, they use the most clay for the size of bead, which is expensive for precious metal clay, and the resulting beads are relatively heavy. However, this is a useful technique for base metal beads or small silver beads.

YOU WILL NEED

Basic tool kit (see page 16)

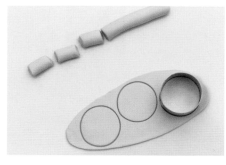

STEP 1 To make several beads of the same size, roll a log of clay and cut equal lengths. Alternatively, roll out a sheet of clay and cut several identical shapes with a cutter. This ensures that each bead is the same size.

STEP 2 For a simple round bead, roll the clay into a ball. Lay the bead on a tile and pierce down from above with a sharp darning needle.

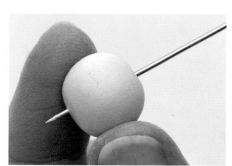

STEP 3 Lift the bead on the darning needle and push the clay farther onto the needle, twisting the needle at the same time to make it slide on more easily.

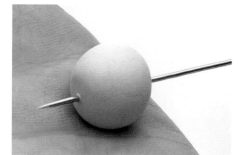

STEP 4 Finally, roll the bead back and forth on your palm to smooth the bead's surface and enlarge the hole.

STEP 5 If the bead shows any cracking on the surface, hold it on the needle and use your finger to slick water over the surface to make a slip that will fill the cracks and smooth the bead.

SOLID BEAD SHAPE VARIATIONS

To make melon beads, roll and pierce a round bead, then press the side of a second darning needle vertically against the side of the bead all round, keeping the spacing even.

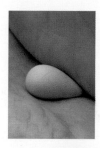

1 To make a heart, roll one side of a ball of clay against your palm to point it into a teardrop shape.

2 Press the teardrop lightly down on to a tile to flatten it, then push a needle into the rounded top to divide it into a heart.

3 Pierce vertically or horizontally using a darning needle.

SOLID BEADS TIP
The warmth from your fingers will dry the clay as you shape the beads, so make sure it is well hydrated before you begin.

Making flat beads from sheets

These simple beads are easy to make from rolled out sheets of clay. They can be decorated in many exciting ways, from texturing and stamping to adding color with enamel or resin. Remember to embellish both sides, because they will flip round when worn.

YOU WILL NEED

Basic tool kit (see page 16)

Texture sheet (optional)

Cutters

Darning needle

STEP 1 Roll out a sheet of clay between 2 p.c. and 4 p.c. (0.5 and 1 mm) thick. You can work fairly thinly to save clay, because the beads will be double the thickness of the sheet. Texture the sheet if you wish and use cutters to cut out pairs of shapes.

STEP 2 Lay one shape, right side down, on your work surface and brush over the top with water. Lay a needle or toothpick across the center of the shape.

STEP 3 Gently press a second piece, right side up, onto the first. Press hard enough to make a good join but not so hard as to damage any texture you have applied. Pat the clay down on either side of the needle and twist the needle so that it moves freely.

STEP 4 Dry, then remove the needle. The fired and finished beads can be threaded onto a cord, or connected with wire and loops, as here, and interspersed with beads of other materials.

Hand-forming solid bicone beads

Make bicone beads using a Perspex sheet or log roller to create the classic shape.

YOU WILL NEED

Basic tool kit (see page 16)

Log roller or Perspex sheet

Wool needle and darning needle

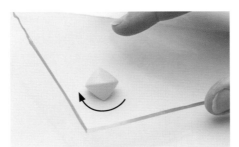

STEP 1 Form a ball of clay and lay it on a tile. Hold the Perspex sheet in your hand and press lightly onto the ball. Rotate the sheet in a small circle to make the ball revolve. You will be able to see it taking shape through the Perspex.

STEP 2 Make indentations in the points with a wool needle and leave to dry for a few minutes to become firmer. Then push the darning needle right through the bead. Apply a water slick to smooth it if necessary.

Making beads with a combustible core

Using a combustible core to make beads gives wonderful design possibilities for larger beads using the minimum amount of clay. It also means that the beads are lightweight for their size. They can be decorated in many different ways once the basic bead has been made over the core, or you can only cover parts of the core to make openwork beads.

YOU WILL NEED

Basic tool kit (see page 16)

Core material

Drill

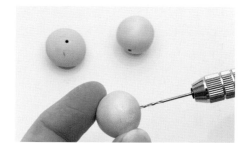

STEP 1 Make the core from your chosen core material (see page 90). To make identically sized beads, roll a log of the core material and cut equal lengths of the required size. Remember that the beads will be slightly larger all over than the core.

STEP 2 Core material can be made into a variety of shapes to cover with metal clay. For covering with sheets of clay, roll the clay into a sheet about 2 p.c. (0.5 mm) thick. Use a thicker sheet if you plan to engrave the bead. Cover the core following the instructions on page 92.

STEP 3 After drying fully, drill bead holes through the clay covering only—there is no need to drill through the core because it will burn away. The piece can now be decorated with syringing, paste, engraving, etcetera. Fire as recommended on page 93.

Making lentil beads using a former

In this technique, sheets of clay are shaped over formers to create the simple lentil shape. This requires a pair of identical round balls as formers (if you do not have two, reuse the same one for each half bead). The fired beads are hollow and lightweight. This is the best technique to use to make hollow core beads if you do not have a kiln, because it avoids burning away a combustible core. It is also a successful technique with base metal clays, because burning the core can be difficult with charcoal firing.

YOU WILL NEED

Basic tool kit (see page 16)

Pair of round formers—here 1" (25 mm) marbles

Round cutter or template in a size to match the former—a 1" (25 mm) former will need a cutter of about the same diameter

Polymer clay scraps to support the marbles

STEP 1 Roll out the clay into a sheet 2 p.c. (0.5 mm) thick. Use a thicker sheet for larger beads over 1" (25 mm) diameter. Cut out two circles using a cutter.

STEP 2 Lightly oil the formers and smooth a circle onto each one, coaxing it down around the sides into a cup shape. Support the formers on scraps of polymer clay to prevent rolling. At this point you can emboss the clay or stamp it. You can also cut out decorative holes in the clay with small cutters.

STEP 3 Dry the clay on the marbles then remove the clay cups from them. If this is difficult, use more oil next time. Running a knife tip around the edge usually works for stuck pieces.

Continued next page ▶

STEP 4 Lay sandpaper on your work surface and rotate each half bead on this to sand the edges completely smooth. Check that the two halves meet neatly, sanding further if necessary.

STEP 5 File across one half to make a notch on each side for the bead hole. Position the notches toward the top of the bead if you want it to hang in one direction.

STEP 6 Apply paste generously around the top of one half, building it up inside and keeping it clean on the outside. Press the other half onto the first and dry.

STEP 7 Sand away any excess paste and use a drill bit to drill the holes neatly.

Tube beads

This is an excellent way to make tube beads of all sizes. You will need a former in the shape of a round cylinder such as a knitting needle, a small rolling pin, a piece of copper tube, or even a large nail.

YOU WILL NEED

Basic tool kit (see page 16)

Cylindrical former

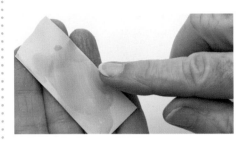

STEP 1 Roll out a sheet of clay, about 2 p.c. (0.5 mm) thick. Cut a rectangle the width of the required bead and long enough to wrap around the chosen former. Lightly wet one side with water so it will stick to the former.

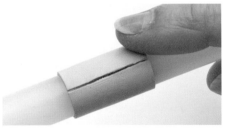

STEP 3 Press the ends together to make them butt together but leave a slight gap. This will make it easier to remove the bead after drying. Dry the piece thoroughly, using heat if the former is heatproof.

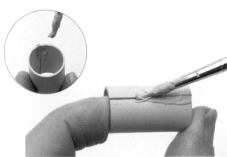

STEP 5 Force paste into the join and press the sides together. Smooth away any paste that wells out and apply more paste to the join inside the bead to strengthen it, then dry the piece.

STEP 2 Lay the wetted side of the rectangle on the former and smooth it round until the ends overlap. Cut through both layers of the overlap with a blade and pull away the excess clay from above and below the cut.

STEP 4 Ease the dried bead off the former.

STEP 6 Roll out another sheet of clay and place on a tile. Apply paste to one end of the bead and press this down onto the sheet. Cut round and remove the excess. Dry on the tile and remove. Repeat for the second end.

STEP 7 Sand the bead smooth and decorate at this point if required.

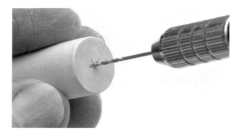

STEP 8 Drill a hole in each end of the bead.

FORMER VARIATION

Hollow oval beads can be made using icing nozzles as formers. Wrap a sheet of clay around the nozzle, joining the ends, and smooth and dry. Make two identical halves and join with paste.

A plastic icing nozzle used as a former

Two half beads, dried and ready for joining

The joined halves after joining with paste and sanding

TUBE BEAD NECKLACE,
JULIA RAI
A striking necklace made with tube beads that were dry constructed and textured with paste.

Molding beads

This is an easy way to make highly decorated or smooth and regular beads with a minimum of effort. You can use a bead you have made yourself as the master, or replicate an existing bead or small object that can be turned into a bead.

YOU WILL NEED

Putty silicone (see page 72)

Existing bead as a master

Ball tool

STEP 1 Make up the molding compound and push the master bead into it, just over halfway. The mold can be made using the top of the bead or one side, whichever is the most suitable according to the decoration. Leave to set for five to ten minutes, then remove the master.

STEP 2 To use the mold, form a ball of clay that is about half the size of the cavity of the mold and oil it lightly on one side.

STEP 3 Press the oiled side of the clay into the mold. Use your fingertip or a blunt tool such as a ball tool to push the clay firmly into the mold and work it up the sides. Aim to make a hollow cup about 4 p.c. (1 mm) thick that reaches up to the top of the mold cavity.

Continued next page ▶

Beads can be molded in a wide variety of shapes. These metal clay beads were made using simple one-part molds of both silicone and polymer clay. Molding beads is far less time consuming than other methods and with the hollow form, also uses less clay.

STEP 4 If the clay becomes too thin or a hole appears, press more clay into the mold to reinforce it. Trim off the clay at the top of the mold all round.

STEP 5 Leave the clay to dry in the mold, or apply some heat with a heat gun or hair-dryer. Finally, flex the mold and upend it to let the molded half bead fall out. Repeat for the other half and dry both halves.

Assorted metal clay beads and their molds

STEP 6 Sand the halves by rubbing them on a sheet of sandpaper, then join them together with generous amounts of paste. Dry and sand away excess paste.

STEP 7 Drill a hole through the bead to finish.

Bead caps

Metal clay gives you the freedom to create your own embellishments for beads of all kinds. Bead caps are placed on either end of feature beads and look gorgeous made in either precious or base metals to frame a semiprecious stone or lampwork bead.

STEP 1 To make bead caps for a specific bead, use small cutters such as circles, stars, or flowers to cut out metal clay shapes from a textured sheet. Press them onto a marble of a similar diameter to the beads they are intended to embellish. Make a small hole in the center of each bead cap and leave to dry.

STEP 2 After firing and polishing, the caps are threaded on either side of the feature bead to accentuate it. These copper bead caps had small balls of clay pressed into the center of each before piercing.

YOU WILL NEED

Basic tool kit (see page 16)

Small cutters

Texture sheet

Marbles

Bead cones

Bead cones are used at the ends of multistrand necklaces to make a neat finish. They can be plain or decorated, as required for the design of the necklace.

YOU WILL NEED

Basic tool kit (see page 16)

Drawing compass

Thin cardstock

Adhesive tape

Wire

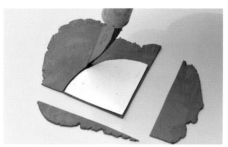

STEP 1 To make a template, set the arms of a drawing compass at about 1" (25 mm) radius, and with the point at the corner of the cardstock sheet, draw a quarter circle. Cut out the shape. Roll out a 2 p.c. (0.5 mm) thick sheet of clay and use the template to cut out the quarter circle in clay.

STEP 2 Draw another quarter circle on the card of 2" (50 mm) radius and cut out as before. Roll this around a pencil to shape into a cone for a former. Overlap the edges and tape in place. Shape the clay quarter around this former, placing it just above the top of the point. Apply paste and press the edges together, overlapping slightly. Leave a hole in the top of the cone. Dry and repeat for a second cone.

STEP 3 To use bead cones, several strands of beads are knotted to wire and drawn into the cone to conceal the ends. The protruding wire is made into a loop for attaching a clasp.

Making buttons

Metal clay buttons add flair to all kinds of handmade garments, and can also be used as jewelry elements in their own right. They can be made from cutout shapes, sculpted pieces, or be molded. Fired buttons will last a lifetime and can be machine washed.

YOU WILL NEED

Basic tool kit (see page 16)

Ball tool

Cutters

STEP 1 Roll out an 8 p.c. (2 mm) thick sheet of metal clay and lay on a tile. The example here has been textured with a texture sheet made from tree bark. Use cutters or templates to cut out shapes of the size required. Make a small indentation in the center of each shape with a pencil end or large ball tool.

STEP 2 Make two or four holes in each dent with a blunt wool needle. Push the needle down until it touches the tile, then rotate it slightly in the hole to enlarge it. After drying the holes can be enlarged neatly with a drill bit if necessary.

BUTTON VARIATION

Shank buttons are made by embedding a loop of wire into the back of a molded button before firing.

Filigree and syringe techniques

Metal clay in a paste or slip form can be piped in thin lines from a syringe to create a form of filigree. While this does not fully simulate traditional wire filigree, it is a superb art form in its own right, with beautiful flowing lines forming delicate openwork of all kinds.

This technique is more challenging than many other metal clay techniques and requires a steady hand, as well as the ability to draw while pressing the plunger of the syringe to extrude the paste line at a regulated speed. You will need to coordinate the movement of your hand with the pressure on the plunger. Once the basic technique is mastered, the varieties of filigree that can be created are richly decorative and well worth the effort of learning the technique.

Filigree can be applied to a clay background as a decoration, or created as openwork on a separate surface—such as a ceramic tile—from which it is removed after drying. It can also be applied to a combustible core and different nozzle thicknesses are available.

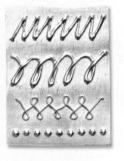

**Repeating patterns
on a clay sheet backing**
From the top:
Zigzag line made with a medium nozzle.
Looped line made with a medium nozzle.
Figure eight line made with a fine nozzle.
Dots made with a medium nozzle.

Landscape
Drawn with a fine nozzle on a clay sheet backing. See page 122.

TOOLS FOR SYRINGING

These are the essential tools that are required for creating syringed filigree.

1 Syringe with metal clay
2 Nozzles
*Fine nozzle—0.5 mm: This gives the most delicate filigree and is usually used for random syringing because it is more difficult to control. With practice, however, you will find that you can create controlled lines with the fine nozzle.
See the trees on page 122.*

Medium nozzle—1 mm: This is the easiest to use for controlled shapes. It is best to work from side to side across a drawing, or toward you. Turn the piece as you work to avoid pushing the syringe away from you.

Thick nozzle—1.5 mm: This is used for structural elements in a larger design and for framing finer work.

3 Acetate and tiles: Used as work surfaces.
4 Syringe caps—shown on the syringe, capping the blue nozzle. This prevents the paste in the nozzle drying out.
5 Fine paintbrush for minor adjustments.

Openwork filigree
Linked openwork elements and trapped gemstones. See page 122 and Gemstones, page 153.

Filigree with hollow forms
Left: controlled lines made with a medium nozzle.
Right: random lines made with a fine nozzle.
See Hollow core techniques, page 90.

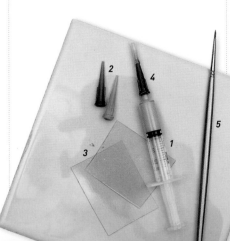

Holding the syringe

This method of holding a syringe gives far more control than most other methods. Practice using a syringe on a ceramic tile so that the paste can be recycled into a paste pot. Alternatively, fill an empty syringe with toothpaste to give yourself practice without wasting any clay.

YOU WILL NEED

Basic tool kit (see page 16)

Syringe with medium nozzle

STEP 1 Fix a nozzle onto the syringe. Hold it in your working hand as you would a pen. Use your other hand to grip the syringe and depress the plunger. This means that the hand that is drawing does not have to apply pressure, and therefore has more control.

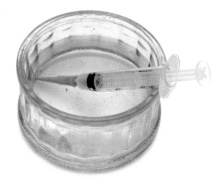

STEP 2 When you need to pause in your work, set the tip of the syringe in a water pot to prevent it drying out. If the nozzle becomes blocked, push a fine needle into the end of the syringe to clear the nozzle.

Using a syringe

Practice using a syringe on a ceramic tile so that the paste can be recycled.

YOU WILL NEED

Basic tool kit (see page 16)

Syringe with medium nozzle

Dots

Evenly sized dots can be created as random decoration or in lines.

Dab down and squeeze as you dab. Lift the syringe up sharply to make the dot.

Extruding a line

Straight lines are relatively easy to syringe because you can stretch the clay line to straighten it before letting it drop into place.

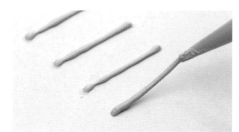

Begin by pressing out a small ball of paste and dab it down lightly onto the surface. This will anchor the line. Continue to press the plunger gently and lift the syringe so that the line of paste extends from the surface upward.

Move the syringe across slowly so that the line does not break but also does not sag unduly. Finish with a dab to secure and end the line cleanly.

Zigzags

Zigzags, stars, and other straight-sided designs are all syringed in the same way, with a dab to hold the line whenever the direction is changed.

Anchor the beginning of the line with a downward dab and extrude a clay line of the required length, then dab down to anchor the line. Continue extruding and move the syringe in the opposite direction to create the next line in the same way.

Curved lines

Curved lines are more difficult to execute than straight lines, because the clay line will need to be dropped into place in a curve rather than stretched to make a straight line.

Draw the required line on the clay or tile surface with a pencil. Dab down to start the line and extrude a line about ½" (13 mm) long. Allow the extruded length to drop down in a curve following the drawn line.

Drawing with a fine nozzle

This technique demonstrates using a fine nozzle to draw landscape images. The same technique is used for trees, mountains, and other subjects. The line is applied with the nozzle tip touching the surface to help with line control.

YOU WILL NEED

Basic tool kit (see page 16)

Syringe with fine nozzle

STEP 1 Draw the tree in pencil. Dab the tip of the syringe down at the top of the tree and draw swift curved zigzags to outline the tree, with the tip of the nozzle just skimming the surface to give more control over the line.

STEP 2 Make shorter zigzags down the middle of the tree to fill in the center and build up a more three-dimensional shape. Finally, draw the trunk of the tree. Use a hair dryer or a heat gun to dry the syringing and prevent the lines from spreading.

IF ...,
SACHIYO KOMAI
Superbly syringed filigree flowers in this lovely necklace are attached to a knotwork green cord.

Repeat elements

Repeated elements are created using acetate as a work surface, so that a pattern can be placed under the acetate and the syringing repeated as many times as needed to create identical pieces. Use a medium nozzle.

YOU WILL NEED

Basic tool kit (see page 16)

Pencil

Acetate

Syringe with medium nozzle

STEP 1 Trace the design and tape it to a tile. Tape a piece of acetate over the design.

STEP 2 Syringe over the lines of the design first to make a base layer, then repeat for more layers as required. If you pipe two layers and then dry the piece, a third layer can be piped on the back to strengthen it. Three layers usually give sufficient strength for openwork filigree elements.

STEP 3 Remove the syringing on its acetate and set aside to dry. Do not use artificial heat to speed drying because the acetate may cockle. Tape another piece of acetate over the design and repeat to make as many identical elements as required.

Infilling with openwork

Syringing combines well with cutout sheets of clay.

YOU WILL NEED

Basic tool kit (see page 16)

Syringe with medium and fine nozzles

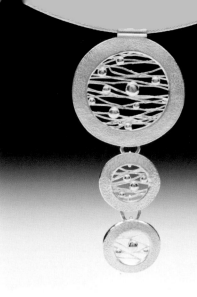

WEB OF LIFE PENDANT,
CHRIS PATE
A dramatic openwork pendant with waving lines of filigree within textured rings.

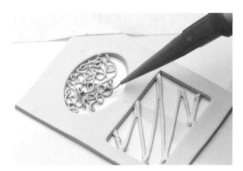

STEP 1 Roll out a sheet of clay and lay it on a tile. Cut out the shape and any internal shapes that you will fill with filigree. Dry on the tile. Anchor the dried piece on the tile with masking tape. Syringe your patterns into the cutout areas. Here, a fine syringe extrudes a random pattern. Build up at least a double layer of lines for strength, working to the edges all around.

STEP 2 A medium syringe is best for straight lines. Make sure that the syringing touches the edges of the dried clay piece at the end of each line for strength. If you make a mistake, the soft syringed lines can be wiped away without damaging the dry surround.

Refilling syringes with slip

This is remarkably successful if you use only very smooth slip that is newly purchased, or recycled slip made from ground up clay that has been sifted.

YOU WILL NEED

Slip in a small container

Empty syringe

STEP 3 Use a dot of clay to secure the ends of lines where they touch the edges of the dry clay. Build up a reasonable thickness of lines, but not so many that the filigree becomes too solid. Dry the piece again on the tile.

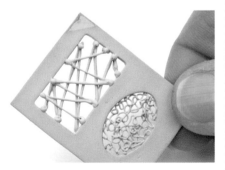

STEP 4 The piece will come free from the tile after drying. Be aware that the filigree lines are very fragile until fired.

Push the tip of the syringe into the slip so that it is well below the surface. Pull back the plunger so that the slip is drawn into the syringe. Be careful not to let the syringe tip come above the surface of the slip, otherwise air may be drawn in. Wipe the tip and cap it or fit a nozzle.

Paper clay techniques

Silver metal clay is available in more varieties than any other metal clay, and a paper or sheet form is one of them. This material was developed for origami or paper folding techniques, but a wonderful variety of other papercrafts can be used to make lightweight and unusual jewelry.

The main advantage of paper or sheet clay is that it behaves like paper or card and does not dry out while you work. It can be cut out with scissors or a sharp knife, folded, twisted, braided, and shaped. You can draw on it with a pencil and rub out mistakes with an eraser.

Although paper clay was developed for origami techniques, these can be a rather extravagant use of the material. Origami involves folding a sheet into a three-dimensional form, but requires a lot of paper for a small object. This is fine for a cheap material like paper, but is costly for silver clay sheet. Other forms of paper sculpture, such as paper cutting, quilling, kirigami, and palm weaving, are all successful techniques for paper clay, and use far less material.

EARRINGS,
SUE HEASER
The ancient craft of flax folding (palm weaving) from New Zealand has been adapted to make silver paper clay earrings.

Paper shapes
Shapes cut out using paper punches. See page 126.

Origami
Origami folding techniques. See page 126.

Kirigami
Paper clay cut and shaped into three-dimensional pieces. See page 128.

Paper sculpture
Shapes cut out, scored, and folded. See page 129.

BRANDS

The two brands available, Art Clay Silver Paper (left) and PMC sheet (right) have similar kiln firing requirements but a different handling quality. Art Clay is stiffer, more like thin cardstock, and is good for pieces that need to hold their shape, such as paper sculpture and kirigami. PMC sheet is softer and can take more folding, so is good for origami and draping effects. Both types can be used for quilling and palm weaving.

Quilling
Strips of paper clay coiled and assembled in the style of the Victorian papercraft. See page 129.

Palm weaving techniques
Adapting palm weaving from various cultures to silver paper clay. See page 129.

Paper cutting
The ancient technique of paper cutting transferred to silver. See page 129.

PMC sheet

Art Clay Silver Paper

Paper clay basics

Working with paper or sheet clay is very similar to working with ordinary paper. The sheet does not dry out as you work so you can take your time making your piece.

YOU WILL NEED

Basic tool kit (see page 16)

Paper or sheet clay

Pencil and sharp scissors

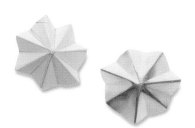

STEP 1 First design your piece using ordinary paper or thin cardstock. If paper clay is folded and refolded it can begin to fracture, so practice first with paper. When you are happy with your paper piece, you can use it as a template for the silver sheet.

STEP 2 Draw cutting lines on the paper clay accurately, with a good point on the pencil. Do not use a very sharp pencil that may damage the sheet.

STEP 3 Cut out the shape with sharp scissors or a knife. Again, be very accurate so as to avoid wastage. Save unused pieces for other projects—they will keep in their wrapper for some time.

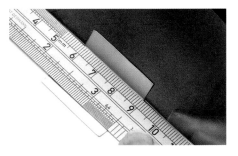

STEP 4 Fold the sheet accurately and neatly. It is a good idea to lay a ruler along the fold line and make the fold by pushing up with another straight edge. This ensures accurate folding along the line.

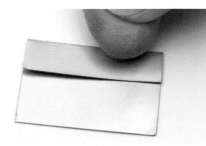

STEP 5 Run your fingernail along each fold to crease it firmly.

STEP 6 If the paper cracks along the fold, as here, it is likely to be old stock and too dry for folding. Use it up for paper cutting or quilling. Any small cracks can be mended after firing with oil paste.

TIPS FOR WORKING WITH SILVER PAPER CLAY

- Be very accurate when cutting out shapes and drawing fold lines, as small errors will result in ill-shaped pieces.
- Fired paper clay is relatively fragile and best used for pendants and dangling earrings. For stronger pieces, use a lump clay backing. Folded origami shapes are more durable due to the folded layers.
- Water should not be applied to the sheet since it may disintegrate. A small amount of paste can be used to join elements and add findings, but this should be kept to a minimum.
- White stick glue can be used to join pieces temporarily while you work. Use paste for the final sticking so the pieces fuse together when fired.
- Paper clay does not require drying before firing, and any small amounts of paste will dry as the kiln warms up.

TIPS FOR FIRING A PAPER CLAY PIECE

- Fire paper clay in a kiln, although small pieces added to lump clay as embellishments can be stovetop or torch fired.
- Place pieces in a cold kiln and bring up to temperature. Fire at the highest temperature recommended by the manufacturer for maximum strength.
- Support shaped pieces when firing with fiber cloth, since they may sag.
- Use stainless steel dressmaking pins pushed into a fiber kiln board to hold folded pieces in shape during firing.

FINISHING TIPS

- After firing, brush as usual and burnish if required. Polish gently because the sheets are very thin and may crack.
- Cracks should be repaired with oil paste and the piece fired again.
- Findings can be added using oil paste after firing, and the piece fired again. Soldering fired paper clay is difficult because it is so thin and can melt.

Cutout embellishments

Simple cutout shapes make attractive embellishments on silver clay jewelry, and can be pasted onto plaster-dry clay.

YOU WILL NEED

Basic tool kit (see page 16)

Paper clay

Paper punch

Plaster-dry silver clay piece

STEP 1 Use a paper punch to cut out shapes from the paper clay. Use the punch upside down so you can position the sheet of paper clay carefully to avoid wastage.

STEP 2 Press down on the punch and the shape will pop up as it is cut.

STEP 3 Use a fine ball tool or point to mark any details on the shape, such as leaf veins. These will be visible after firing. You can also pinch the lines to add shape.

STEP 4 Apply a thin coat of paste to the plaster-dry piece to be decorated. Do not use too much paste because the paper clay may become wet and break up.

STEP 5 Press the paper clay shape down on the paste. Fire soon afterward, otherwise the piece may become detached as the paste dries. If you fire with a torch, avoid aiming the flame too directly at the paper clay decoration.

Origami

Many of us learned origami as children: folding a square or rectangle of paper into paper shapes and toys. There are many good books available on the art of origami, which make excellent sources of inspiration and designs. Choose designs that require the minimum amount of folds for the most effect. This demonstration shows making a tiny boat for a charm or for earrings—each one takes less than half a sheet of paper clay.

YOU WILL NEED

Paper clay

Paper

Sharp scissors

Stick glue

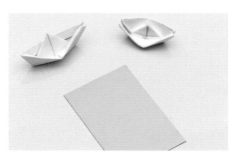

STEP 1 Cut a rectangle of paper clay that is half as long again as it is wide. Here, a rectangle 1¼ x 1⅞" (30 x 45 mm) is laid next to two little boats made in paper for practice. Measure the rectangle very accurately for the best results.

STEP 2 Fold the rectangle in half. Fold in half again in the other direction and open out to give a center line.

STEP 3 Fold the two top corners down to meet in the middle at the center line.

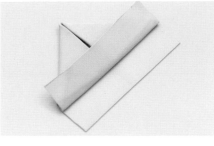

STEP 4 Fold up the protruding flap at the bottom. Crease all folds well with your fingernail.

ORIGAMI PENDANT
RACHEL AZULIE
Neat paper folds are set off by a gorgeous pearl in this oxidized pendant.

STEP 5 Flip the piece and fold up the other flap to match the first. Push your finger into the bottom of the piece between the two folded up flaps (as indicated by the arrow) to open it out into a triangular shaped hat.

STEP 6 Fold the sides into the center and flatten the hat again. Apply a little stick glue to the point where the flaps cross over each other to hold them firm while you complete the piece.

STEP 7 Fold up the pointed flap at the front to meet the top. Flip the piece and repeat on the back.

STEP 8 Carefully open the piece up again as before and flatten it with the sides in the center. Now pull the two ends down to open it up into a little boat.

STEP 9 Pinch the shape so that the sides are vertical and the little sail stands up in the middle.

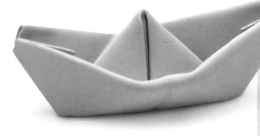

STEP 10 Fire in a kiln and cool for a while before quenching to avoid cracking. Add a loop with oil paste after firing, or drill a hole to attach a jump ring for hanging.

Kirigami

This technique is a combination of paper cutting and folding. There are many different ways of doing this, from elaborate snowflakes cut from folded circles of paper to a simple line of dancing dolls cut from pleats. Paper clay is relatively thick so this example, with the paper cut first and then shaped into a little lantern, is a more successful approach.

YOU WILL NEED

Basic tool kit (see page 16)

Paper clay rectangle,
1¼ x 1 ½" (30 x 40 mm)

Pencil

Firing board

Stainless steel
dressmaking pins

Kirigami earrings
Square pieces of paper clay are cut and then curved into stylish earrings.

STEP 1 Draw a ⅛" (3 mm) border all around the rectangle in pencil. Draw vertical lines across the inner rectangle about ⅛" (3 mm) apart. Use a ruler and sharp blade to cut along the vertical guidelines, taking care not to cut into the border area.

STEP 2 Fold the cut sheet in half horizontally but do not crease hard. It needs to open into a gentle curve.

STEP 3 Roll the sheet around a pencil to curve it into a tube. Apply paste along one edge and press the other edge firmly over it.

STEP 4 Push the ends toward each other to make the folded center bulge outward into a lantern shape.

STEP 5 Remove the pencil and place the lantern upright on a firing board. Use three steel dressmaking pins to hold the bottom in a circle. This will prevent it springing apart during firing. Fire and cool slowly.

STEP 6 To attach a hanging loop, slip the lantern back onto the pencil and drill a hole on either side of the top band. Brush and polish and attach a handle of silver wire. This can now be strung on a cord or chain using a jump ring, or be attached to an earwire to make a drop earring.

Other paper techniques

There are many other paper techniques from cultures all over the world that can be adapted to paper clay. Books on these subjects are widely available as well as information on the web.

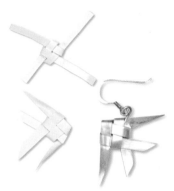

Palm weaving or flax folding

This craft comes from New Zealand and is a form of braiding with palm leaves. Paper clay sheet works well instead of palm leaves, and the results are as strong as origami because of the woven strips.

Paper sculpture

Dimensional forms in paper clay make beautiful relief pieces from simple shapes. First, make the prototypes in thin cardstock by drawing open spirals and curved or geometric shapes. Cut these out and score along the center of each. Fold the sides downward along the central lines then pinch to make the shapes. Now make the pieces in paper clay. For firing, hold the pieces in place on a fiber kiln board with pins, and add loops after firing.

DESTINY BROOCH,
JULIA RAI
This striking silver clay pin is embellished with silver paper clay strips, which were attached on-end to the surface to create the symmetrical geometric patterns.

Quilling

This ancient papercraft makes delicate filigree effects in paper clay. Cut strips of clay from the sheet about 1/8" (3 mm) wide and as long as the sheet. Roll each strip up into a coil around a cocktail stick then leave to relax and open a little. Paste the ends in place and pinch into teardrops and ovals. Assemble the coils using dabs of paste between them.

Paper cutting

This is an ancient craft with European and Far Eastern origins. First, draw the design on the sheet of paper clay and use a pointed knife to cut out the shapes. Fire flat and mount in a polymer clay frame.

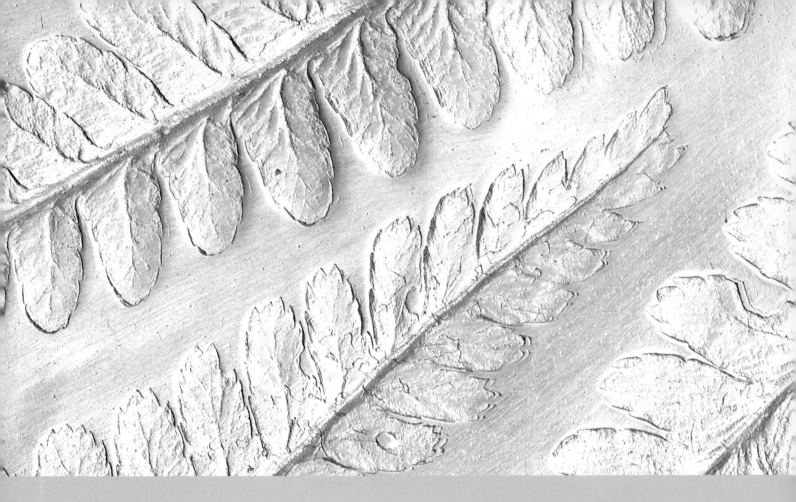

3

Bangle and ring making techniques

Ring making is a popular metal clay technique, and there is nothing more satisfying than making your own rings to the design and style of your choosing. Bangle making uses similar techniques on a larger scale.

Bangles and cuffs

The advent of cheaper base metal clays means that making larger pieces, such as bangles and cuffs, is becoming more popular.

Bangle mandrels are available, but they are expensive, so the steps on these pages show how to make a simple bangle and cuff using a paper template or a soft drinks can. However, if you enjoy making these larger pieces, a larger mandrel is a good investment.

SALAMANDER BANGLE,
XUELLA ARNOLD
The molded bronze clay twigs contrast with the silver lizard.

Simple carved bronze bangle
See opposite.

Copper cuff decorated with stamped images
See pages 75 and 134.

CLAY QUANTITIES FOR BANGLES AND CUFFS

An average woman's bangle, with a diameter of 2 ⅜" (61 mm) and ¼" (6 mm) thick all round, will need about 50 g of metal clay.

For an average-sized cuff, which is 1" (25 mm) wide and ¹⁄₃₂" (1 mm) thick, you will need about 50 g of clay to allow you to roll out the shape. Some of this will be cut away and can be used for another project.

Sizing bangles

Bangles are far less critical than rings when allowing for shrinkage. Make bangles 10 percent larger than required—this is an adequate allowance for all main clay types that shrink between 8 and 15 percent. If in doubt, go up a size in the table below.

To find your bangle size, use a piece of string and measure around the widest part of your hand—the widest point that

the bangle will have to pass over. Then spread out the string and check the measurement. This is the inner circumference of the bangle. Add ½" (13 mm) to this measurement for comfort and find the measurement above this in the table. This will give you the diameter of template to use to make the bangle, allowing for shrinkage of about 10 percent.

AVERAGE BANGLE SIZES AND ALLOWANCE FOR SHRINKAGE

Size	Inner circumference	Inner diameter	Inner diameter to allow for 10% shrinkage
Small	7" (17.8 cm)	2 ³⁄₁₆" (5.6 cm)	2 ½" (6.4 cm)
Medium	7 ½" (19 cm)	2 ⅜" (6.1 cm)	2 ¹¹⁄₁₆" (6.9 cm)
Large	8" (20.3 cm)	2 ½" (6.4 cm)	2 ¾" (7.1 cm)
Extra large	8 ½" (21.6 cm)	2 ¹¹⁄₁₆" (6.9 cm)	3" (7.6 cm)

Making a bangle

This simple bangle is formed from a log of clay, and can be made using any metal clay. If the type of clay you are using must be fired in charcoal, make sure your firing container is large enough before you begin.

Bangles can also be made on a soft drinks can, using the technique described in Making a cuff (see page 134).

YOU WILL NEED

Basic tool kit (see page 16)

Pair of compasses

Pencil

Paper

Plastic hammer

Bangle mandrel or rolling pin

STEP 1 Use the table on page 132 to calculate the size that you need to make your bangle. To draw a circle of that diameter, set a pair of compasses to half the diameter.

STEP 2 Roll a log of metal clay a little thicker than required to allow for shrinkage. Here, the clay is rolled to ⅜" (10 mm) thick. Lay the clay log on the template and shape it to match the drawn circle. You can push opposing sides in to make the bangle more oval-shaped for comfortable wear.

STEP 3 Cut through the overlap at an angle then use paste to join the two ends, squashing them together for a strong join. Smooth out the join. Dry on the paper so that the bangle is not distorted by moving.

STEP 4 Sand and refine the join and decorate the bangle as you wish. Here, the bangle is being carved with a file.

STEP 5 After firing and cooling the bangle should lie flat. If it does not, hammer it on a flat surface. You can also tap it on a bangle mandrel—or improvise with a rolling pin for a mandrel—to correct any distortion.

BANGLE VARIATIONS

Cut a strip of clay from a thick sheet and twist it to make a decorative strip. Wrap this around a drinks can wrapped in paper. Do not join the ends but let them overlap a half turn and add decorative ends. The bangle size can be adjusted after firing.

Texture a strip of clay and wrap it around a drinks can. Decorate the join with added pieces of clay to disguise it. This copper bangle has been oxidized with heat.

Making a cuff

A cuff has open ends and so is more forgiving for sizing, and can be shaped after firing to ensure a good fit.

YOU WILL NEED

Basic tool kit (see page 16)

Pencil

Paper

Scissors

Aluminum can, covered with paper secured with tape

Plastic hammer

Bangle mandrel or rolling pin

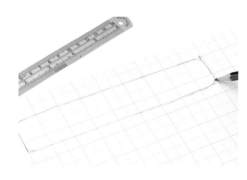

STEP 1 Draw a rectangle 7 x 2" (180 x 50 mm) on paper, for a template. Cuffs are adjustable and this is an average size. Add 1" (25 mm) in length for larger sizes. Curve the corners and cut out.

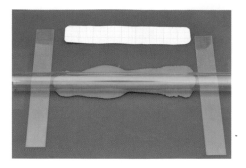

STEP 2 Form a log of clay and roll it lengthwise to 4 p.c. (1 mm) thick using two pairs of rolling guides placed end to end to give the length required. Use a long roller to roll across the width as well.

STEP 3 With the clay sheet still on a nonstick surface, lay on the template and cut around it with a craft knife.

STEP 4 Stamped decoration looks good on cuffs, and here a wooden fabric stamp is oiled and pressed into the clay surface. Do not press too hard as this will make holes in the clay sheet.

STEP 5 Apply a thin film of water to the underside of the cutout sheet and press this side onto a paper-covered aluminum can. The clay should stick to the paper and not slip off. Dry and remove from the can.

STEP 6 Sand the edges of the cuff to smooth them. Be gentle with the piece since it may crack under its own weight if handled too much. Fire and quench.

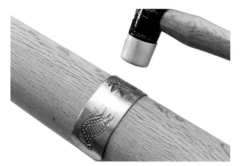

STEP 7 Before polishing, check that the cuff fits well and, if necessary, use your hands to adjust the gap by bending the metal gently. You can also tap over the cuff with a plastic hammer over a rolling pin or bangle mandrel to correct any warping.

Ring making

Ring making stretches back in time for several thousand years, and ancient rings from many and varied cultures are found all over the world. Making rings with metal clay continues this fascinating tradition, and gives you the freedom to create your own designs.

There are many different ways of making rings in metal clay, and the following pages focus on techniques that are tried and tested. The main concern with ring making for the metal clay artist is the fact that the clay shrinks during firing, so allowance has to be made for this when constructing the rings.

ROBOT RINGS,
X-RIO
These quirky rings in silver clay have moving parts and added brass components.

Engraved silver band ring
The band ring is decorated with engraving. See pages 137 and 146.

Silver band ring
The design was molded onto the band before making the ring. See pages 137 and 139.

Decorated silver band ring
This time, a band ring has been decorated with syringing and added small leaves. See pages 120 and 137.

Silver half-round ring
This half-round ring features embedded artificial gemstones. See pages 139 and 154.

Bronze half-round ring
Bronze half-round ring with carved decoration and embedded artificial gemstones. See pages 139, 147, and 149.

Copper half-round ring
Copper half-round ring with molded setting added before firing. See pages 77 and 139.

Silver swivel ring
The band has been forged and a glass bead riveted onto the shank with sufficient play to allow the bead to swivel. See pages 142.

Silver forged ring with molded setting
See pages 77 and 141.

Silver stone-set ring
A classic half-round ring with an embedded stone setting. See pages 139 and 155.

Silver free-form ring
Silver ring made from a long clay log wrapped around the mandrel, finished with an embedded stone. See pages 140 and 149.

Copper free-form ring
See page 140.

Copper forged ring
A band ring made with textured copper clay and forged after firing. See pages 72 and 142.

Silver signet ring
A half-round shank with an engraved heart-shaped setting. See pages 139 and 141.

Silver riveted ring
Half-round ring with a glass bead setting. See pages 103, 139, and 141.

Sizing rings and calculating shrinkage

Rings can be made with any of the different metal clays, but since these clays all shrink by varying amounts when fired, it is important to calculate how much larger a ring should be made to accommodate this.

Metal clay shrinks in length, width, and depth, so a calculation of the circumference of the ring is always an approximation. Also, clay shrinks more for larger rings, for wider bands, and if fired longer and hotter. However, the table on page 143 will give you a starting point from which you can develop your own measurements. The table gives ring sizes used in different countries and the equivalent circumference measurement in millimeters, which is the most accurate way of measuring rings, as well as the approximate measurement required to allow for the shrinkage of most available clays.

When measuring for your ring ensure you make allowances for knuckles, warm hands, and the width of the ring to be made: wider rings should be made about a half size larger.

YOU WILL NEED

Ring sizer—either an adjustable strap type or a ring sizing set—or a length of wire or string and a ruler

Pencil

Paper

Ring mandrel

CLAY QUANTITIES FOR RINGS

The amount of clay you need to make a ring depends on its style and size. An average woman's band or classic half-round ring will need 7 g of clay. A large, heavy, and chunky style man's ring can use as much as 15 g.

BRONZE AND PEARL RING,
SABINE ALIENOR SINGERY
Textured sheets of bronze clay capture a pearl in this unusual ring.

STEP 1 Depending on the ring gauge you are using, use columns 2–4 on the table on page 143 to locate your ring size. Then select your metal clay type (from columns 5–8) and find the measurement that corresponds to your ring size. Next, find the closest millimeter measurement in column 1 to the one you have just found in columns 5–8. Finally, it's back to columns 2–4 to find your ring size with the shrinkage factored in.

STEP 2 Set the sizer to this larger measurement, push it onto a ring mandrel, and mark a line at that point. This is the point on the mandrel to make your ring. Below is an example of how to find your ring size with the shrinkage allowance included.

STEP 3 If you do not have a ring sizer, measure round your finger with some wire, then pull it straight and measure in millimeters. Find the closest measurement to this in column 1 in the table on page 143. Look across to columns 5–8 to find the measurement required to make your ring.

STEP 4 This measurement includes the allowance for shrinkage. Mark it on a strip of paper and wrap that around the mandrel, sliding it up and down to find the exact position to make your ring.

US size 6 ½ (UK size N): the length (circumference) required for Art Clay Silver = 58.0mm

The closest measurement to this in column 1 is 57.8mm, which is US size 8 ½ (UK size Q ½)

Making a band ring

This is the simplest type of ring to make, and the one that beginners usually start with.

YOU WILL NEED

Basic tool kit (see page 16)

Ring mandrel

Pencil

Memo note

Plastic hammer

STEP 1 Calculate the ring size and mark it on the mandrel. Cut a 1" (25mm) wide strip from a memo note with the sticky part at one end. Wrap the strip round the marked point on the mandrel, securing it with the sticky end. Test that the strip can move freely on the mandrel to allow removal later.

STEP 2 Roll out the clay to 4 p.c. (1 mm) thick. This is a good thickness for band rings and should provide sufficient strength even for fine silver rings. To roll a long strip, shape the clay into a log, lay it between rolling guides, and roll it lengthwise.

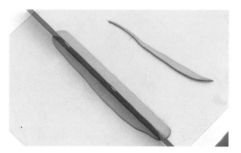

STEP 3 Use a long slicer blade to cut one edge of the sheet straight, then cut the other side to make a band about ³⁄₈" (10 mm) wide. You can make the ring wider or narrower if you wish. Use a ruler to cut the strip to about ³⁄₁₆" (5 mm) longer than the total calculated length.

STEP 4 Flip the strip over and use your finger to spread a thin film of water over the clay surface. This will help the ring stick to the paper on the mandrel.

STEP 5 Lay the clay strip, wetted side down, on the paper on the mandrel. Turn the mandrel so that the clay strip is wrapped right around it, keeping it straight and overlapping the ends.

STEP 6 Check that the clay is touching the paper all round: if not, reapply the strip. This will ensure that the ring is the correct size. Use the slicer blade to cut through both layers of clay.

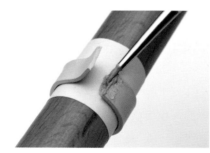

STEP 7 Peel back the strip and remove the excess clay. Apply paste generously to the two ends and press them together firmly to make a butt joint. Apply paste over the join, leaving it proud. It will be sanded away after drying.

STEP 8 Surface-dry the ring—about two minutes with a hair-dryer or 15 seconds with a heat gun. This will give the clay sufficient strength to remove it from the mandrel. Do not let the mandrel get too hot, because it will swell and prevent the removal of the ring. If this does happen, leave it to cool down before the next step.

Continued next page ▶

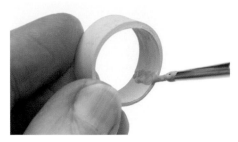

STEP 9 Carefully slip the memo note off the mandrel with the ring on it and stand it on end on a ceramic tile or baking sheet. Dry fully in an oven.

STEP 10 When the ring is dry, remove the paper by easing it away from the inside of the ring. Apply paste to the join inside the ring to strengthen it, and dry again.

If the ring is too tight, you can increase the size by at least a half size by tapping it further on the mandrel. Pull it toward you firmly while you rotate the mandrel and tap with the hammer. Do not continue for too long however, since it may split. To enlarge it further, reheat it to pale orange with a blowtorch, stovetop, or kiln and, after quenching, tap again. The reheating will soften (anneal) the metal so you can enlarge it further.

   If the ring is too large, try firing again at the hottest temperature for the clay. This can make it shrink further. Alternately, paint the inside with Art Clay Silver Overlay Paste and fire again to make it tighter.

STEP 11 Sand the sides of the ring by rubbing it on sandpaper laid on a flat surface. This will correct any irregularities on the edges of the ring. Use fine-grit sanding pads to sand over the join—you should be able to make it invisible. Take care not to sand too much inside the ring, which may make it too large. Sand the inside edges to chamfer them and make the ring more comfortable to wear.

STEP 12 The ring is now ready to be fired as required for the clay type used. It is best to fire silver clay rings in particular at the highest temperature and the maximum time recommended, because they will get more wear than most forms of jewelry.

USING RING PLUGS

STEP 13 When the ring has been fired and quenched you can strengthen it further by putting it back on the mandrel and tapping it all round with a plastic hammer. This will also make it perfectly round.

If you have problems with sizing rings, you can use a ring plug to prevent a ring shrinking too much during firing. Insert a plaster ring plug of the required finished ring size inside the ring and fire as usual. After firing, immerse the piece in water and the plaster will dissolve away. Plaster plugs are available from metal clay suppliers, or you can make your own using molds and investment plaster.

DECORATING BAND RINGS

A plain band ring can be decorated in many different ways.

◀ A simple decorative technique is to texture the clay before cutting the strip. When joining the ring, avoid spreading paste too far around the join. You can disguise the join when the ring is plaster dry using engraving tools to continue the lines of a pattern.

▶ You can cut out shapes from the strip of wet clay with tiny cutters before putting it on the mandrel. These can also be cut from the edge of the strip.

▶ A mold can be used to make a landscape or story ring. Here, a polymer clay mold was made from shapes cut out of thin cardstock and glued to more card. The rolled clay is pressed onto the mold and trimmed before placing it on the mandrel.

▲ Filigree decoration can be added using a syringe.

▶ Lettering or symbols can be engraved into the ring.

Making a half-round ring

A half-round ring has a D-shaped cross section and is a timeless classic. Once the basic shape is mastered the ring can be embellished in many different ways, or be given a variety of settings.

While you can buy ring molds to make classic half-round rings, you will need to buy a different mold for each size of ring you want to make. Therefore, learning how to make your own rings on a mandrel is a useful process, and one that will give you far more versatility. With practice, you will be able to make a ring shank far quicker than when using a mold.

YOU WILL NEED

Basic tool kit (see page 16)

Ring mandrel

Memo note

Log roller

Hammer

Setting (or the head)

Shoulder

Shank

STEP 1 Prepare the mandrel as usual. Roll a log of clay about ⅛" (3 mm) thick and about ⅜" (10 mm) longer than the circumference of the ring required. Use a log roller to smooth it into an even log.

STEP 2 Press the log roller down lightly on the log to flatten it evenly all along its length. It should now be about ³⁄₁₆" (5 mm) wide and 8 p.c. (2 mm) thick.

STEP 3 Wet the surface of the clay band and place the wetted side onto the paper on the mandrel. Wind it around until the two ends overlap as shown. Use a blade to cut through both ends and remove the scrap clay. This ensures that you can make an accurate butt join.

Continued next page ▶

STEP 4 Apply paste to the two ends and press them together firmly, straightening the ring shank as you do so. Add more paste as necessary to ensure a strong join. If you are adding a setting, this is the place to add it so that the join is covered. If you are making a plain band, the join will need to be smoothed away completely by sanding and pasting when plaster dry.

STEP 5 Wet your finger and smooth it over the surface of the ring, pressing down lightly as you do so to shape it into a D-section. Flatten the area that will be the bottom of the shank to make the ring more comfortable to wear.

STEP 6 Dry the ring on the mandrel, then remove it from the mandrel on its paper. Dry fully in an oven and remove the paper from inside the ring.

▼ **CYGNET RINGS,**
XUELLA ARNOLD
Lyrical silver rings of sculpted cygnets with gold leaf keum-boo embellishment. The eyes are green tourmalines.

STEP 7 Sand the ring to refine the D-shape and smooth the join. To add a setting, use a large file to file across the top of the ring where the setting will be attached to make a flat area.

STEP 8 After firing the ring can be tapped on the mandrel to make it round and stronger. If you have added a setting, only tap up to it on each side.

HALF-ROUND VARIATIONS

Integral setting
Roll the clay into a thicker log tapered at each end. Wet the clay and press onto the mandrel, overlapping the tapered ends to join them on the underside of the ring. The thicker part can now be shaped as a setting and inset with stones or carved.

Free-form ring
Create a long, thin log using an extruder or by rolling. Wind this around the mandrel several times and twirl into a decorative shape for the setting. A fireable gemstone can be set into the coils.

Open-ended ring
Taper the ends of the log and wrap around the mandrel but do not join the ends. They can be turned outward into a scroll.

Forged ring with added setting

One way of avoiding the problems of shrinkage is to make and fire a ring shank as a flat piece to be forged into a ring after firing. This works well with silver and copper clays, however bronze clay is difficult to forge successfully with light tools.

The best thickness for forging is about 4 p.c. to 6 p.c. (1 to 1.5 mm). Thicker rings are possible but are harder to shape.

This type of ring has a forged shank to which the setting is added and the ring fired again. The shank does not make a closed ring, but is left open to embed in the underside of the setting. When making the shank, remember to still allow for shrinkage, and any excess can be cut off with cutters if required. The steps show forging a ring from a strip, but you can also forge rings from a flattened log for a half-round shank.

YOU WILL NEED

Basic tool kit (see page 16)

Ring mandrel

Plastic hammer

METALWORK TOOLS

Because you will be working with fired metal, you will need a pair of good-quality wire cutters for cutting ring bands to length. Cheaper wire cutters will work, but may leave a ragged edge that needs filing smooth.

STEP 1 Roll out metal clay to 4 p.c. (1 mm) thick and cut a strip for the ring shank. This should be about ³⁄₁₆" (5 mm) wide and the correct length for the size of ring required, allowing for shrinkage. Fire the shank, firing hot and as long as recommended for maximum strength. Quench the shank but do not brush it, since it needs to be as soft as possible for bending

STEP 2 Lay the shank across the mandrel at a point for a slightly smaller size than required, and bend it round the mandrel with your hands—it should be soft enough for you to do most of the shaping by hand.

STEP 3 Using a plastic hammer, tap the shank gently all around at the correct point on the mandrel so it is snug on the mandrel and there is a gap of about ³⁄₁₆" (5 mm) between the ends. You can adjust the gap to make the ring fit. Trim with wire cutters if necessary. Use pliers to bend the ends of the shank up to embed into the setting.

Continued next page ▶

Add a fireable stone

Mount the stone in metal clay and dry (see page 155). Make a shank on a mandrel and cut a space of the appropriate size for the mounted stone. Paste the mounted stone to the ends of the ring shank.

Signet ring

Cut a small heart shape—or any suitable shape—out of a 8 p.c. (2 mm) sheet of clay and dry it. Engrave the initials in the surface (see page 146). After drying, paste it to the filed top of a plaster-dry ring.

Rivet setting

Embed a rivet in the top of the ring shank (see page 103). After firing, rivet on a glass bead and a decorative washer.

STEP 4 Make a small rectangle of fresh clay to span the space between the two shank ends. It should be 8 p.c. (2 mm) thick and large enough for the two prongs of the shank to be embedded. Lay the rectangle face down on a tile and push the upturned ends of the shank into the soft clay. Trim if necessary, dry, and apply paste to fill any gaps next to the fired metal.

STEP 5 Attach the setting, here a molded shell, to the rectangle using plenty of paste to make it very secure—otherwise it can pull away while firing because of the fired shank. Fire again then finish as desired.

STEP 6 The finished ring after firing. This technique is a quick way to make rings with different settings but the same shanks. You can make and fire shanks of different lengths in advance. They are then ready to have settings added when required.

FORGED AND SETTING VARIATION

A swivel ring can be made in a similar way. Make and fire the shank and drill a hole in each end. File the ends into a rounded shape. After firing, shape as above and turn up the ends of the shank to accommodate a bead. Secure the bead with a rivet with a small washer on the outside of each end (see page 102).

Forged band rings
The two ends of a forged ring can be soldered or pasted together to make a continuous band ring.

YOU WILL NEED

Basic tool kit (see page 16)

Ring mandrel

Plastic hammer

Soldering equipment or oil paste

STEP 1 Calculate the size of the ring allowing for shrinkage and adding about ³⁄₁₆" (5 mm). Form the band as you would when making a band ring, but fire it flat.

STEP 2 Bend the fired band around the mandrel, at first a little too small to create the shape, then hammer it at the correct size for the finished ring.

STEP 3 When the ring is the correct shape, trim it to just ¹⁄₃₂" (1 mm) larger than required with wire cutters. These should cut through the thin metal easily.

STEP 4 File the ends to make a tight join that meets all along the edge. If your intention is to solder, the join must fit perfectly with no gaps.

FORGED BAND VARIATIONS

STEP 5 Solder the ends together (see page 64)—here, a pallion of solder is positioned on the fluxed join before heating with the torch. Alternatively, join with oil paste and fire again.

STEP 6 The resulting join should be almost invisible. Tap the ring on the mandrel again to work harden it and correct any distortion.

Leaf rings
Silver clay leaves made from paste can be forged around a mandrel and then soldered or joined with oil paste to make unusual, naturalistic rings.

Recycled rings
Small fired-silver cutout shapes that were rejected for other projects can be soldered together into a strip to make a ring shank to shape around a mandrel.

RING SIZES TO ALLOW FOR SHRINKAGE OF DIFFERENT CLAYS

1 Circumference (mm)	2 US	3 Britain, Australia, and New Zealand	4 Japan	5 Art Clay Silver circumference (mm) 8% shrinkage	6 Fast-firing base metal clays circumference (mm) 10% shrinkage	7 PMC minimum circumference (mm) 12% shrinkage	8 PMC maximum circumference (mm) 15% shrinkage
46.5	4	H ½	7	51.1	51.6	52.8	54.9
47.8	4 ½	I ½	8	52.5	53.1	54.3	56.4
49	5	J ½	9	53.8	54.4	55.7	57.8
50.3	5 ½	L	11	55.2	55.8	57.1	59.4
51.5	6	M	12	56.5	57.2	58.5	60.8
52.8	6 ½	N	13	58.0	58.6	60.0	62.3
54	7	O	14	59.3	59.9	61.3	63.7
55.3	7 ½	P	15	60.7	61.4	62.8	65.3
56.6	8	Q	16	62.1	62.8	64.3	66.8
57.8	8 ½	Q ½	17	63.5	64.2	65.7	68.2
59.1	9	R ½	18	64.9	65.6	67.1	69.7
60.3	9 ½	S ½	19	66.2	66.9	68.5	71.2
61.6	10	T ½	20	67.6	68.4	70.0	72.7
62.8	10 ½	U ½	22	69.0	69.7	71.3	74.1
64.1	11	V ½	23	70.4	71.2	72.8	75.6
65.3	11 ½	W ½	24	71.7	72.5	74.2	77.1
66.7	12	Y	25	73.2	74.0	75.8	78.7
68	12 ½	Z	26	74.7	75.5	77.2	80.2
69	13		27	75.8	76.6	78.4	81.4

This example uses the table above to find the correct ring size, allowing for shrinkage.

US size 6 ½ (UK size N): the length (circumference) required for Art Clay Silver = 58.0mm

The closest measurement to this in column 1 is 57.8mm which is US size 8 ½ (UK size Q ½)

4 Embellishing

Fired metal clay is solid metal, and as such can be embellished using traditional metalworking methods. However, the embellishing process can begin before the clay is even fired, by preparing the piece for the planned embellishments. This is clearest in techniques such as enameling or decorating with resin.

Engraving, carving, and etching

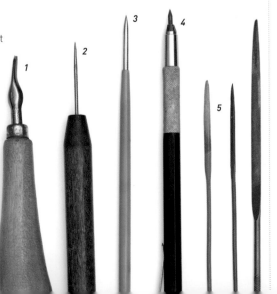

Engraving on solid metal is a skilled technique and one of the areas in which metal clay has a serious advantage over conventional metalworking. Plaster-dry metal clay can be engraved or carved as easily as a piece of chalk, and those with drawing skills will find this technique especially enjoyable.

Engraving is an ancient craft that involves scribing lines to decorate a surface, whether delicately engraved words and images or dramatic slashes and textures.

Carving is a heavier form of engraving that can be used to embellish surfaces or emphasize the shapes of a piece, while etching consists of masking part of the plaster-dry surface then removing the unmasked areas with a wet sponge to make relief designs.

ON SILENT WINGS,
LYNDA CHENEY
Carving enhances the flowing lines and vibrant shape of this silver owl pendant.

Engraving on silver clay
Engraved decoration displaying: a repeat pattern, hatching and cross hatching, and a leaf with two weights of line.

Engraving on copper clay
Engraved decoration showing (top to bottom): copperplate lettering, leaf scroll, and a simple bird.

Carving on bronze clay
Carved decoration with (top to bottom): hatching and cross hatching, curved lines, and stars.

Water etching on silver clay and on copper clay
See page 148.

BE PREPARED

Pieces that are to be engraved or carved need to be prepared well to avoid breakages and disappointing results. The clay should be thick enough to take the engraving and the surface sanded smooth before you begin.

TOOLS FOR ENGRAVING, CARVING, AND ETCHING

Plaster-dry metal clay is a relatively soft surface to engrave or carve, so there is no need for specialist engraving tools. A small burnisher with a good point or a needle tool in a handle will suffice. Metal clay suppliers stock clutch pencil-type holders with a carbide tip that are ideal. It is also worth looking for micro V-shaped wood engravers, which make good deep grooved lines on dry clay. Small needle files are the best tool for carving clay. You will also need a pencil to draw your designs and a soft paintbrush to brush away the powder from engraving.

1 Micro V-shaped wood engraver
2 Needle tool
3 Burnisher
4 Clutch pencil holder with carbide tip
5 Needle files

Engraving

Some plaster-dry clays are easier to engrave than others—most silver clays have a hard surface while bronze clay is much softer. Errors are easily corrected with paste and sanding.

YOU WILL NEED

Plaster-dry clay piece, sanded smooth

Pencil

Eraser

Engraving tools

STEP 1 Use a pencil to draw your design onto the clay surface. Any mistakes in your drawing can be sanded away or lightly removed with an eraser.

STEP 2 Draw along a small section of a line with the engraving tool to make a slight groove. Then go over the line again—the tool should keep to the line because it will follow the groove.

STEP 3 Brush away any resulting powder as you work and scribe along the line again until it is clearly marked.

STEP 4 Now repeat for the next section of the line. This is easier than trying to engrave a long line in one stroke. Any errors can be repaired with paste.

STEP 5 A small V-shaped woodcutting tool will cut a V-shaped line and can be used to emphasize and deepen dominant lines in the design. However, it is difficult to make it curve around corners.

STEP 6 Once the main outlines of the design are engraved, you can infill with areas of hatching or other details with lighter lines.

Carving

A half round file is a good tool for carving, or any fine needle file. The surface to be carved needs to be convex so this technique is especially suited to rings and bangles.

YOU WILL NEED

Basic tool kit (see page 16)

Plaster-dry clay piece, sanded smooth

Pencil

Eraser

STEP 1 Mark the lines of your design with pencil. Lay the edge of the file along the line and saw back and forth (do not lift the file or you will lose your place). Tilt the file around the piece to extend the line.

STEP 2 Filed carving is good for large and chunky pieces. As long as the surface is curved, you can carve delicate details with the tip of a needle file.

Water etching

Traditional etching involves using acids on metal. This metal clay technique uses water on plaster-dry clay. Areas of the clay surface are masked with nail polish and the unprotected areas are simply sponged away. This technique can be used with base metal as well as silver clays.

Etched pieces can show delicate results. These pieces are less than 1" (25 mm) across. The details of the face were engraved through the nail-polish resist before firing. Etched pieces can be further embellished with enamel and resin.

Etched pendants

YOU WILL NEED

Basic tool kit (see page 16)

Pencil

Plaster-dry clay piece

Clear nail polish (must not be a metallic variety—this can cause discoloration)

Small piece of sponge

STEP 1 Draw your design on the plaster-dry clay, then paint around the edges of the piece with nail polish to prevent them being eroded during the etching.

STEP 2 Use a fine paintbrush to paint over the areas to be masked, ensuring that you paint a thick layer of polish. Dry thoroughly—a heat gun does this in a matter of seconds.

STEP 3 Wet a small sponge and ring it out, then dab at the piece repeatedly to remove a thin layer of clay. Do not continue too deep, otherwise the edges will become undercut and break down.

STEP 4 Dry again thoroughly before firing.

STEP 5 After firing, the etched surface is lightly textured, while the masked areas remain smooth.

Incorporating gemstones

Gemstones and jewelry are natural partners, and stones set in your metal clay designs will add color, sparkle, and interest. This section covers some of the many techniques you can use to embellish your metal clay jewelry with gemstones.

Gemstones have been incorporated into jewelry for thousands of years, and metalworkers have developed hundreds of beautiful ways to do this. Metal clay has only been in existence for a fraction of that time, but artists have already developed many techniques for setting stones into clay both before and after firing. A lovely stone may inspire a piece or add just the right touch to complete it.

Faceted stone and purchased bezel
Stone mounted in dry clay. See page 154.

Faceted stone and purchased bezel
Stone mounted in a purchased bezel. See page 156.

Faceted stones and metal clay bezels
Stones set in metal clay bezels. See page 155.

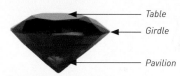

STONE SHAPES

Natural and artificial stones come in many different shapes, and it is useful to have a working knowledge of the terminology.

Table
Girdle
Pavilion

Facet cut
Facet-cut stones are cut with flat areas to make them sparkle, and have a terminology all of their own, as illustrated above. The pavilion gives the stone depth and adds to the refraction or sparkle, but raises the question of how to set the stone. Facet-cut stones are best set so that light can shine into the stone from below.

Cabochon and wire
Cabochon mounted in a flat wire bezel strip. See page 158.

Cabochon and claws
Oval cabochon mounted in metal clay heart-shaped claws. See page 159.

Cabochon and clay strip
Cabochon mounted in a handmade metal clay strip. See page 157.

Cabochons
Cabochons are flat-backed stones with a smooth domed top. They are usually round or oval, and their flat back makes them easy to set. Semiprecious stones that are opaque can be set directly onto the metal clay; they do not need light to enter from below.

Cabochons

Rough cut
Stones and crystals that are rough cut display their natural surfaces and have great appeal. They can be tumble polished or left with their natural finish.

Rough cut, tumble polished

Paua shell and claws
Irregular paua shell mounted in metal clay claws. See page 159.

Pearl and wire
A half-drilled pearl mounted on embedded wire.

Paua shell and wire prongs
Irregular paua shell mounted in balled wire prongs. See page 159.

Rough cut, unpolished

TYPES OF STONE AND HOW TO USE THEM

A wonderful variety of gemstones is available to embellish metal clay jewelry. If setting stones before firing it is essential to use fireable stones that will not be destroyed by heat. After firing, any type of stone can be set using conventional stone setting techniques.

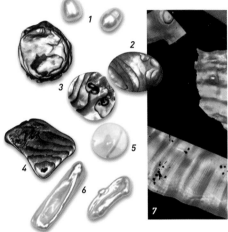

Natural stones

Semiprecious and precious stones make fabulous embellishments for jewelry and are available in a wonderful array of shapes, colors, and sizes. Natural stones are best set in metal clays after firing because they can be unpredictable when heated. While a few can be fired safely in the clay, many cannot. Major jewelry suppliers now give this information beside the stones on their websites. See the table on page 151 for indications of which stones can be fired.

1 Leopard-skin jasper tumbled stone 2 Turquoise cabochon 3 Bornite (Peacock ore) rough stone 4 Tiger's eye cabochon 5 Lapis lazuli cabochon 6 Snowflake jasper tumbled stone 7 Rose quartz rough stone 8 Jade cabochon 9 Moonstone cabochon 10 Amber cabochons.

Man-made gemstones

There is a huge variety of artificial gemstones available, and they vary in quality from plastic and glass right through to crystal, and industrial diamonds. Synthetic stones that are created in a laboratory are the kind normally recommended for use in metal clay jewelry. These are of a high quality and are difficult to tell from genuine stones. They are mostly available as facet-cut stones (see Stone shapes, page 149), but smooth cabochons are also to be found. These stones have many names, such as lab-created gemstones, cubic zirconia, CZs, or artificial gemstones.

This type of stone can be embedded in metal clay before firing, and stones labeled as "fireable" by suppliers will be safe to fire. Do not buy if there is no indication, since they may discolor during firing.

1 Corundum ruby red 2 Spinel aquamarine blue 3 Spinel dark blue 4 Cubic zirconia champagne 5 Assorted cubic zirconia 6 Corundum ruby red 7 Cubic zirconia emerald green.

Natural materials

These beautiful materials display fabulous colors and textures from the natural world. Pearls are available in many different natural shapes, from perfect rounds through to irregular freshwater pearls. Mother-of-pearl, shell, and coral can be cut into shapes, chips, and flat cabochons. Mother-of-pearl is also sold as a thin sheet for inlay (see Using resin, page 169, for how to use mother-of-pearl sheet). None of these types of material are fireable.

1 Freshwater pearls 2 Black-lip shell oval 3 and 4 Assorted paua shell shapes 5 Mother-of-pearl flat, round bead 6 Stick pearls 7 Mother-of-pearl sheet for inlay.

FIRING STONES IN SILVER CLAY

Silver clay with embedded stones can be fired in a kiln, on a stovetop, or with a blowtorch with the following restrictions:

- Stones greater than 5 mm diameter should be fired in a kiln.
- Do not quench, but cool pieces with embedded stones slowly after firing: quenching will shatter the stones.
- Low-fire natural stones (see Fireable gemstones, below) should be fired only in a kiln.
- Do not fire damaged or cracked stones, check them carefully for irregularities before firing.

FIRING STONES IN BASE METAL CLAYS

Fireable stones can be fired buried in charcoal, so they can be embedded in copper and bronze clays before firing. The charcoal firing excludes oxygen and provides some protection for the stones. The fireable natural stones listed in the table right can be fired in charcoal up to a maximum of 1560°F (850°C), but again, proceed cautiously, because firing conditions and individual stones vary.

TURQUOISE INLAY,
KATSUHIKO SUZUKI
Pieces of turquoise, green turban shell, and coral inlaid into fired silver clay create this striking mosaic pendant.

FIREABLE GEMSTONES

While laboratory-created gemstones can be purchased with a fireable label, natural stones are not so simple. Some are destroyed by the firing process, while others become damaged. The following table lists popular natural stones that are either not fireable or have been found to be fireable at the temperatures shown. Do not fire if there are any obvious fractures in the stone, since it may crack. This table is for guidance only, and natural gemstones vary a lot. If in doubt, set the stone after firing. It is not worth attempting to fire a stone if you are not sure: if it is spoiled in the firing, it will have to be drilled out of the solid metal—not an easy task.

NATURAL STONES FIRING CHART

Low fire 1200°F (650°C) Kiln fire only	High fire 1560°F (900°C) All firing methods	DO NOT FIRE	
Amazonite	Alexandrite	Agate	Malachite
Garnet	Cat's eye chrysoberyl	Amethyst	Onyx
Labradorite	Chrysoberyl	Aquamarine	Opal
Moonstone	Corundum	Carnelian	Pyrite
Obsidian	Hematite	Chalcedony	Quartz
Peridot	Ruby	Diamond	Topaz
Sunstone	Sapphire	Emerald	Tourmaline
Tanzanite	Spinel	Jade	Turquoise
Tourmaline—green		Lapis lazuli	

This table is for guidance only. Do not fire stones that are valuable or irreplaceable. Natural stones vary considerably and each one is unique.

Embedding in soft clay

There are several ways of embedding fireable stones in soft metal clay, and some of the most successful methods are detailed here. The stones used are all lab-created stones.

YOU WILL NEED

Basic tool kit (see page 16)

Gemstone

Ruler

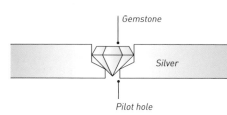

Gemstone

Silver

Pilot hole

STEP 1 First you need to establish the depth of the stone to determine how thick the clay should be to hold it securely. Place the stone, table downward, on a flat surface and stack rolling guides on either side. Use a ruler to check that the stone is below the level of the guides. The clay will shrink during firing, so add at least an extra 1 p.c. (0.25 mm) to the thickness that the clay should be rolled out to.

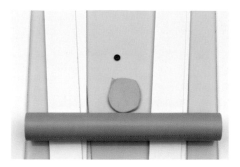

STEP 2 Roll out the clay to the calculated thickness on a tile using the same stack of rolling guides. This is a 4 mm stone that needs at least 20 p.c. (5 mm) depth of clay. For very deep stones you can add to the pile with playing cards.

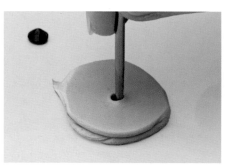

STEP 3 Pierce into the center of the clay sheet with a blunt needle and rotate the needle while holding it vertically, to make a hole just smaller than the size of the stone. If you have trouble judging this, make a notch the width of the stone in a piece of card and lay this on the clay where you make the hole.

STEP 4 Place the stone, pavilion down, into the hole and push it down with a paintbrush handle or similar tool, until the table is just below the clay surface. The stone will create a perfect round hole for itself as it is pushed down into the clay.

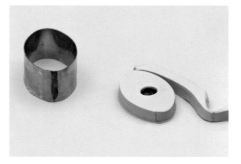

STEP 5 Cut out the clay as required. It is best to set the stone before cutting the shape to avoid distortion. Dry the piece on the tile. The stone will become caught in the clay with the slight shrinkage of drying. The piece can now be further embellished or have findings added. Clean the surface of the stone of any dust before firing, since any left will fire onto the surface.

EMBEDDING VARIATION

For thicker stones, to avoid having to make the whole clay piece very thick, add a smaller cutout piece of clay where you will set the stone. Smaller stones are shallower than larger ones; the 3 mm stones on the right can be set in a much thinner sheet of clay than a 5 mm stone.

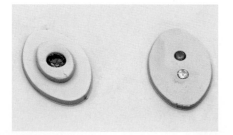

Setting with syringing

Fireable gemstones can look beautiful in filigree, and can be added during syringing. This technique shows how to add small stones of 5 mm or less. The technique is also useful for differently shaped stones.

YOU WILL NEED

Basic tool kit (see page 16)

5 mm gemstone

Pencil

Syringe with a medium nozzle

STEP 1 Draw the shape of the piece to be syringed on a ceramic tile and the outline of where the gemstone will be set.

STEP 2 Using a medium nozzle, syringe a line of paste over the drawn design to make the first layer. Syringe a small circle of the appropriate size where you want the stone to be set.

STEP 3 Use a hair-dryer or a heat gun to dry the syringing and prevent the lines from spreading or slumping.

STEP 4 Syringe again over the first line, taking care to match it as accurately as you can. Clean up any errors with a damp paintbrush. For larger stones, you may need to syringe another layer.

STEP 5 Use tweezers to place the stone, pavilion side down, into the setting.

STEP 6 Now syringe a third layer, trapping the girdle of the stone with the line of paste to ensure it is securely held in the filigree. Make sure that it is trapped on at least two sides by the line of clay. Syringe the rest of the design to complete the layer.

STEP 7 Correct any mistakes with a damp paintbrush. Dry the piece and make sure that there is no unwanted clay on the surface of the stone. Sand gently to smooth any rough areas before firing.

STEP 8 The filigree holds the stone securely. Repeated elements such as this one make delicate jewelry.

Embedding in plaster-dry clay

This technique gives a more refined finish than embedding stones in soft clay. It is used for setting small stones of 5 mm or less.

YOU WILL NEED

Plaster-dry clay piece: while the clay is still soft, make sure it is thick enough to take the stone to be embedded and make a pilot hole where the stone is to be mounted

Gemstone, here 5 mm

Pin vise

Drill bit smaller than the stone to be set, in this example 2 mm for a 5 mm stone

Stone-setting bur or drill bit the same size as the stone

Toothpick

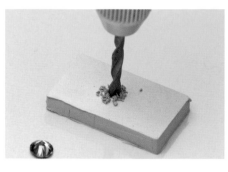

STEP 1 Use the 2 mm drill bit to drill a hole right through the plaster-dry clay: the pilot hole will make this process easier. The hole through the clay will allow light to hit the stone from below.

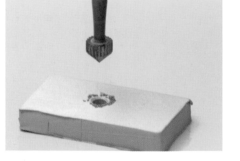

STEP 2 Now use the stone-setting bur to drill into the hole again to shape it to take the stone. The bur will make a ledge all around for the stone to sit on (see diagram on page 152).

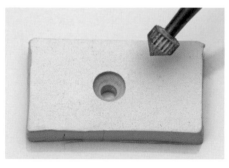

STEP 3 The shape of the hole that the bur creates mirrors exactly the pavilion of the stone. The girdle of the stone must sit below the clay surface so that it is caught firmly in the clay when fired.

STEP 4 Keep testing the hole by trying the stone in it, and continue drilling until it sits neatly with the table just below the surface of the clay.

STEP 5 Before firing, clean the surface of the stone of any dust, which will otherwise become fired on and spoil the stone. A dampened toothpick works well.

STONE-SETTING BURS

These drill bits are specially made for setting round, facet-cut stones and match the shape of the pavilion for each size. They come in different sizes for different stones, the most useful being 2, 3, 4, and 5 mm. You can use an ordinary drill bit of the appropriate size instead, although it will not match the shape of the stone so well.

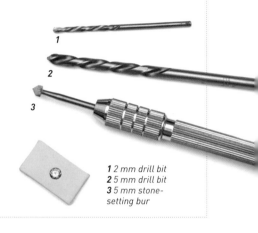

1 2 mm drill bit
2 5 mm drill bit
3 5 mm stone-setting bur

RUBEN'S PIN,
EMMA BAIRD
A beautifully mounted ruby trillion (triangular shaped stone) tops this pin.

Polishing pieces with embedded gemstones

After gemstones have been fired into metal clay, the piece will need polishing. This should be done with care to avoid damaging the embedded stone.

YOU WILL NEED

Basic tool kit (see page 16)

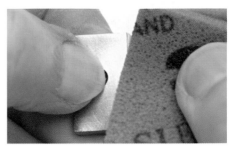

STEP 1 After firing, the gemstone will be securely held in place by the clay's shrinkage. Brush over the metal part of the piece but avoid brushing the stone, because the stainless steel bristles can damage even these hard stones.

STEP 2 When sanding the metal around a stone, cover the gem with your thumb so that the sanding does not damage it. Masking tape over the stone is an alternative method.

Creating metal clay bezels for faceted stones

This technique is used for setting larger stones in their own metal clay bezels. The piece is then used as a piece of jewelry in its own right, or added, when plaster dry, to a ring shank or other piece of jewelry. The stone is fired in the bezel, which shrinks around it to hold it firmly. The stone used here is a 13-mm long marquise stone.

YOU WILL NEED

Basic tool kit (see page 16)

Brush protector, drinking straw, or small round cutter to remove clay in the stone cavity

Gemstone

STEP 1 Calculate the depth of the stone following the instructions in Embedding in soft clay (see page 152). Shape a ball of clay, press it down onto a ceramic tile, then roll it to this thickness between the two stacks of rolling guides.

STEP 2 Press the stone, table down, into the clay until the girdle is just below the clay surface. This will make a cavity of the same shape as the stone.

STEP 3 Ease the stone out with the point of a needle. Try not to mark the surface around the cavity.

STEP 4 Use a brush protector to cut out the clay from the cavity, about 1/16" (2 mm) in from the edge all round. Alternatively, use a tiny round cutter or a drinking straw. It does not have to be the same shape as the stone, but needs to look neat. This hole will allow light to come through the stone.

STEP 5 Replace the stone, this time with the pavilion downward, and push it down until the girdle is 1/32" (1 mm) below the clay surface.

Continued next page ▶

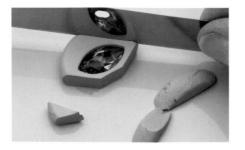

STEP 6 Trim away the excess clay 1/16" (2 mm) from all round the edge of the stone with a craft knife or slicer blade, cutting in straight lines—the shape will be refined by sanding after drying.

STEP 7 Dry the piece, then sand all around to refine and smooth the shape. If the stone drops out it will be easier to refine the piece and the stone can be replaced in the bezel just before firing.

STEP 8 Use a needle file to smooth the edges of the hole in the bottom of the cavity.

Drop earrings made from a pair of stones mounted in metal clay bezels. The loops to attach the earwires were pasted on before firing.

Mounting in purchased bezels

Fine silver and base metal bezels are available for pushing into soft clay. Some have a blade protruding from the setting for pushing into the clay, while others are just pushed down. After firing, stones that cannot be fired can be set in the bezel.

YOU WILL NEED

Basic tool kit (see page 16)

Stone

Purchased bezel to match stone

STEP 1 The clay needs to be thick enough for the bezel to be pushed into it and still leave at least 1/32" (1 mm) below the bezel. Push the bezel into the clay just up to the top of the bottom bar. Dry and fill any cracks between the clay and the bezel, otherwise the clay may crack during firing.

STEP 2 Bezels with blades can be pushed sideways into the clay. Alternatively, you can cut off the blade and set them in the clay as in Step 1.

STEP 3 After firing, place the stone in the bezel, pulling the prongs open with pliers, if necessary, to seat the stone. Squeeze the prongs alternately with pliers to secure the stone. Marquise bezels have only two prongs for attachment. The stone should be held firmly with no sign of movement.

Making bezel strips

You can make your own bezel strips out of very thinly rolled clay. The stones are set after firing, so this technique is suitable for any type of stone.

Roll out a sheet of clay 1 p.c. (0.25 mm) thick. Lay the sheet on a ceramic tile and cut strips of various widths. Small stones need ⁵/₃₂" (4 mm) bezels, larger stones will need ³/₁₆" (5 mm) or even ¼" (6 mm). Dry and fire the strips, but do not brush or polish them. You can make a selection of bezel strips to use in your work so you always have some ready.

BEZEL STRIP VARIATIONS

Use a texture sheet to texture the clay before cutting the strips to be used for decorated bezels.

A scalloped-edge bezel can be made by cutting along one end of a strip of soft clay with a cutter or wavy blade.

Embedding a bezel in soft clay

These steps show the metal clay bezel made previously can be used to set a semiprecious cabochon. You can use a purchased fine silver bezel strip instead.

STEP 1 Ensure the metal clay or purchased bezel strip is wide enough to reach just above the beginning of the curve of the side of the stone plus ¹/₃₂" (1 mm) for embedding in the clay. Bend the bezel strip around the stone. It needs to be slightly loose to allow for easy setting.

STEP 3 Roll out a sheet of clay at least 8 p.c. (2 mm) thick. If it is too thin, the bezel will act like a cutter and the clay may split beneath it during firing. You need at least 4 p.c. (1 mm) of clay under the bezel once it is pushed in. Cut out any shape required and press the bezel into the clay, keeping it exactly horizontal.

STEP 2 Cut the strip with wire cutters allowing for an overlap of about ¹/₃₂" (1 mm). File the ends so that they meet exactly in a butt joint and check again that it fits around the stone loosely. Extra space is not a problem, but a bezel that is too tight after firing makes it impossible to set the stone.

STEP 4 Dry the piece then apply paste all around the join between the bezel and the dry clay. Any gaps may open up and cause cracks during firing. Paste the join in the bezel—Art Clay Silver Overlay Paste works well for this, or you can use ordinary paste. Dry and sand to smooth any rough areas. Fire the piece and set the stone (see Setting a stone in a fired bezel, page 158).

Adding a bezel to fired clay

A bezel strip can be shaped round a stone and then added to fired silver metal clay using Art Clay Silver Overlay Paste. The advantage of this is that there are no problems with shrinkage. Alternatively, you can use solder for attaching bezels to any type of fired metal clay.

Use Art Clay Silver Overlay Paste to attach the fired bezel to a fired silver piece. Add extra paste inside the bezel for a strong join and fill any cracks. Fire again and set the stone (see Setting a stone in a fired bezel, below).

Setting a stone in a fired bezel

This type of setting, with a continuous bezel, is called a rub-over setting.

FINE SILVER HALF LENTIL AMMONITE BEADS,

MARY ANN NELSON

A citrine cubic zirconia is embedded with syringing in one of the beads. Photopolymer plates were made of ammonites to create the texture.

STEP 1 Place the stone inside the bezel and check its position. If it is too high you may be able to file the back of the stone to lower it. If it is too low the bezel may cockle as you rub it over the stone, but a piece of bezel strip placed under the stone can correct this.

STEP 2 Use a burnisher to push the bezel toward the stone at the top and bottom, then at the two sides. Only push the bezel a little way inward.

STEP 3 Now continue on the diagonals, pushing the opposite sides toward the stone. Repeat several times, working around the bezel and pushing it over a little further with each repeat until the top edge of the bezel is against the stone.

STEP 4 A large file is useful for the final pressing over of the bezel, which will become harder as you work. Finally, burnish around the edge of the bezel to smooth out any irregularities. The finished bezel should be smooth and continuous all the way around and hold the stone securely.

Mounting stones using claws or prongs

A claw setting has spikes of metal that are bent over a stone to hold it securely in place. There are many elaborate ways of making these, but for the metal clay artist it is an excellent way of setting irregular stones or cabochons after firing. The claws can be made as long or short as necessary to hold the stone. The stone should have a relatively flat back so that it will lie on the metal clay backing.

YOU WILL NEED

Basic tool kit (see page 16)

Cardstock

Pencil

This silver setting has been designed to mirror the shape of the stone

STEP 1 To make claws that are the correct length for your stone, make them first in cardstock and mock up the piece to check that it will hold the stone securely. You will need three or more claws, depending on the shape of the stone.

STEP 2 Make the piece and dry it on a ceramic tile. Lay the stone on the clay and draw around it with a pencil about 1/32" (1 mm) away from the edge of the stone. This allows for shrinkage and gives you a guide to positioning the claws.

STEP 3 Roll out a sheet of clay 2 p.c. (0.5 mm) thick and cut diamond shapes for the claws. You need to allow only 1/8" (3 mm) of the claw length for attaching to the piece. Mark across each claw and bend 1/8" (3 mm) of the attaching end up at right angles. Leave the claws on the tile and dry.

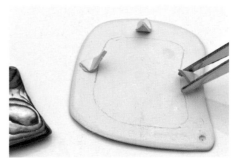

STEP 4 Use paste to attach each claw in place on the backing piece. Dry thoroughly.

159

INCORPORATING GEMSTONES

STEP 5 Fire the piece and quench. Do not brush, so that the claws are as soft as possible while fitting them over the stone. Bend the claws upward further so that you can position the stone between them.

STEP 6 Use a small file to press the claws over the stone to secure it in position. The piece is now ready to brush and polish, but take care not to sand or brush over the stone, which may get damaged.

CLAW VARIATION

Ball the ends of short lengths of wire and embed these in the piece instead of adding claws. After firing, bend the balled ends of the wire over the stone.

Adding gold

Gold has fabulous qualities that have fascinated people for thousands of years, and adding gold to your metal clay jewelry gives richness and quality. Gold is very costly, but by adding it in thin layers and as accents, you can make the most of small amounts.

The soaring price of gold in recent times has made gold metal clay beyond the reach of many artists. However, there are cost-effective ways to add touches of real gold to your jewelry. Keum-boo is an ancient Korean technique that permanently fuses gold leaf to the surface of fine silver. It is not difficult to do and produces gorgeous results. Alternatively, gold powder in the form of a paste can be applied to the surface of fired fine silver metal clay. When fired again, the gold bonds to the silver to give a gold coating or accents.

Keum-boo dragonfly
Textured silver clay. Oxidized to accentuate the gold.

Gold paste butterfly
Gold paste painted in a loose design and oxidized increasingly from left to right.

Keum-boo diamond
Design on textured and oxidized silver clay.

ADDING GOLD TO BASE METAL CLAYS AND STERLING SILVER

Sterling silver and base metal clays are difficult to gild because the copper in the metal oxidizes, which stops the gold fixing. Sterling silver can be gilded, but must first be depletion silvered, also known as depletion gilding (see Further reading, page 186).

Stamped silver clay
Gold paste accents the raised flowers.

Gold paste
Gold paste applied to fired silver clay as a coating and then scraped off in places (top). Gold paste brush strokes (bottom).

Heart-shaped silver clay piece
Silver clay piece with keum-boo leaf, oxidized.

Molded silver fish (above right)
Silver fish embellished with gold paste.

WHICH GILDING METHOD SHOULD I CHOOSE?

To help you choose the gilding method best suited to your design, consider the advantages and disadvantages of each.

Keum-boo
Use for flat, lightly textured, or smooth areas, and where you want the applied gold to have sharply defined edges.

Advantages
- Clear edges achieved with cutout pieces of gold leaf.
- Neat geometric shapes are possible.
- Enhances rather than obscures surface texture.
- Repeat shapes are possible with the use of paper punches.

Disadvantages
- Difficult to apply to strong relief and deeply cut areas.
- Difficult to use on very curved surfaces.

Gold paste or paint
Use where you want to gild particular areas of a piece, such as the beak of a bird or a raised relief area. Also for looser marks such as brushstrokes, fine lines, or random patches.

Advantages
- Easy to apply as small details, such as spots and thin strokes.
- Can be applied to recessed areas.
- Easy to apply to curved surfaces.
- Easy to apply as required to follow the detail of surfaces that are textured or sculpted.

Disadvantages
- Can obscure fine texture on the silver.
- Needs to be applied smoothly, otherwise brushstrokes will show.

POD RING,
JULIA RAI
Hand-sculpted silver and gold clays textured with paste create this ring.

Keum-boo technique
This is a method of bonding pure gold leaf to the surface of fine silver. The surfaces of the silver and gold form an alloy where they meet, to produce permanent gold plating. The process is carried out here using a gas stovetop, but can also be done using a kiln or an electric hot plate. A blowtorch, however, is more difficult to control and may overheat the piece.

Low-relief texturing on the piece to be embellished will produce more opulent results.

YOU WILL NEED

24k (can be 23.5k) gold leaf
Tissue paper
Pencil
Scissors or paper punch
Silver metal clay piece, fired but not brushed, lightly textured if desired
Cup of cold water
Rag
Baking soda, optional

STEP 1 The 24k gold leaf comes as a small rectangle. To control the leaf while you cut out shapes, sandwich it in a folded sheet of tissue paper.

STEP 2 Draw guidelines on the tissue paper and cut out the shape through all the layers. Work in from the edge of the sheet of gold leaf to avoid waste. Choose shapes that will complement the texture. Simple triangles and strips work well.

Continued next page ▶

STEP 3 You can also punch-out shapes in the leaf using a paper punch. Work with the punch upside down and again punch through the leaf inside the folded tissue paper.

STEP 4 Lay the fired silver piece on a firing mesh on a gas stovetop and use tweezers to place the leaf on top. You can use saliva to stick the leaf in place.

STEP 5 Turn on the stovetop and wait until the silver glows pale orange. This is the same temperature as for stovetop firing silver clay.

STEP 6 Turn off the gas and hold the piece steady with the tweezers. Immediately tap the center of the gold leaf with a burnisher to attach it lightly to the silver. Now burnish the gold leaf with a firm circular motion, moving from the center outward to smooth away any air pockets.

STEP 7 If the gold sticks to the burnisher it has become too hot. Dip the burnisher in water to cool it, mop on a rag, and continue burnishing. If the gold has not stuck fully and you can see unattached areas, turn on the stovetop again to reheat and repeat the process once more.

STEP 8 Leave the piece to cool naturally and check for full adhesion. If there are any tears or holes, patch them up with small pieces of gold leaf and heat and burnish as before. After cooling, brush the piece with a stainless steel brush or a mild abrasive such as baking soda rubbed on with your finger. The light texturing is accentuated by the gold.

STEP 9 Here, a gold leaf shape has been cut out using a paper punch and applied to a silver heart impressed with a real leaf.

DOUBLE-SIDED FISH PENDANT,
MILICA BUBANJA
Keum-boo is used to luscious effect in this pendant and is combined with patina, a pearl setting, and a handmade chain.

KEUM-BOO VARIATIONS

You can fire keum-boo in a kiln, but it is more laborious. Heat the unadorned piece in the kiln to 1470°F (800°C). Remove the piece with tongs on its board and immediately use tweezers to place the gold leaf on the surface of the silver. Tap and burnish as usual. When the piece cools down, replace it in the kiln for a few moments to reheat and continue the burnishing process until the gold leaf is firmly attached.

Firing with an electric hot plate is similar to using a gas stovetop. Test the hot plate first to find what setting you need to keep the silver glowing pale orange.

A liver of sulfur patina will color the silver and bring out the contrast between the two metals.

Painting with gold

Proprietary gold pastes consist of pure gold powder mixed with a binder to help them stick. They are usually painted onto freshly fired silver metal clay which is then fired again to fix the gold.

Each brand comes with its own instructions, and because these vary you should follow them carefully. The type demonstrated here is Art Clay Gold Paste.

STEP 1 The gold paste should be the consistency of thin yoghurt. If it is too thick, add a little distilled water and mix with a needle, wiping the needle clean with the brush to avoid waste. The paste comes with a bottle of medium for diluting it when using it on ceramic or glass, but this is not used when applying to silver.

STEP 2 Paint over the parts of the piece that you want to gild. Aim to make a thin, even layer, no thicker than 1/64" (0.5 mm). Thicker layers may crack or peel off. You can also apply in two thin coats, drying between each.

STEP 3 The gold will look dark on the silver and will lighten as it dries. Air dry the piece for at least 15 minutes. You can speed up drying with a hair-dryer, but only use gentle heat. Fire the piece for five minutes on a gas stovetop and cool naturally without quenching. Alternatively, fire in a kiln at 1470° F (800°C) for ten minutes, remove, and cool naturally.

STEP 4 Check the piece and if the gold is a pale color you can apply another coat of gold and fire again. Brush lightly with a stainless steel brush, then sand with fine-grit sandpapers or burnish.

163

ADDING GOLD

Decorative paste techniques

Metal clay in paste or slip form is an excellent decorating device in its own right. Use it on plaster-dry clay to make textures and for stenciling.

Paste is often seen as purely utilitarian for metal clay techniques, used for joining, mending, and attaching. However, it is also an excellent material to use for surface decoration.

◄ Stenciled maple leaves decorate a simple silver clay band ring.

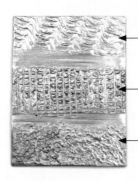

Combed paste in wavy swirls

Combed paste in a grid

Random paste dabbed and dried

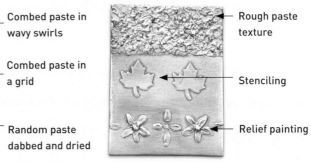

Rough paste texture

Stenciling

Relief painting

Paste as texture

Metal clay paste can be painted onto dried clay surfaces and worked in various ways to produce surface patterns and texture.

YOU WILL NEED

Basic tool kit (see page 16)

PASTE TEXTURE VARIATION

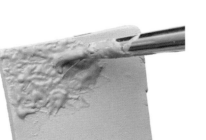

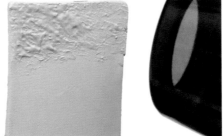

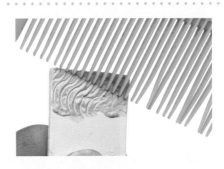

STEP 1 Apply paste liberally to the plaster-dry clay surface, dabbing and stippling with the brush to raise the paste into an interesting texture.

STEP 2 If you partly dry the paste as you work, using a hair-dryer or heat gun, the paste will not slump back into a smooth surface. The partly dried paste can then be worked further for more interesting effects.

As a coating of paste is just beginning to dry, draw a comb across the surface to give ridges and furrows. Dry briefly with hot air to set the markings. You can also make a grid by drawing the comb across the clay in one direction then again at right angles.

Relief painting

You can use paste to add your own designs to the clay surface.

YOU WILL NEED

Basic tool kit (see page 16)

Pencil

STEP 1 Draw your lines with pencil on the sanded, plaster-dry surface.

STEP 2 Load a paintbrush with fairly liquid metal clay paste and paint over the designs. Dry and then paint over again to build up the image. Continue applying layers and drying in between. You will need at least four or five layers for sufficient definition.

STEP 3 After firing, the finished piece has a pleasing, impressionist quality. If you make a texture sheet from the surface, you will be able to repeat the image many times.

Stenciling

Paste can be stenciled onto the surface of dried metal clay.

YOU WILL NEED

Basic tool kit (see page 16)

Masking tape

Shiny paper backing used for peel-off labels

Paper punch

Plaster-dry metal clay piece

STEP 1 Press a strip of masking tape onto a piece of paper backing. Use a small paper punch to cut out shapes through both thicknesses. Alternatively you can cut out your own shape with a craft knife.

STEP 2 Remove the backing plastic and press the masking tape down firmly onto the plaster-dry surface of the metal clay.

STEP 5 Peel off the tape to reveal the pattern.

STEP 3 Use a small spatula or brush to spread several layers of paste over the design, drying between each layer until the cavities in the masking tape are flush with the top surface of the tape.

STEP 4 Sand over the masking tape until you can see the design appearing again.

Using resin

Resin is a fabulous embellishing material, and particularly suitable for metal clay jewelry. It requires no special equipment and simulates the beautiful effects of enamel, without the need for a kiln.

Modern resins are safe, easy to use, and extremely durable after curing. They can be transparent or opaque, but the crystal-clear transparent colors are the most exciting to use on all types of fired metal clay, because the textured or smooth shiny metal shows through the resin. Manufacturers supply pigments for coloring the resin, although good-quality artists' oil paints can be used to color epoxy resin and provide a vast palette of colors.

Resin can be used as a clear or colorful coating on metal, or to fill cavities to suggest deep pools of color. Different colors can be swirled together or layered. Clear resin can be domed over dry and delicate small objects—such as dried flowers, photographs, sequins, charms, and glitter—placed in metal clay locket shapes, and the doming gives a wonderful magnifying effect.

Resin-filled motif
Stamped image filled with colored resin. See opposite and page 168.

Resin-filled cavities
The cavities of a textured clay surface have been filled with colored resin. See pages 72 and 168.

Resin-filled recesses
Resin fills the recesses of a molded copper clay pendant. See opposite and page 77.

Rock pool
Hand-sculpted silver clay rock pool pendant with a deep pool of resin for the water.

Bezel
Bezel cup made in silver clay with polymer clay cane slices and filled with domed clear resin. See opposite.

Plique-à-jour
Syringed filigree silver clay piece with resin used to simulate plique-à-jour enamel. See pages 120 and 169.

Resin and mother-of-pearl
Mother-of-pearl inlay with resin. See page 169.

Resin over engraving
Resin in a thin layer over engraving and syringed filigree. See pages 121, 147, and 168.

TYPES OF RESIN

There are two main types of resin available. The following techniques are demonstrated using epoxy resin.

Epoxy resin
Epoxy resin is a crystal-clear liquid that is set by mixing with a hardener. It has a working time of about 30 minutes and sets after about 24 hours at room temperature. The result is extremely hard, durable, and crystal clear with a glasslike surface. Well-applied resin will last indefinitely.

UV resin
This gel type of resin is set by exposure to an ultraviolet light source in a box. While this takes only minutes, the light boxes are quite expensive to buy. After setting, there is normally a sticky residue on the surface that must be cleaned off with a solvent. The surface may also have to be sanded smooth.

Resin is applied after firing and polishing, and needs to be kept level, otherwise it will flow off a piece. It can be applied to flat surfaces and recessed areas, but not to curved rings or bangles. Here are some ideas for how to add resin to metal clay pieces.

Impressing with paper shapes

Texture the clay with cutout paper shapes and fill the impressions with colored resin.

Stamps

Stamp the clay with a motif and fill the depressed areas with colored resin.

Framed textures

In this example a metal clay sheet was textured with a polymer clay mold taken from a piece of antique jewelry, then framed with a strip of metal clay. Resin fills the cavities.

Embedding

Make a locket back and fill with baked polymer clay cane slices, charms, beads, photographs, or dried flowers. Fill the cup with clear resin to cover the added objects and dome it slightly above the top of the bezel.

Cloisonné effects

Take a mold from an original sculpt in polymer clay that has depressed areas. Mold pieces in metal clay and apply resin to the recessed areas. This simulates cloisonné, which is an enameling technique.

RESIN TOOLS AND MATERIALS

Using resin requires a handful of specific tools and materials.

1 Ceramic tile for mixing
2 Artists' oil paints
3 Denatured alcohol (methylated spirits) and cotton swabs for cleaning the surface
4 Mixing cups—use small graduated medicine cups from a pharmacy
5 Blunt wool needle for applying resin
6 Spatula for stirring and mixing colors

7 Syringes for measuring resin and hardener in tiny quantities. Label each one to keep it exclusively for resin or hardener. Alternatively, you can pour directly into the measuring cup

TIPS FOR WORKING WITH RESIN

Resin is an irritant, so try to keep it off your hands when working to avoid an allergic reaction. Wearing a pair of light latex or plastic gloves is advisable.

Clean up any mixed resin with denatured alcohol (methylated spirits) before it sets: it will be impossible to remove once set. Apply resin to thoroughly clean surfaces: any dust or fibers can float upward and spoil the glassy surface.

How to use resin

Mixing, coloring, and applying two-part resin is a simple process. There is usually about 30 minutes of working time before the resin begins to set, so it is best to mix up small quantities at a time. The usual proportion is 1 part resin to 1 part hardener but this varies between brands so check the instructions and measure carefully.

YOU WILL NEED

Basic tool kit (see page 16)

Epoxy resin

Two syringes

Measuring cup

Artists' oil paints in colors of your choice (or use resin pigments)

Cotton swab

Denatured alcohol

Glass tumbler

STEP 1 Use a syringe to put 2ml of resin into a measuring cup, or pour to the 2ml mark. Now add the hardener using another syringe or by pouring.

STEP 2 Stir thoroughly for at least one minute until all the streakiness has gone, scraping the mixture from the sides of the cup. Set aside for a few minutes for the bubbles to disperse.

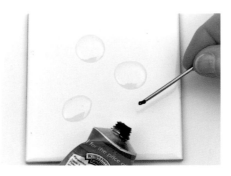

STEP 3 Scoop up some resin on the spatula and make several small pools on the tile, one for each color you need. Use a blunt wool needle to take a dot of oil paint from the tube and place it next to a pool of resin.

STEP 4 Mix the color into the pool of resin, crushing any flecks of paint until the color is uniform. Do not add too much or the resin may not set well. Add colors to the other pools as required in the same way.

STEP 5 Clean the silver piece well with a cotton swab soaked in alcohol and allow to dry. Scoop up some resin on a blunt needle and use the needle to apply it to the area to be colored. Use the needle to push the resin to the edges of the recess and into corners.

STEP 6 Add further colors as required. The adjacent resin colors should remain separate or you can draw them into each other with a fine needle. You can dome the resin slightly but do not add too much or it will flow out.

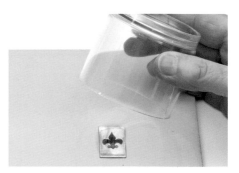

STEP 7 Blow gently on the piece to disperse any bubbles or pop them with a fine needle. Leave the piece to set on a level surface in a warm place for at least 12 hours or as recommended in the instructions. Cover with an upturned tumbler or bowl to protect it from dust.

SETTING TIP
Put a small pool of resin on a piece of paper and leave it to set with the resin-decorated metal piece. You can then test to see if the resin is set without touching your piece.

Clean up

Scrape any remaining resin out of the measuring cups before it sets, and clean them out with denatured alcohol. Clean other tools by wiping with alcohol.

Plique-à-jour

This beautiful enameling technique resembles miniature stained glass and can be simulated with openwork metal clay filigree and resin.

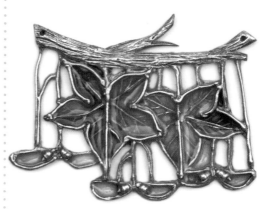

First you must create the piece in openwork filigree by syringing on a ceramic tile (see page 120). Press the fired and polished piece onto a rolled out sheet of soft polymer clay. Apply resin in the usual way, leave to set and then scrape away the polymer clay backing. Clean away any traces of polymer clay with alcohol.

Mother-of-pearl mosaic

Tiny triangles cut from a thin sheet of mother-of-pearl and inlaid into metal clay pieces are covered with a protective coating of resin. An undercoat of black paint enhances the effect.

YOU WILL NEED

Basic tool kit (see page 16)

Fired metal clay piece with shallow recessed area

Thin sheet of mother-of-pearl

Black acrylic paint

Clear varnish or glue

Rubber block

Clear resin

STEP 1 Cut the mother-of-pearl sheet into tiny triangles by pressing down on it with a sharp blade. Wet the sheet as you work to prevent the pieces jumping.

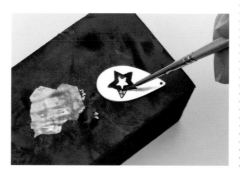

STEP 2 Paint a thin coat of black acrylic paint over the recessed area on the silver piece. Use clear varnish or glue to fix the mosaic pieces in a regular pattern in the recess. Allow to dry, then apply a coating of clear resin and leave to set.

Enameling

The ancient technique of enameling is a time-honored way of adding color to metal. Enamel is actually powdered glass that is fused onto metal with heat—an apt material with which to decorate metal clay. You will need a small kiln for firing enamel: a metal clay kiln is ideal.

Fine silver is one of the best metals for enameling because it can be heated without producing firestain. Fired silver clay is relatively porous so the areas to be enameled should be well polished or burnished to prevent salts from the silver discoloring the enamel.

Base metal clays are more difficult. They need pickling to remove firestain and the porous fired metal clay will absorb the pickle causing problems with the enameling. Therefore, it is easier to use other embellishments, such as resin or gemstones, on base metal clays.

These pages represent an introduction to the subject, and use only the simplest of equipment. For more information, see Further reading, page 186.

Wet-packed enamel
Textured piece with random wet-packed enamel and added silver wire spirals. See page 172.

Sifted enamel
Sifted enamel over a piece impressed with a fern leaf. See page 173.

Cloisonné
Cloisonné landscape with silver wire outlines, wet-pack enamel, and silver leaf. See page 172.

CHOOSING ENAMELS

There is a bewildering number of enamels available from various manufacturers. Lead-free enamels are recommended for safety reasons, and the following points will help you to choose which to use.

- Enamels can be opaque, transparent, or opalescent. Transparent enamels will give the added interest of seeing the silver background through the enamel, and are the kind demonstrated here.

- Enamels are available in lump or powder form. Start with powder, because they are easier to use and need no grinding.

- Start with a few colors, concentrating on the easy blues and turquoises.

- Red and pink enamels are difficult to use on silver, since they can discolor or become cloudy.

Lump enamels

Powdered enamels

- Use soft enamels that are fired between 1380 and 1500°F (750 and 815°C), which is below the melting point of silver.

ENAMELING TOOLS

You will need the following as a basic kit for using wet pack enamel on silver.

1 Small jelly jar with a lid
2 Fine paintbrush
3 Small spoon
4 Denatured alcohol (methylated spirits) and cotton swabs for cleaning
5 A mesh with the sides bent downward to place on the kiln shelf
6 Gloves and tongs for handling the hot mesh
7 Safety goggles

If you wish to sift enamels as well you will need the following:

8 Small sieve: 80-mesh is a good all-round size
9 Spray bottle with enamel adhesive
such as Klyr-Fire or enameler's gum
10 Stilt for firing counter enamel

EMBELLISHING

170

LARK IN A MEADOW,
JOY FUNNELL
This lyrical bird pendant
is embellished with
warm enamel colors.

Preparing the silver piece

Enamel can be applied to recessed areas or to the whole piece. Fire silver clay well for a dense metal. It is best to embed fine silver findings in silver clay—if you solder findings, use hard or enameling solder.

YOU WILL NEED

Basic tool kit (see page 16)

Dishwashing liquid

Soft brush

STEP 1 Brush the piece and polish or burnish it well to compact the surface.

STEP 2 Scrub the piece thoroughly using dishwashing liquid and a soft brush. The water should cling to the surface without beading.

Preparing the enamel

The enamel powder must be washed to remove the fine particles that will cloud transparent enamel.

YOU WILL NEED

Small jelly jar with lid

Enamel powder

STEP 1 Put a little enamel powder in a small jelly jar and cover it with water.

STEP 2 Put the lid on the jar and swish the water and enamel around. The water will become cloudy as the fine particles are mixed into the water.

STEP 3 The coarser particles will slowly sink to the bottom of the jar like fine sand. These are the grains you want.

STEP 4 Pour off most of the cloudy water. Add more water and repeat until all the cloudy water is removed and the water is clear. Put the lid on and keep the enamel covered with water for wet packing.

STEP 5 Lump enamels must be ground in a pestle and mortar. The resulting powder is then washed in the mortar.

Applying the enamel: wet pack

This type of application is called wet pack, and requires a minimum of equipment: a teaspoon and a fine brush. It is applied in several thin layers, firing between each one.

YOU WILL NEED

Prepared enamel

Teaspoon

Prepared silver clay piece

Kitchen paper

Mesh with sides bent down

Enamel grinding stone, optional

FIRING STAGES

Enamel goes through several different stages during firing.

Granular
The enamel looks like sugar granules, but has fused to the surface of the silver.

Orange peel
The enamel has begun to melt and appears glossy, but still has some texture. Stop at this stage for the first layers of enamel, because the rough surface is easier to add another layer to.

Fully fired
The enamel has become a continuous shiny coating. This is the stage to reach in the final firing.

Overfired
This piece has been overfired in a kiln that was too hot. The turquoise enamel has discolored and burnt before the enamel melted fully.

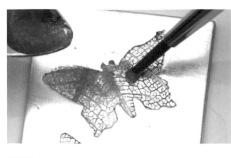

STEP 1 Scoop up some enamel and water in a small teaspoon. Use the fine brush to push grains of enamel and a little water onto the piece and spread it evenly. Aim for a thin layer, about one grain thick, all over the area to be enameled. Use the water to help move the enamel grains around.

STEP 2 Add another color, butting it up to the first. Continue, working your way across the area to be enameled.

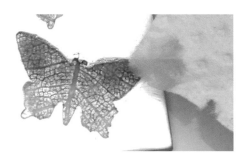

STEP 3 Use the corner of a sheet of kitchen paper to absorb excess water from one edge of the enamel. Leave to dry on top of the hot kiln for about five minutes.

STEP 4 Heat the kiln to 1560°F (850°C). The ideal temperature to fire soft enamel is about 1500°F (815°C), but the temperature drops as soon as you open the kiln door, so it is best to keep the kiln hotter and keep an eye on the temperature. If you have a larger kiln that holds heat well, set it at about 1500°F (815°C).

STEP 5 Place the piece on the mesh and hold it in the open door of the kiln briefly to be sure it is fully dry. Place it inside the kiln and shut the door. Watch the temperature. When it returns to about 1470°F (800°C), or after about 30 seconds, open the door and check the enamel.

STEP 6 If it is not melting, close the door and fire for another 15 seconds, then check again. When it has an orange peel texture (see Firing stages, left), remove the mesh from the kiln and allow it to cool down. The color will change as it cools.

STEP 7 Apply another layer of enamel and fire again to orange peel. Repeat to make at least three layers, filling gaps as necessary and until you are pleased with the result. The final firing should be continued until the enamel is shiny all over.

STEP 9 An angled view of the piece shows a glassy surface on the enamel, which has been slightly domed. You can use an enamel grinding stone, available from enameling suppliers, to grind the surface flat if you wish. After grinding, fire the enamel again to make the surface glassy.

Counter enamel

If you are enameling a metal piece thinner than 4 p.c. (1 mm) you will need to enamel the back of the piece to prevent cracking the top enamel. Apply several sifted layers to the back of the piece first. Then enamel the top of the piece and fire in a stilt to prevent the counter enamel sticking to the mesh.

Applying the enamel: sifting

Another way of applying enamel is to sift it dry onto the piece. This gives an even, thin coat of enamel. It is also used when a piece needs counter enameling (see below). Dry washed enamel in a jar on top of the kiln or in a slow oven—180°F (80°C).

STEP 1 Spray the prepared silver clay piece evenly all over with enamel adhesive spray.

STEP 3 Wipe under the piece to remove any enamel and fire as for wet-pack application. Repeat to make several layers.

YOU WILL NEED

Prepared metal clay piece

Enamel adhesive such as Klyr-Fire in a spray bottle

Paper

Small sieve, or improvise with a fine coffee strainer

Paper

Prepared enamel

Cotton swab

Mesh with sides bent down

STEP 2 Put the piece on a clean sheet of paper and sift the dried enamel over it.

ENAMEL VARIATIONS

Try using snippets of gold or silver leaf in your enamel. Add them at the last layer and coat with sifted clear enamel to set them. Add tiny coils of fine silver or gold wire in the same way.

An enameled fish pendant decorated with gold leaf and silver wire

Embellishing with polymer clay

Polymer clay is easy to use and is a wonderful way to add color to your metal clay jewelry.

Polymer clay is a fine-grained modeling clay that combines beautifully with metal clays. It is available in many colors that can be mixed to make a seemingly infinite palette, and it can be modeled, shaped, extruded, and sculpted into an incredible variety of objects and embellishments. It remains soft until hardened permanently in a home oven.

Transfer
Polymer clay transfer in a bronze metal clay frame. See page 177.

Marbling
Silver paper-clay cutout framed in marbled polymer clay. See page 129.

Micromosaic
Polymer clay micromosaic framed in silver clay. See Further reading page 186.

Appliqué
Polymer clay appliqué picture framed in textured silver clay.

Faux stones
Polymer clay faux stones in a molded bronze clay brooch. See page 176 and Further reading page 186.

Transfer
Polymer clay transfer in a silver clay frame. See page 177.

Marbling
Marbled polymer clay in a silver clay frame.

Malachite marbling
Marbled polymer clay in malachite colors in a silver clay frame.

POLYMER CLAY TOOLS

Tools for polymer clay are similar to those used for metal clays.

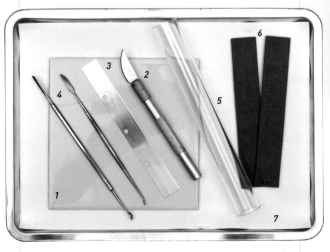

Types of polymer clay
There are many brands of polymer clay, and the following techniques are suitable for any of them. Fimo, Premo Sculpey, and Kato clay are popular brands for jewelry making, and are widely available from craft and hobby supply stores.

1 Ceramic tile
2 Craft knife
3 Slicer blade
4 Modeling tools
5 Roller: this needs to be heavier than for metal
clay, so improvise with a sturdy bottle
6 Rolling guides
7 Baking sheet lined with paper to bake pieces on, optional

Marbling polymer clay sheets

By marbling polymer clay you can produce glorious patterns of color for the inside of a frame or for shaping into cabochons or beads.

YOU WILL NEED

Basic tool kit (see page 16)

Polymer clay, several different colors, including black

Fired and polished metal clay frame with a central cutout, here drilled as a pendant

Strong glue or epoxy glue

STEP 1 Condition the polymer clay and shape each color into a log about ⅜" (10 mm) thick.

STEP 2 Press the logs together and roll into a single log. Twist the log to begin the marbling.

STEP 3 Fold the log in half and roll again. Repeat the process of rolling and folding four or five times.

STEP 4 Form the log into an S-shape and lay it down on your work surface, pressing it together to flatten it into a pancake. Roll out the pancake between rolling guides—2 mm (8 p.c.) is a good thickness—and watch the gorgeous swirls appear.

STEP 5 Place a fired and polished metal clay frame on the marbled sheet, trying different areas to see what looks best. When you are happy, cut out the section roughly with a craft knife.

STEP 6 Roll a thin sheet of black polymer clay and lay it on the tile. Press the marbled sheet on top and place the frame on the desired point. Press down so that the clay bulges up slightly into the frame opening.

STEP 7 Trim all around the outside of the frame and remove the scrap polymer clay. Make a hole with a needle through the hanging hole in the frame. Bake the whole piece on the tile according to the manufacturers' instructions. The temperature will not affect the metal clay.

STEP 8 When the piece is cool, slide a blade under it to remove it from the tile. Test that the polymer clay is firmly attached to the metal clay and, if not, prize it off and glue it down with strong glue.

▲ Polymer clay simulates semiprecious stones realistically. These beads show amber, jade, lapis lazuli, and turquoise all made with polymer clay.

▲ Use polymer clay to frame metal clay creations.

◄ Add color to your metal clay jewelry with polymer clay. Here, faux amber beads are combined with oxidized silver clay beads.

► Press ovals of soft polymer clay onto a metal clay piece and bake: much easier than setting stones.

► Use polymer clay to back openwork filigree pieces. This protects the delicate silver filigree and provides gorgeous colors.

TIPS FOR WORKING WITH POLYMER CLAY

- Knead each piece of clay in your hands before starting. This will condition the clay and soften it for easy working. Cut off small pieces and roll them into logs, folding and rolling until the clay does not crack where folded.
- Keep wet wipes handy to clean your hands between colors.
- The clay remains soft indefinitely until baked, giving you all the time you need to create your pieces. Store in a tin or other dustproof container at room temperature wrapped in baking parchment or waxed paper—do not use plastic food wrap or plastic bags, which become sticky.
- Bake pieces on a ceramic tile or paper-lined baking sheet at the temperature recommended by the manufacturer.
- Test your oven first by baking small 4 p.c. (1 mm) thick strips of clay. After baking and cooling, try to break them. They should bend into a U-shape before breaking. Polymer clay hardens on cooling but thin sheets remain flexible.

MARBLE VARIATION

Instead of rolling the marbled clay into a sheet, cut across the marbled log with a sharp blade (1). Open out pairs of slices (2) and push them together side by side (3), matching the patterns revealed for a mirror-image effect. This works best with only light marbling, so the shapes inside the log are not too tiny.

1

2

3

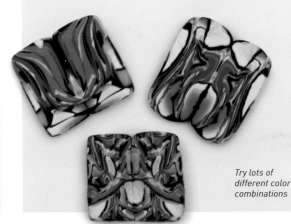

Try lots of different color combinations

A matched pair has been framed inside a locket with a hinged door

Polymer clay transfers

Polymer clay can be used to make durable and detailed transfers from laser printers or toner-based copiers, and these can be used to add photographs, text, and images to metal clay pieces. The finished polymer clay transfers can be pressed into fired metal clay pieces while they are still soft or baked first and then mounted like gemstones.

YOU WILL NEED

Basic tool kit (see page 16)

Scissors

Polymer clay: white and black

Polymer clay tools (see page 174)

Printed image of a suitable size for the frame—ordinary copier paper is fine

Fired and polished metal clay frame

Superglue

TRANSFER TIPS

- You will need an image printed by a laser printer, or photocopied using a toner-based copy machine. Inkjet printers do not work, but any type of toner printer does.
- Use any brand of light-colored polymer clay.
- The transferred image will be reversed, so flip any images that include text before printing them.
- Use a computer or the copier to resize the image to fit the required size.
- All types of image can be transferred: color images, black and white, grayscale, sepia, line drawings, photographs, etc.

STEP 1 Roll out a sheet of white polymer clay about 4 p.c. (1 mm) thick and lay it on the tile. Cut out the printed image with a small border around it.

STEP 2 Place the image face down on top of the clay and burnish it on firmly with the tip of your finger.

STEP 3 Dip your finger in water and wet the back of the paper. Allow it to soak in for a few seconds.

STEP 4 Now rub over the back of the paper with your finger. The paper will begin to disintegrate as you rub. Continue rubbing and removing the threads of paper. Work slowly and be patient so that you don't smudge the underlying print.

STEP 5 Add a little more water if the paper gets too dry. Eventually all the paper will be removed and the image is left on the clay surface. Leave to dry. Any white areas indicate traces of remaining paper and should be lightly wetted and rubbed gently.

STEP 6 Lay the metal clay frame over the image and trim away the excess polymer clay. Bake the frame and the clay on the tile, following the manufacturer's instructions. Back it with a sheet of black polymer clay if you would like a black back to the frame.

Using glass and ceramics

Glass and ceramics combine beautifully with metal clays. Both can be fired with low-fire silver clay to create exciting mixed-media jewelry. Base metal clays cannot be fired with glass and ceramics, but they can be combined with glass by adding mounts after firing.

Kiln firing is necessary when firing silver clay with glass and ceramics, because both materials need to cool slowly to avoid cracking, which is not possible with torch or stovetop firing.

Silver clay can be wrapped around glass cabochons and fired in a kiln to make complete pieces of jewelry. If you do not have a kiln, you can still make your own silver clay mounts to attach to purchased glass cabochons.

CHARTREUSE RING,
ERNA PIECHNA-SOWERSBY
Fused iridescent glass contrasts beautifully with the silver metal clay surround.

Mounted glass
Fused-glass cabochon mounted in silver clay. See page 180.

Fused glass and flexible clay
Fused dichroic glass wrapped in flexible clay and fired. See page 181.

Openwork glass
Openwork glass piece with silver mount. See page 181.

Mounted ceramic
Ceramic piece mounted in silver clay. See page 182.

Layered glass
Dichroic cabochon with fine silver wire bail trapped between the layers. See page 181.

Decorated glass
Dalle de verre glass, decorated with Art Clay Silver Overlay Paste and attached to a bail. See page 181.

Clay sandwich
Silver clay sheet and thin copper sheet cut out with paper punches and sandwiched between two layers of glass. See page 181.

TYPES OF GLASS

Use high quality fusing glass from a reputable manufacturer that is less likely to discolor during firing than other glass. Always use glass with the same COE (expansion rating) number so the pieces are compatible. The glass comes in sheets of different thickness and the best for small cabochons is 2 to 3 mm thick.

Different kinds of glass available for fusing into jewelry

1 Plain colored and opalescent glass
2 Multicolored glass
3 Plain, clear glass
4 Dichroic patterned glass
5 Dichroic textured glass

TOOLS FOR GLASS FUSING

1 Glass cutter: the pistol grip type shown is easy to control
2 Breaking pliers
3 Safety goggles
4 Graph paper to help cut straight lines in the glass
5 Felt-tip pen to mark the glass
6 Ruler

Denatured alcohol (methylated spirits) and cotton swabs for cleaning

Ceramic shelf paper to cover the kiln board

Making cabochons

The instructions and firing times given here are for making small cabochons 1" (25 mm) long or less.

YOU WILL NEED

Ruler

Glass cutter

Fuseable glass COE 90

Cotton swab

Denatured alcohol

Ceramic shelf paper

A selection of fused-glass cabochons

STEP 1 Cut the pieces of glass into small rectangles, strips, or triangles of 1" (25 mm) long or less. Mark cutting lines with a felt-tip pen and score the glass using a ruler and a glass cutting tool.

STEP 2 With the convex side of the jaws upward, align the breaking pliers centrally over the score line and ⅜" (10 mm) from the edge of the glass. Squeeze to snap the glass along the score line.

STEP 3 Try arranging separate pieces of glass into other shapes too. You can cover dichroic glass with a larger piece of clear glass. Ensure you clean all the pieces with denatured alcohol to remove fingerprints. Place the pieces on a kiln shelf covered in ceramic shelf paper. Leave a space of at least ½" (13 mm) between pieces.

STEP 4 Put the shelf in a cold kiln and heat at full ramp to 1560°F (850°C). When the kiln reaches this temperature open the door and check the pieces. They should be rounding well into cabochons.

Continue heating for between five and ten minutes. When you are satisfied with the shapes, turn off the kiln but leave the temperature display on. Prop open the kiln door and let the temperature drop to 1020°F (550°C)—called crash cooling. Do not let the temperature drop below this.

STEP 5 Shut the kiln door and leave until the internal temperature reaches room temperature. Remove the shelf and wash the dust from the ceramic paper away from the glass cabochons.

KILN TEMPERATURES

Low-fire silver clays, such as Art Clay Silver 650 or PMC3, can be used with glass and ceramics. The kiln temperatures and times given here are for fusing glass in a small jewelry kiln with a chamber approximately 8" cubed (200 mm cubed) or less. Larger kilns will need lower temperatures because their longer ramp time will cause the glass to overheat. Check your kiln instructions.

OVERLAY PASTE

Art Clay Silver Overlay Paste is specifically made for decorating glass and ceramics with silver. It can be applied with a fine brush, used with stencils, or brushed over a piece and scratched back. It is also useful as a glue when attaching silver clay to glass for mounting. Firing is similar to the schedules detailed here, but read the accompanying instructions before you begin.

Art Clay Gold Paste can be used in the same way to decorate glass and ceramic.

Silver and gold pastes fired onto glass cabochons

SAFETY

Wear safety goggles when cutting glass, and take care with the small glass shards that are inevitably produced. Work on newspaper so that when you have finished you can gather up the paper with any glass shards and dispose of them safely.

Mounting glass in silver clay

This simple setting technique can be adapted for many different designs.

YOU WILL NEED

Basic tool kit (see page 16)

Low-fire silver metal clay

Glass cabochon, cleaned with denatured alcohol

Cutters

Ceramic shelf paper

Denatured alcohol

Cotton swab

Toothpick

STEP 1 Roll low-fire silver clay into a 4 p.c. (1 mm) sheet and texture if required. Cut out a shape to complement the cabochon and press the cabochon into the soft clay.

STEP 2 Remove the cabochon and use a fine needle to cut around the impressed shape, just inside the outer line. Remove the clay. This is to give a clear back to the cabochon so it is lit from behind.

STEP 3 Cut further shapes and paste these to the backing, trapping the cabochon in place. Dry and drill a hole or add a bail for a pendant if required.

STEP 4 Use a cotton swab and denatured alcohol to clean the glass surface of any dust or fingerprints, which will spoil the surface during firing. A dampened toothpick will clean hard-to-reach areas. Place on ceramic shelf paper on a kiln shelf and set the kiln to fire at full ramp to 1470°F (800°C). When the temperature is reached, crash cool immediately (no holding time). Leave to cool as before.

STEP 5 The glass piece will be trapped by the silver clay. Finish by brushing and polishing as required.

Wrap open-fused triangles of glass in silver clay for hanging pendants, and fire as shown opposite.

Make triangular cabochons and wrap the widest part in silver clay to make pendants.

If you do not have a kiln, simple, flat bails, decorated and fired, can be glued to the back of cabochons after firing. E6000 glue or epoxy glue is recommended.

Cutouts of silver paper clay or copper sheet metal can be trapped between two pieces of glass before firing.

Make a loop of fine silver wire and trap it between two pieces of glass for an embedded loop.

Dalle de verre, or billet glass, comes in large pieces that can be broken up with a hammer into attractive chunks. Fire lightly in a kiln before mounting to remove the sharp edges. Decorate with Art Clay Silver Overlay Paste and mount using a simple bail fired onto the piece.

SOUND OF LEAVES,
NOBUKO YUNOMURA
Glass and silver clay combine to make a beautiful, naturalistic necklace and pair of earrings.

Decorative pieces of
ceramic from beach finds

YOU WILL NEED

Basic tool kit (see page 16)

Small piece of broken ceramic

Denatured alcohol

Cotton swab

Paper

Pencil

Low-fire silver clay

Ceramic shelf paper

Mounting ceramics

Silver clay can be used to mount ceramics in the same way as glass. Ceramics tolerate a higher firing temperature than glass but they may have glazes that are damaged by too high a temperature. For this reason, a slightly lower firing temperature is advisable.

This technique shows how to mount irregular-shaped pieces of broken ceramic. Those shown here are beach finds of nineteenth-century crockery. If your piece shows cracks or flaking glaze, either reject it or do a test fire.

STEP 1 Clean the ceramic piece all over with denatured alcohol. File off any sharp edges with a metal file. This is not difficult to do and most crockery is relatively soft.

STEP 2 Measure around the piece with a long strip of paper and mark where it joins. This will give you a guide as to how long the silver surround strip needs to be.

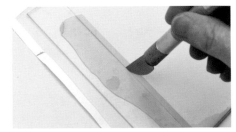

STEP 3 Roll the low-fire silver clay into a long sheet between 2 p.c. rolling guides (0.5 mm). Use a straightedge and craft knife to cut the strip. It should be the same width as the thickness of the piece of crockery.

STEP 4 Wet one side of the clay strip and press it all around the edge of the crockery piece, smoothing it on.

STEP 5 Overlap the ends and cut through both layers. Remove the excess strip and press the ends together firmly, securing with paste. The join must be strong otherwise it may open during firing.

STEP 6 Dry the piece then add a loop. Here, a pointed log of clay is looped and joined with paste to the clay strip.

STEP 7 ◄ Place on ceramic shelf paper on the kiln shelf and heat at full ramp to 1400°F (760°C). Hold for 15 minutes then crash cool to 1020°F (550°C). Shut the kiln and leave until it reaches room temperature.

CERAMIC MOUNTING VARIATION

Buttons can be art in miniature, and when mounted in metal clay make delightful pieces of jewelry. Here a simple set of prongs with an attached bail has been made from silver clay for a ceramic button. After firing, the prongs are bent round the button to secure it.

Patinas

The world of patinas and oxidation is an easy and enjoyable one to explore, especially if you like your pieces to look antique, or are looking for exciting and vibrant effects for your metal surfaces.

A patina is a surface color that develops on metal, either naturally over time or artificially induced with chemicals and/or heat. It is also called oxidation. Silver, copper, bronze, and their alloys can all be oxidized successfully. The results give a suggestion of aging but can also produce glorious colors.

MAYAN CALENDAR,
STANLEY MICALLEF
This exotic bronze clay pendant is gorgeously colored using heat patinas.

Torched copper
Copper has been torched to give the patina, then quenched and the raised areas polished. See page 185.

Silver and liver of sulfur
Silver oxidized with liver of sulfur to give orange, blue, purple, and black. See page 184.

Ammonia and sawdust
Copper placed in a jar of sawdust with ammonia and vinegar overnight. See page 185.

Baldwin's patina
Bronze combined with copper and swabbed with Baldwin's patina. See pages 108 and 185.

Polished-back liver of sulfur
Silver oxidized with liver of sulfur and polished back. See page 184.

Liver of sulfur
The lower part of this bronze piece has been oxidized with liver of sulfur. See page 184.

Ammonia and sawdust
Bronze placed in a jar of sawdust with ammonia and vinegar overnight. See page 185.

Ammonia and sawdust
Bronze placed in a jar of sawdust with ammonia and vinegar but only left for two hours. See page 185.

Liver of sulfur
Samples of silver and liver of sulfur. See page 184.

Using liver of sulfur

Used to oxidize both silver and base metals, liver of sulfur (potassium sulfide) is available in lump form or as a liquid or gel. It has an unpleasant smell but produces gorgeous colors on silver and more muted colors on base metals.

The results are variable and depend on water temperature, the strength of the solution, and the length of time the piece is immersed. If you do not like the color from oxidation, remove it by refiring the piece briefly.

The technique for using liver of sulfur is demonstrated here with silver.

For an antique effect, polish the piece with silver polish so that only recessed areas remain dark. There is no need to protect the surface in this case because the recesses are unaffected by wear.

YOU WILL NEED

Basic tool kit (see page 16)

Fired and polished silver clay piece

Cotton swab

Dishwashing liquid

Liver of sulfur, here as a solution

Hot water

Ceramic or glass cup

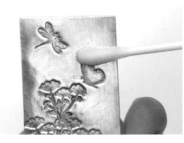

STEP 1 Wash the fired and polished metal piece in a strong solution of dishwashing liquid to clean it thoroughly, otherwise the patina will be patchy.

STEP 2 As a rough guide, use a few drops of liver of sulfur in a quarter cup of hot (not boiling) water. If you are using lump liver of sulfur, use a pea-sized piece. Dissolve the liver of sulfur in the hot water and stir.

STEP 3 Grip the metal piece in tweezers and swirl it in the solution, pull it out after a few seconds to inspect progress.

Copper darkens to a dull brown in liver of sulfur. Polishing back gives light copper highlights.

STEP 4 On fine silver, golden colors appear first, then coppers, blues, purple, and black. If you want to progress to full black, rinse the piece occasionally to prevent any buildup which may flake off.

STEP 5 When the piece is the required color, rinse thoroughly in clean water. You can use the same liver of sulfur solution for more pieces, but when it becomes cloudy and pale it is spent and is safe to pour away down the drain.

Liver of sulfur turns bronze a rich, golden brown.

EMBELLISHING

Baldwin's patina

Baldwin's patina is a proprietary solution that will darken copper and not silver or bronze. It is therefore useful to show up the different metals in mixed pieces.

Rub the solution directly onto the piece using a cotton swab, rinsing in warm water between applications.

PRESERVING THE PATINA

Surface patinas will be removed by wear, so preserve the colors by coating with any varnish suitable for metal, or use Renaissance wax, which is a microcrystalline Wax polish. Any coating knocks back the colors slightly.

Ammonia and sawdust

This technique colors copper and bronze wonderful blues and greens.

YOU WILL NEED

Basic tool kit (see page 16)

Jelly jar with lid

Sawdust

Teaspoon

Vinegar

Household ammonia

Wooden skewer

Fired copper or bronze clay piece, washed thoroughly with dishwashing liquid to de-grease.

STEP 1 Half fill a jar with sawdust. Mix one teaspoon of vinegar with three teaspoons of ammonia and pour onto the sawdust. It should dampen it thoroughly. Mix well with a wooden skewer.

STEP 2 Place your metal piece into the jar and cover it in the mixture using the skewer. Replace the lid tightly to contain the smell. Leave for one or two hours or overnight. The longer you leave it the more the colors will develop.

STEP 3 Use tweezers to remove the piece from the mixture and wash thoroughly with water. Copper will produce lovely blues and blacks, bronze will become speckled with green.

Heat treatment

Copper and bronze can also be given lovely colors with a blowtorch.

YOU WILL NEED

Fired copper or bronze metal clay piece

Blowtorch

Fire brick

Run the flame lightly over the piece and see the colors develop. Copper will become multicolored, bronze a deep gold. Quench to hold the color.

Resources

Suppliers

USA

www.artinsilver.com
Hadar's Clays

www.bronzclay.com
Bronzclay and Copprclay worldwide suppliers

www.cooltools.us
Tools and equipment plus clays, embellishing products, and kilns

www.gemresources.com
Gemstone specialists

www.metalclays.com
Metal clays, tools, and accessories

www.metalclaysupply.com
Metal clays, tools, and accessories

www.riogrande.com
Metal clays, jewelry findings, resins, enamelling supplies—also scrap metal dealers

www.wholelottawhimsy.com
Metal clays, molding compounds, resins, gemstones, enamels, tools, and accessories

UK

Creative Glass UK
www.creativeglassshop.co.uk
Art Clay clays, tools, accessories, and glass fusing supplies

www.craftworx.co.uk
Hadar's clays

www.cjresins.co.uk
Resins

www.diamondcz.co.uk
Gemstone specialists

www.cooksongold.com
Findings, wire, tools, enamels, resin, soldering materials, metal clays—also scrap metal dealers

www.fredaldous.co.uk
Siligum putty silicone molding material, resins, and polymer clay

www.metalclay.co.uk
Art Clay clays, CopprClay, BronzClay, polymer clay, tools, and accessories

www.palmermetals.co.uk
Findings and wire—fine silver and sterling, plus soldering materials

www.thepmcstudio.com
PMC clays, Creative Copper and Bronze clays, tools, and accessories

AUSTRALIA

www.ceramicandcraft.com.au
PMC clays, tools, and accessories

www.eclecticstudio.com.au
Metal clays, findings, wire, resin, molding materials, tools and accessories, enamels, and polymer clay

www.metalclay.com.au
Metal clays, tools, and accessories

www.polymerclay.com.au
PMC clays, polymer clays, tools, findings, and accessories

NEW ZEALAND

www.artclaynz.co.nz
Metal clays, tools, accessories, enamels, resin, glass, gemstones, molding materials, findings, and wire

www.beadaholic.co.nz
Silver clays, polymer clays, and findings

www.zigzag.co.nz
Art Clays, polymer clays, resin, molding materials

Recommended reads

BOOKS ON METAL CLAYS

Metal Clay Beads: Techniques, Projects, Inspiration
Barbara Becker Simon
Lark Books, 2009

The Art of Metal Clay—Revised and Expanded
Sherri Haab
Potter Craft, 2008

Magical Metal Clay Jewelry
Sue Heaser
Krause Publications, 2008

Setting Stones in Metal Clay
Jeanette Landenwitch
Brynmorgen Press, 2009

PMC Technic
Tim McCreight
Brynmorgen Press, 2007

Sculptural Metal Clay Jewelry
Kate McKinnon
Interweave Press, 2010

Metal Clay Rings
Irina Miech
Kalmbach Books, 2010

Metal Clay Fusion
Gordon Uyehara
Lark Crafts, 2012

BOOKS ON RELATED TOPICS

Metalworking 101 for Beaders: Create Custom Findings, Pendants & Projects
Candice Cooper
Lark Books, 2009

The Art of Enamelling
Linda Darty
Lark Crafts, 2006

Keum-Boo on Silver
Celie Fago
Celie Fago, 2007

The Art of Resin Jewelry
Sherri Haab
Potter Craft, 2008

The Encyclopedia of Polymer Clay Techniques
Sue Heaser
Running Press, 2007

Kiln-Formed Glass: Over 25 Projects for Fused and Slumped Designs
Gillian Hulse
St. Martin's Griffin, 2010

Soldering Made Simple
Joe Silvera
Kalmbach Books, 2010

USEFUL WEBSITES

www.sueheaser.com—Sue Heaser's website with information, projects and more resources

www.artinsilver.com/blog/—information on Hadar's clays and combining metal clays

www.thegoldsmiths.co.uk/assay-office/—information on hallmarking in the UK

www.hallmarkingconvention.org/—information on international hallmarking laws

www.hobbymaxistore.com—information on Prometheus clays

www.metalclayacademy.com—large site with all kinds of information

www.metalclayguru.com/—tips and projects from metal clay artists round the world

www.pmccblog.blogspot.co.uk/—an informative blog by metal clay artists

www.squidoo.com/preciousmetalclay—many different articles on using metal clays

MAGAZINES

http://art.jewelrymakingmagazines.com/

www.metalclayartistmag.com/

www.metalclaytoday.com/

Index

A

Acar, Elif *Bangle of the Bride* 93
ammonia and sawdust 183, 185
appliqué 108, 111
Arnold, Xuella *Cygnet Rings* 140
    Salamander Bangle 132
    The Strawberry Thief 82
Azulie, Rachel *Origami Pendant* 127

B

bails 56, 60, 102
    soldering 65
Baird, Emma *Chain Bracelet* 105
    Ruben's Pin 154
Baldwin's patina 183, 185
bangles 131, 132–133
    bangle mandrels 18, 19
base metal clays 12–13, 160
    firing 49, 111, 151
    firing containers 20, 21, 49
beads 70, 112–119
    bead caps 112, 118
    bead cones 112, 119
    combustible core 115
    flat beads 112, 114
    lentil beads 112, 115–116
    molding beads 112, 117–118
    solid bicone beads 112, 114
    solid round beads 113
    tube beads 112, 116–117
blowtorches 20, 21, 44, 185
    blowtorch firing 45–46
    copper and bronze 185
box forms 94–95
braiding 84
brass brushes 22, 23, 54
breadcrumbs 90
bronze clays 12, 13, 33, 64
brooches 12, 70, 77
    brooch pins 56, 62
brushes 18, 19
brushing 51
Bubanja, Milica *Double-Sided Fish Pendant* 162
buffing wheels 22, 23
burnishing 18, 19, 50, 53
buttons 119

C

candle wax impressions 72
caning 108, 109
card 90
carving 146, 147
catches 96

locket catch 101
ceramic shelf paper 20, 21
ceramics 16, 17, 182
    mounting ceramics 182
chains 104, 107
charcoal 20, 21
Cheney, Lynda *Folded Pendant* 87
    Midnight Feast 78
    Not even a mouse 2
    On Silent Wings 146
clay cords 84, 85
clay quantities for jewelry 12, 132, 136
combining clays 108, 111
construction techniques 94–95
copper clays 12, 13, 33, 64
cork clay 90, 92
craft knives 16, 17
crumpling 86
cufflinks 12, 63, 77
cuffs 12, 132, 134
curling 86
cutters 16, 17, 70–71
    lockets 94, 95
    making cutters 71
    paper cutters 75
cuttlefish impression 72

D

drilling tools 18, 19, 22, 23, 42, 54–55
    stone-setting burs 154
drying equipment 18, 19
drying techniques 39–40
    air drying 39
    avoiding warping 40
    domestic ovens 39
    food dehydrators 39
    hair-dryers 40
    heat guns 40
    hollow core 93
    hot plates 39
    kilns 39
    mug warmers 40

E

earrings 70
    earwires 56, 61
    stud earrings 61
enamel 14, 15, 145, 170–173
    counter enamel 173
    preparing enamel 171
    preparing silver piece 171
    sifting 173
    wet pack enamel 172–173
engraving 146–147
epoxy resin 166
extruders 16, 17, 30

F

feathering 108
    copper and silver 110
felt polishing wheels and points 55
fiber blanket/cloth 20, 21
fiber box, making 49
file pockets 16
files 18, 19
filigree 92, 120
filing 50, 52
findings 14, 15, 56–63
    brooches 56, 62
    cufflinks 63
    earwires for drop earrings 56, 61
    head pins 56, 58
    jump rings 57
    loop-and-peg findings 59
    pendants 60
    stud earrings 61
    toggle-and-ring clasps 56, 63
    U-loops 60
finger gauges 18, 19
fingerprint jewelry 75
finishing techniques 25, 50–55
    brushing 51
    burnishing 53
    filing 52
    hammering 55
    hobby drills 54–55
    pickling 51
    sanding 53
    silver paper clay 125
    tumbling 52
firebricks 20, 21
firing 44–49
    base metal clay 12, 44
    blowtorch firing 45–46
    combined clays 111
    enamel 172
    firing boards 20, 21
    firing containers 20, 21
    gas stovetop firing 20, 21, 44, 47
    gemstones 151
    glass 179
    hollow core 93
    kiln firing 48–49
    precious metal clays 10–11, 44
    silver clays with copper/silver alloys 111
    silver paper clay 125
    testing 46
flexible clay 29
flowers 83
forging 89
formers 86, 87, 91, 115, 117
freeform sheets 86
Funnell, Joy *Lark in a Meadow* 171

G

Gage, Holly *If I Could Fly* 102
gas stovetop firing 20, 21, 44, 47
gemstones 14, 15, 149–157
    adding bezel to fired clay 158
    bezel strips 157
    bezels for faceted stones 155–156
    embedding bezel in soft clay 157
    embedding in plaster-dry clay 154
    embedding in soft clay 152
    mounting in purchased bezels 156
    mounting stones using claws or prongs 159
    polishing pieces with embedded
        gemstones 155
    setting stone in fired bezel 158
    setting with syringing 153
    stone shapes 149
    types of stone 150
glass 14, 15, 178–181
    making cabochons 179
    mounting glass in silver clay 180
    overlay paste 180
gloves 20, 21
glycerin 12, 13
goggles 20, 21
gold clay 10, 11, 44, 160–163
gold, embellishing with 160–163

H

hallmarking 50
hammering to strengthen 55
hammering warped pieces 55
hammers 22, 23
hand polishing 50
head pins 56, 58
Heaser, Sue *Earrings* 124
    Kestrels Necklace 74
    Pea Pod Necklace 88
    Turtle Lagoon Pendant 74
hinges 96–101
    book hinges 99
    flat hinges 98–99
    hinge pins 99
    hinge tubes 97
    locket hinges 100–101
hollow core techniques 90–93
    covering core with clay sheet 92
    covering core with filigree 92
    covering core with paste 92
    creating core 91
    drying and firing 93
    materials 90

I

impressing clay 72
    fine materials 73

fingerprints 75
paper cutters 75
soap and wax 76
stamps 75
stencils 75
texture sheets 74, 76
thicker materials 73
inlay 108, 111

J

Jacobson, Hadar *Mirror Image* 55
    My Primary Colors 108
jars 16
jump rings 57

K

keeping clay workable 31–33
    rehydrating 31–32
    storing clay 33
    wet clay 33
keum-boo 160, 161–163
kilns 20, 21, 39, 44
    kiln firing 48–49
    kiln shelves 20, 21
knotting 84, 85
Komai, Sachiyo *If...* 122
Kovalcik, Terry *Buzz Box* 38
    Food Chain 83
    Panel Ring 101

L

lace impressions 72
leaf impressions 83, 88–89
leaf replicas 88–89
links 104–107
    joining with jump rings 105
    joining with wire 106
liver of sulfur 183, 184
lockets 94, 96
    catch 101
    hinge 100–101
    making with cutter 94, 95
log roller 16, 17
loop-and-peg findings 59
loops 85

M

materials 10–15, 73, 90, 167
Micallef, Stanley *African Drum Beads* 112
    Mayan Calendar 183
modeling tools 16, 17
mokumé gané effect 108
molds 16, 17, 77–81
    one-part molds 77, 78–79
    sprigs 81
    two-part molds 77, 79–80

N

necklace clasps 56, 63
needles 16, 17, 96
Nelson, Mary Ann *Cuff* 34
    Fine Silver Half Lentil Ammonite
        Beads 158
    Lapis Lazuli 6
    Tree of Life 4

O

oil paste 10, 11, 38
olive oil 12, 13
overlay paste 10, 11
oxidizing materials 14, 15, 183–185

P

paintbrushes 16, 17
paper clay 10
pasta formers 90, 93
paste replicas 88–89
paste techniques 37–38
    gold paste 160, 161, 163
    homemade oil paste 38
    joining soft clay with paste 38
    making paste 37
    paste as texture 164
    relief painting 165
    silver oil paste 38
Pate, Chris *Chinese Pendant Reverse* 76
    Running Horses Brooch 108
    Web of Life Pendant 123
patinas 183–185
    preserving 185
pendants 12, 70, 77, 90
    bails 56, 60
    pendant holes 58
    pendant loops 56
photopolymer sheets 76
pickling 51
Piechna-Sowersby, Erna *Chartreuse*
    Ring 178
plastic wrap 16
playing cards as rolling guides 27
pliers 22, 23
PMC 10
polish 18, 19
polishing 54–55, 155
polishing cloths 18, 19
polymer clay 14, 15, 76, 77, 174–177
    marbling polymer clay sheets 175–176
    polymer clay transfers 177
power tools 22, 23, 50
pre-finishing techniques 25, 41–43
    allowing for shrinkage 42
    caulking 43
    drilling 42

filing 42
    joining dried clay with paste 43
    mending with paste 43
    sanding 41
precious metal clays 10–11
putty silicone molding compound 14, 15, 76, 77, 78–81

R

radial bristle disks 22, 23, 54
Rai, Julia *Destiny Brooch* 129
    Pod Ring 161
    Tube Bead Necklace 117
reclaiming clay 34
reconstituting clay 35
recycling fired silver 36
recycling soft clay 36
rehydrating clay 32
relief painting 165
resin 14, 15, 145, 166–169
    how to use 168–169
    mother-of-pearl mosaic 169
    plique-à-jour 169
Reuben, Suzanne *Blue Moon Bracelet* 96
    Textured Tile Bracelet 104
rings 102, 131, 135–143
    band rings 137–139
    clay quantities 12, 136
    forged band rings 142–143
    forged ring with added setting 141–142
    half-round rings 139–141
    ring mandrels 18, 19
    ring plugs 138
    sizing 136, 138, 143
rivets 102–103
    captured rivet 103
rolling tools 16, 17
rubber blocks 18, 19
rubber stamps 16, 17, 72, 75

S

safety 44, 180
Sanderson, Hattie *Pod Necklace* 56
sanding 41, 53
    sanding disks 22, 23, 54
    sanding pads 18, 19
    sandpaper 18, 19
seedhead replicas 89
sheet construction 94
sheet clay 10
shrinkage 42, 45
    bangles 132
    base metal clay 12
    precious metal clays 10–11
    rings 136, 143
silicone polishers 22, 23, 54

silver alloy clays 10, 11, 44
silver clay paste 10, 11
silver clays 10, 11, 44, 48
    firing 48, 151
    soldering 64
silver paper clay 10, 11, 124–129
    basics 125
    cutout embellishments 126
    flax folding 129
    kirigami 124, 128
    origami 124, 126–127
    palm weaving 124, 129
    paper cutting 124, 129
    paper sculpture 124, 129
    quilling 124, 129
silver sheet clay 10, 11
Singery, Sabine Alienor *Bronze and Pearl Ring* 136
    White Bronze Headband 106
slicers 16, 17
soft clay sheets 86–87
    cutting and shaping 87
soft clay techniques 25, 26–30
    cutting strips 28
    flexible clay 29
    logs by hand 29
    making balls 28
    ovals 29
    rolling sheets 27–28
    teardrops 29
    using extruder 30
    using syringe 30, 90, 92
soft sculpture techniques 82–83
soldering materials 14, 15
soldering techniques 64–67
    solder strip and flux 67
Sperling, Barbara *Mixed Material Necklace* 34
    Rockstack Necklace 1
sprigs 81
Spurgin, Tracey *Textured Bead* 34
stamping 72, 75
stencils 75
sterling silver clay 10
sterling silver findings 14, 57
storing clay 33, 92
Suzuki, Katsuhiko *Turquoise Inlay* 151
syringe-type silver clays 10, 11
syringes 16, 17, 30, 90, 92
syringing 90, 92, 120–123, 153
    curved lines 121
    dots 121
    drawing with fine nozzle 122
    extruding a line 121
    holding syringe 121
    infilling with openwork 123
    refilling syringes with slip 123

    repeat elements 122
    using syringe 121
    zigzags 121

T

templates 71
text impressions 72
texture 72–76
    texture sheets 16, 17, 72, 74, 76
thick sheets 86
tissue blades 16, 17
tongs 20, 21
tools 16–17
    basic tool kit 16
    dedicated tools 27
    enameling 170
    engraving, carving, and etching 146
    firing equipment 20–21
    glass fusing 178
    polymer clay 174
    pre-finishing, drying, and finishing 18, 19
    resin 167
    ring and bangle making tools 18, 19
    shaping tools 22–23
    soldering 64
    syringing 120
    working with different metals 50
tumbling 52
tweezers 20, 21

U

U-loops 60
UV resin 166

V

vegetable oil 12, 13
vermiculite 20, 21

W

waste, avoiding 109
water etching 146, 148
weaving 84, 85
wire 14, 15, 96
    balling wire 66
    sweat soldering wire 66
    wire cutters 22, 23, 141
    work hardening wire 59
wood clay 90, 92
work surfaces 16

X

X-Rio *Robot Rings* 135

Y

Yunomura, Nobuko *Sound of Leaves* 181

Credits

Picture credits

Quarto would like to thank the following artists and photographers for kindly submitting images for inclusion in this book:

Acar, Elif, at Prometheus Experimental Studio, www.hobbymaxistore.com, p.93tr
Alienor Singery, Sabine, http://www.sabinealienor.com, p.106b, 136t
Arnold, Xuella, www.xuella.co.uk, Photography by Simon Chapman, p.82bl, 132tr, 140cr
Azulie, Rachel, p.127tr
Baird, Emma, emmmabaird.wordpress.com, p.105tr, 154br
Bubanja, Milica, 162br
Cheney, Lynda, www.silverclaywithlynda.co.uk, p.2, 78, 87tc, 146t
Funnell, Joy, www.joyfunnell.co.uk, p.171
Gage, Holly, p.102t
Jacobson, Hadar, www.hadarjacobson.com, p.55, 108t
Komai, Sachiyo, p.122tr
Kovalcik, Terry, www.terrykovalcik.com, Photography by Corrin Jacobsen Kovalcik, p.38, 83tr, 101tr
Micallef, Stanley, Dragon Glass/Art Clay Silver South Africa, p.112, 183
Nelson, Mary Ann, Photography by Paul Mounsey, www.paulmounsey.co.uk, p.4, 6, 34bl, 158bl
Pate, Chris, www.touchmark.co.uk, Photography by Paul Mounsey, p.76b, 108br, 123tr
Piechna-Sowersby, Erna, Photography by Brian Laughlan, p.178
Rai, Julia, www.juliarai.co.uk, Photography by Paul Mounsey, p.117, 129tr, 161tr
Reuben, Suzanne, www.suzannereuben.com, p.96b, 104b
Sanderson, Hattie, www.hattiesanderson.com, p.56tr
Sperling, Barbara, www.barbarasperling.com, Photography by Robert Diamante, p.1, 34
Spurgin, Tracey, www.craftworx.co.uk, p.34cr
Suzuki, Katsuhiko, p.151
X-Rio, p.135
Yunomura, Nobuko, p.181

All step-by-step and other images are the copyright of Quarto Publishing plc. While every effort has been made to credit contributors, Quarto would like to apologize should there have been any omissions or errors—and would be pleased to make the appropriate correction for future editions of the book.

Author's acknowledgments

I am indebted to many people who have helped me during the long and difficult journey of writing this book. In particular:

- Aida Chemical Industries Co. Ltd., Japan and Creative Glass AG, Switzerland for supplying all the Art Clay Silver clays and Art Clay Copper used in this book.
- Hadar Jacobson for supplying her copper and bronze clays as well as fulsome information on how to use them.
- Bill Struve for supplying Fastfire BronzClay.
- Mehmet Aykoc for supplying Prometheus bronze and copper clays.
- Tracey Spurgin for sending me Baldwin's patina.
- Margaret Schindel for her excellent information lenses on Squidoo.
- Maria Alexandrou for discovering and sharing her polymer clay transfer technique.

And all the wonderful people who work in metal clays and then share their techniques on the web, in books, and magazines and through conferences. This book is a joint effort by you all.

Want more jewelry projects and expert techniques?

Check out these must-haves from Interweave

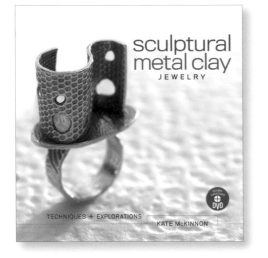

**SCULPTURAL METAL
CLAY JEWELRY**
Techniques + Explorations
Kate McKinnon
ISBN 978-1-59668-174-3
$26.95

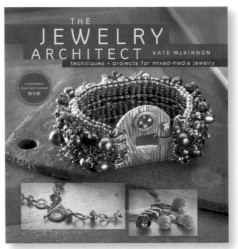

THE JEWELRY ARCHITECT
Techniques + Projects
for Mixed-Media Jewelry
Kate McKinnon
ISBN 978-1-59668-176-7
$26.95

ENLIGHTENED POLYMER CLAY
Artisan Jewelry Designs
Inspired by Nature
Rie Nagumo
ISBN 978-1-59668-634-2
$19.95

LAPIDARY JOURNAL JEWELRY ARTIST

Check out *Jewelry Artist,* a trusted guide to the art of gems, jewelry making, design, beads, minerals, and more. Whether you are a beginner, an experienced artisan, or in the jewelry business, Jewelry Artist can take you to a whole new level.

jewelryartistmagazine.com

Jewelry Making Daily is the ultimate online community for anyone interested in creating handmade jewelry. Get tips from industry experts; download free step-by-step projects; check out video demos; discover sources for supplies, and more!

Sign up at jewelrymakingdaily.com.

 Jewelry Making **Daily** *Shop*
shop.jewelrymaking.com